STUDIES IN THE CULT OF SAINT COLUMBA

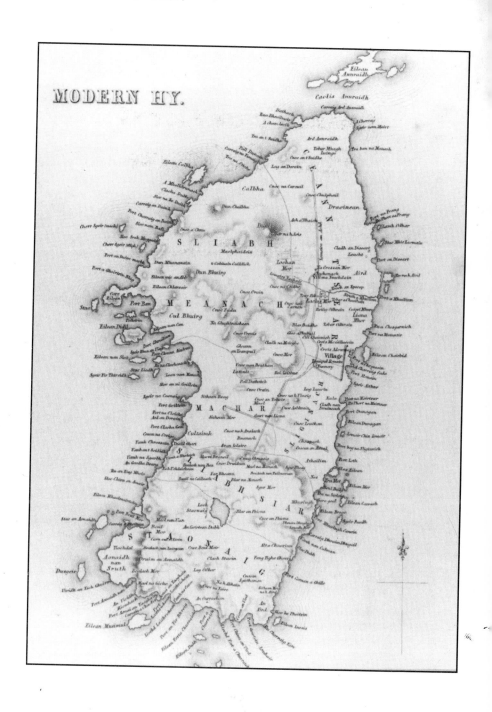

The map of Iona from William Reeves (ed),
The Life of St. Columba, Founder of Hy (Dublin/Edinburgh 1857).

Studies in the Cult of
Saint Columba

Cormac Bourke

Editor

FOUR COURTS PRESS

This book was typeset
in 10.5 on 12.5 point Ehrhardt for
FOUR COURTS PRESS
55 Prussia Street, Dublin 7, Ireland
e-mail: fcp@ indigo.ie
and in North America for
FOUR COURTS PRESS
c/o ISBS, 5804 N.E. Hassalo Street, Portland, OR 97213.

A catalogue record for this title
is available from the British Library.

ISBN 1-85182-268-2 hbk
ISBN 1-85182-313-1 pbk

Printed in Great Britain by Hartnolls Ltd, Bodmin, Cornwall.

Contents

Contents

Ro-fess i n-ocus, i céin,
Columb coich boí, acht ba oín,
tindis a ainm amail gréin,
ba lés i comair cach oín.

Acknowledgements

It is my pleasant duty, and not for the first time, to thank the Director and Trustees of the Ulster Museum for support freely afforded to academic endeavour. I must also thank my colleagues Anne Abernethy and Michael Comiskey for their technical help, Bill Porter, Michael McKeown and Bryan Rutledge for providing many of the illustrations and Jackie Hagan for assistance with editing in the final stages. I have been supported *extra muros* by my fellow-contributors, notably by Nollaig Ó Muraíle, who shared the work of indexing and several times gave me the benefit of his advice.

Cormac Bourke

Permission to reproduce photographs and drawings (other than those of the individual contributors) is gratefully acknowledged as follows: *Finbar McCormick* Figs 1, 3, 4 Royal Commission on the Ancient and Historical Monuments of Scotland, Fig 2 Historic Scotland; *Jane Hawkes* Fig 1 Dean and Chapter of Durham Cathedral, Fig 2 The Board of Trinity College Dublin, Fig 5 Ross Trench-Jellicoe, Fig 6 Ian Scott (Crown Copyright Reserved), Fig 7 Paul Gwilliam, West Yorkshire Archaeological Service, Fig 9 Jason Hawkes; *Raghnall Ó Floinn* Figs 1, 7, 8 National Museum of Ireland, Fig 3 Ulster Museum, Figs 4-6 National Museums of Scotland; *Cormac Bourke* (a) Fig 1 Environment and Heritage Service, Dept of the Environment for Northern Ireland, Fig 4 Fitzwilliam Museum, Cambridge, Fig 5 National Museums of Scotland, Fig 7 John Housby, Figs 9-11 National Museum of Ireland; (b) Fig 1a Ulster Museum, Fig 1b Ashmolean Museum, Oxford, Fig 3 National Museum of Ireland, Fig 4 National Museums of Scotland.

EDITORIAL NOTE

Early personal names are cited wherever possible in accordance with the usage of Ó Riain (1985), with a small number of exceptions which are given in received anglicized form. The terms *sub anno*, *sub nomine* and *sub verbo* are denoted by the abbreviations sa, sn and sv respectively. The *Ordnance Survey Letters* (*OSL-*) are referred to by the MS page-numbers; the *Ordnance Survey Name Books* (*OSNB*) are referred to *sub nomine*. Metric and imperial measure are used according to individual preference and illustrations are not to scale except where scales are indicated. Biblical quotations have not been harmonized.

Preface

On a clear day early in 1996 it was possible to see from the top of Knocklayd, Co. Antrim (1695 ft), with unaided eye, a panorama of Scotland: the Mull of Oa and the deep inlet of Loch Indaal on Islay, the colours of the mountains of Jura, the long coastline of Kintyre with a suggestion of low-lying Gigha alongside. The summit of Knocklayd is marked by a prehistoric burial mound, whose builders can only have intended the occupant, or occupants, to survey to eternity a Scottish as well as an Irish hinterland. The intervening sea, known to history as Sruth na Maoile or the Sea of Moyle, was repeatedly crossed.

A diversion to Scotland, *turas in Albain*, is a commonplace in early Irish literature, and Suibne Geilt (Mad Sweeney), half-man half-bird, ranges far and wide over Cooley, the Mournes, Slieve Gullion, Slemish, Binevenagh, Dunseverick, Islay and Ailsa Craig, describing, as it were, navigational chains.

The subject of this book, Columba, or Colum Cille, may never have stood on Knocklayd, but he belonged to a culture disposed to view these islands as an archipelago. The geographical scope of the Columban federation tempers the perception that he _exiled_ himself to Iona. Columba separated himself from family and familiar ground but was never to leave the known ambit. Indeed, such was the power of his cult that the periphery which he chose became the centre. Nor was it so unfamiliar: Atlantic Scotland resembled his native place. By tradition his boyhood was spent within sight of Muckish, Co. Donegal; Ben More on Mull (though a thousand feet higher), seen from Iona, has a not dissimilar profile. Did the mountain remind him of home? Might he have thought it auspicious? Jura, visible from Ireland, is visible from Iona too.

Columba was at home in Scotland and Ireland. Adomnán, author of the *Vita Columbae*, speaks of him in Mull, Ardnamurchan and the Great Glen, in Durrow, Trevet and Terryglass. His account of the saint's visit to Clonmacnoise is the stuff of poetry, music or drama, or of all three. In an appealing allegory of Columba's fame, in the first chapter of his third book, Adomnán tells of a dream experienced by the saint's mother 'after his conception but before his birth', in which an angel shows her a cloak 'of marvellous beauty, decorated with ... the colours of every flower'. Floating in the air the cloak grows ever bigger to overreach mountain, forest and plain, while the angel foretells the birth of a son 'of such flower that he shall be reckoned as one of the prophets'. Adomnán appears to endorse the aesthetic of the contemporary Book of Durrow, in which the symbol of Matthew (shod in the style of 7th-century

Iona) is cloaked in a seeming patchwork of *millefiori*. Indeed Matthew's Gospel opens with the genealogy of Christ, with his conception and with Joseph's dream of an angel foretelling his birth; in the symbol of Matthew in the Book of Durrow might an image of Columba be discerned? That symbol, the man, is often represented as an angel in insular art. Adomnán's Columba is 'angelic in aspect' and is received at Clonmacnoise 'as if he had been an angel of the Lord'. Adomnán's third book is devoted to visions of angels 'revealed to others in relation to the blessed man, and to him in relation to others'. A 7th-century praise poem, the *Amra Coluim Cille*, casts the saint in an angel's role as 'messenger of the Lord' and explicitly mentions 'God's angel', perhaps in allusion to him. The 12th-century life of Columba in the *Leabhar Breac* mentions *a aingel fén*, 'his own angel', referring not to some celestial companion but to the 'angel' Columba had become.

Adomnán, like Columba, was a native of Donegal and from his abbacy in Iona could visit Northumbria and Birr. His visit to Birr in 697 was the occasion of the enactment by a synod of a law protecting non-combatants which bears his name. That the guarantors of the *Cáin Adomnáin* included senior clergy, Irish kings and the kings of the Picts and of Scottish Dál Riata is eloquent of his prestige. Columba had died in 597 and Adomnán returned to Iona to celebrate the saint's feast-day in his 100th anniversary year; his 1400th anniversary year in 1997 is the occasion of our own publication.

A 'prophesy' in the *Baile Bricín*, *Bricín's Vision*, as colourful in its way as Adomnán's allegory or the Durrow picture, predicted that Columba's rule would build a bridge between Ireland and Scotland: *bid droichtech a ríagol iter Érinn 7 Alpain*. And so it transpired.

These essays speak of a civilization with broad horizons; they offer a sense of this, our archipelago, and of a hidden commonwealth.

Living in the Ocean

Thomas O'Loughlin

The sea was a constant factor in the lives of all who were connected with Iona (Map 1). To reach their monastery, Columba and those who followed him had to cross the sea. To travel anywhere from the monastery involved the sea: in one direction lay Ireland, in another Britain, and further away the continent. The sea brought them visitors, guests, books and supplies. It was visible all round them, and its sounds and fury part of their daily lives. When they recited the words of the psalm – *qui descendunt mare in nauibus, facientes operationem in aquis multis, ipsi uiderunt opera Domini et mirabilia eius in profundo*[1] – they probably felt a strange affinity with its sentiments for, unlike the land-orientated psalmist, they knew ships and sailing intimately and saw the wonders of the sea around them. This leaves us with a number of questions: how did the inhabitants of Iona view the relationship of their island home to the surrounding lands; where did they locate themselves in relation to the places they came from, and travelled to? This chapter seeks to explore this topic.

THE PROBLEM

Iona is located on modern maps by the co-ordinates 56°20'N 6°23'W, and is described as a tiny island situated just off the Ross of Mull in Argyll, Scotland, with the Atlantic on its western shore. For us this is an adequate location since it allows us to know where it is on any relevant map with precision, and to have an idea of the sort of place it is: an exposed island on the north-western periphery of Europe. This information also enables us to locate Iona in relation to other places: so it is on the eastern edge of the Atlantic; Ireland is to the south, Iceland is to the north-west, England is to the south-east, and beyond is the European mainland. The consequences of this peripheral location has been the subject of quite an amount of research

---

1 Ps 106.23: 'Those who go down to the sea in ships and have business in its many waters see the works of the Lord and his great deeds in the deep'. (Throughout this chapter all scriptural references are according to the Septuagint/Vulgate numeration. Unless otherwise noted, all translations are my own.)

over the years from several perspectives.[2] But while these investigations reveal to us the range and quantity of Iona's contacts within early medieval Europe, they do not reveal what its early inhabitants thought about their position in relation to other lands, nor how they imagined travel within their world. Reconstructing *their* view of their geographical position is, of its nature, a tentative affair, but sufficient materials survive from Iona to make the attempt worthwhile. The first step is to examine the general views of the period with regard to the islands in the Atlantic. Works for the patristic and early medieval period provide us with what was the 'common knowledge' of the time regarding the location of the islands of Britain and Ireland, and this information serves as a backdrop to more specific investigations regarding Iona. The second step is to examine the geographical materials we know were available on Iona, as well as what information we can glean from the documents produced there. Essentially, this is the information about its position that we can assemble from four works: Isidore's *Etymologiae* (Lindsay 1911) and *De Natura Rerum* (Fontaine 1960),[3] and the *Vita Columbae* (*VC*)[4] and *De Locis Sanctis* (*DLS*) of Adomnán. The third step is to exercise a control of this material by seeing if the resulting picture is consistent with information from other insular sources which convey how the inhabitants of Iona saw their position. We are fortunate here in that Bede was not only roughly contemporary, but was familiar with Adomnán's works, interested in the life of Iona (O'Loughlin 1995a), and concerned about the position of his own island with regard to other lands. Viewed collectively, these pieces of information provide us with an insight into how the monks on Iona viewed their world in the 7th/8th-century period.

The general picture

The first, and most obvious, point to be made about the islands off the north-western coast of Europe is that, unlike islands such as Crete (cf. *DLS* iii. 1.1), Malta (cf. Acts 28.1) or Sicily (cf. *DLS* iii. 6; O'Loughlin 1996), which were in a sea, they were located in the Ocean (*Oceanus*).[5] This expanse

2 James 1982, from an historian's perspective, and Campbell 1996, from that of an archaeologist, are recent examples. 3 For the basis of asserting that both these works were present on Iona, see O'Loughlin 1994a. 4 The *VC* is referred to in the edition and translation of Anderson and Anderson (1961; rev edn 1991). 5 In this paper the concept of the Ocean will be examined solely from the stand-point of how it is described and understood in Christian texts. A fuller study would involve the notion of *Oceanus* in mythology and as a motif in the phenomenology of religion. However, such studies are the province of others. Moreover, in so far as this paper is concerned with how those on Iona conceptually understood their position and envisaged it on the basis of what they believed to be authoritative descriptions of the physical world, taken for example from the Christian Scriptures and the fathers, they are not our concern. For an outline of the mythological background, see Grimal 1986; Konstan 1987; for the role or place of the Ocean in comparative religion, see Wensinck 1918; Borsje & Ó Cróinín 1995.

of water was qualitatively different from other waters in that it was at the very limit of inhabitable reality and its shore marked the point of the separation between the waters and the dry land (Gen 1.9). This was the primeval 'abyss' (Gen 1.2),[6] the home of Leviathan (cf. Job 41.23 for example) (Day 1985; 1992); it was also connected with the abode of demons (Luke 8.31) and Satan (Rev 20.1-3), and from it, at the end of time, the apocalyptic beast would arise to bring destruction to mankind (Apoc 11.7; 17.8). This threatening aspect of the Ocean seems to be present in most biblical references: it is a place of power and darkness, and is always to be treated with caution. Gathering the various references to the sea, names of different monsters (e.g. Leviathan, Rahab, *draco*), and the abyss, a picture emerges of the Ocean as a place where a great struggle between God and evil is taking place (Wensinck 1918; Reymond 1958; Day 1985; Konstan 1987; Borsje 1996). In Christian works from the Mediterranean basin part of the life of the hermit/monk is to go and do battle with the demons. These battles are envisaged as taking place in remote regions of the desert where the demons lurk. The monks of Iona could consider their own island as a similar theatre of operations in the war against the demons: demons were as close to them in the Ocean as they were to St Antony in the deserts of Egypt.[7]

The biblical image of the Ocean was converted into a part of Christian physics in the late 4th- and early 5th-century commentaries on Genesis. Two of these works, one by Ambrose – the *Exameron* (*CSEL* 32 I,1-261), and one by Augustine – the *De Genesi ad Litteram* (*CSEL* 28 III, I, 1-456), were particularly famous and influential.[8] Ambrose, commenting on Gen 1.9 ('Let the waters be gathered into one place'), remarks that we speak of many seas: the Ocean, the Tyrrhenian, the Adriatic, other small seas, and the Atlantic Sea. While these have various names, in reality they form a single body of water. The smaller seas are interlinked and form the 'sea'. Ambrose's terminology lacks precision, but his import is clear: that there is one great body of water – it becomes obvious that this is the Ocean – and some partially isolated parts of this body are the individual seas. The great body of water

6 This is a concept found in many places in the Scriptures in Greek and Latin where it is a 'bottomless pit' and identified as a great mass of water, and which is always threatening in some way (e.g. Job 28. 14; Ps 41. 8; Sir 16. 18; Ezek 31. 4; Jonah 2. 8; cf. Massie 1898; Grether 1992). In the New Testament it is threatening as an abode of the dead (e.g. Luke 8. 31; Rom 10. 7; Apoc 9. 1-2; 11. 7; 17. 18; 20. 1-3; 2 Pet 2.4; cf. Lewis 1992, 105). 7 We know that the Latin version by Evagrius of Athanasius's *Vita Antonii* (a key document within monasticism, where the theme of the monk fighting the demons in the desert was famously expressed) was present on Iona as Adomnán used it in his *Vita Columbae* (Brüning 1917; Kelly 1982). 8 On the background to these Genesis commentaries being used as works of physics, see O'Loughlin 1992a; and on their influence, particularly in the insular area, see Smyth 1986; O'Loughlin 1992b.

from the 'Indian Sea' to the mouth of the Mediterranean (*ad Gaditani oram*). This Ocean – the term used correctly – surrounds the land of the earth at its extremity. Inside this circle of lands there are other regions of the sea which are connected to the Ocean flowing in and out of it (*Exameron* iii. 3. 12-13). Earlier (ii. 3. 12), commenting on the earthly waters (Gen 1.6-7), he noted that some rivers such as the Danube and the Nile flow into particular seas, but the Rhine flows directly into the depths of the Ocean (*in oceani profunda*). Later (iv. 7. 30), commenting on the tides, he identifies the Ocean with the 'Western Sea' (*mare ... occidentale*). Thus, for Ambrose, the Ocean surrounds the three continents of Asia, Africa and Europe.

Augustine, by contrast, in his *De Genesi ad Litteram*, mentions the Ocean only incidentally. At one point he needs an example of seeing a far-distant object, and in the course of his example he points out that the Ocean is beyond both the lands and the seas between the lands. In size, this Ocean is said to be greater than anything else we know (*De Genesi ad Litteram* iv. 34, 54). Elsewhere (v. 10. 25) he notes that it has an annual pattern of tides, and its waters seem to be identical with the 'great abyss' which rises and falls to irrigate the earth (cf. Gen 2.6).

That Augustine and Ambrose represent the widespread general understanding that the inhabitants of Iona would have found in Latin writings can be seen in the works of Orosius and Patrick. Orosius (early 5th century) in his description of the world at the beginning of his *Historia Aduersus Paganos* – which would become a famous source for medieval geography (Jancey 1994) – describes a circular Ocean surrounding the main bodies of land, and in this Ocean just off the north-western edge of Europe are the islands of Britain and Ireland (Baumgarten 1984). These islands are as far from anywhere of importance for Orosius – who focuses on the Mediterranean – as anything can be. Patrick (5th century) in his *Confessio* seems to share a similar general view of the island upon which he laboured. The island of Ireland is in the 'Western Sea' (literally 'the sea of the setting sun') (*Confessio* §23: *qui erant iuxta siluam Vocluti quae est prope mare occidentale*), and this is at the very ends of the earth (§34). Patrick imagines that the people to whom he preaches are situated at the furthest extent from the first place where the gospel was preached (Jerusalem), and that when the Christian message has reached them it has reached every place on earth (§38). Once the island of Ireland has heard its message, it has been preached 'from the rising of the sun to its setting' (§39, quoting Matt 8.11). This view of Ireland as the land furthest from the original 'homeland' of Christianity is supported by three quotations from Scripture (Jer 16.19; Acts 13.47; Matt 8.11) and numerous allusions.[9]

9 These are identified by Conneely (1993, 42), whose edition and translation are referred to here.

ADOMNÁN'S SOURCES AND WRITINGS

Isidore, bishop of Seville (obit 636), can be seen as the link between the earlier writers and Adomnán's Iona. Isidore used Augustine, Ambrose (O'Loughlin 1995b) and Orosius (Baumgarten 1984) in forming his picture of the world in his *Etymologiae* and *De Natura Rerum*. Very soon after their composition these works were available on Iona, and were used by Adomnán in his writings (O'Loughlin 1994a). In them there were descriptions of the Ocean, information on the location of the islands of Britain and Ireland, and sketch-maps of how the three continents of Europe, Africa, and Asia were related to one another.

In the *Etymologiae*, the Ocean was treated in the book *On the World and its Parts* (xiii. 15). The Ocean marks the limits of the land-mass for it flows around and encircles the land. Its tides swell up and down – to a far greater extent than is the case with seas (cf. xiii. 18) – and it absorbs the waters of the seas and sends them out again.[10] Like the sky it is purple, and is called by different names according to the named areas of land or sea that are close to it. So the Ocean beyond the Pillars of Hercules is called 'Gaditanum' after the names of the Straits of Gibraltar (*Gaditanum*). In this final point Isidore uses one of his linguistic tools (an object getting a secondary name from some other object lying close to it) to clear up the confusion in Ambrose, who was one of his sources in this section. In the next chapter Isidore moves on to describe the lands that circle the Mediterranean: starting from Gibraltar, he mentions Spain, Gaul and Italy, until he arrives back at his starting point. The reader on Iona would also have found in the *Etymologiae* (xiv. 6) a description of Ireland as a narrow land located close to the island of Britain, north of the oceanic coast of Spain, and whose southern parts touched the 'Cantabrian Ocean'. This description of Ireland was destined to become part of Irish tradition.[11]

Reading the chapter on the Ocean in the *De Natura Rerum* (ch xl) would have provided a far less clear picture to our insular monastic reader. In it Isidore tries to reconcile different theories about the swelling and ebbing (the tides) of the Ocean that he finds in the 'philosophers' (i.e. the pagan poets) with what he finds in Ambrose, and to a lesser extent Augustine.[12] Was the

---

10 This notion of the Ocean accepting the water from the rivers and seas and sending them out again is a much larger theme than is our concern here. It is found in both classical and Christian cosmology, and in the latter case is often thought to have biblical support in the text of Qo 1.7 (*Omnia flumina intrant mare et mare non redundat, ad locum unde exeunt flumina reuertuntur ut iterum fluant*) which is used by Isidore in *De Natura Rerum* xli; cf. also Sir 40.12. 11 This description of Ireland, its geographical presuppositions about compass points, and its 'afterlife' in Irish tradition have been examined by Baumgarten (1984). 12 Fontaine notes (1960, 305-9) the influence of the following: Solinus (through Minucius Felix), Cicero – possibly directly, but certainly through Ambrose (the *Exameron*),

Figure 1   T-O map relating to the *Etymologiae*
(from the *editio princeps*, Augsburg 1472).

Ocean like an animal breathing, was its swelling caused by the winds, or by
the heavenly bodies, or their annual rotation? Ultimately, Isidore concluded,
the answers to such questions are beyond us and are known to God alone!
Isidore's final remark was that the Ocean was incomparable in its extent and
impassable.[13] Our island reader may well have taken this as confirming his
own feelings of the Ocean as mighty and mysterious.

   In each of Isidore's works our monastic reader would have found a sketch-
map (a so-called 'T-O map') which was intended to make clear the geography (literally 'writing about land') in the text.[14] In both of these maps (Figs
1, 2) the Ocean is the large circle surrounding the lands. East is at the top,
Europe is in the lower left-hand quarter of the circle, and the reader could
extrapolate that Ireland, Britain and his own Iona were narrow specks just off
that continent (Fig 3). The circumference of the whole sphere[15] was declared

Lucan (and possibly Servius) and Augustine (*De Genesi ad Litteram*), who possibly drew
on Origen through Rufinus. 13 There is a hint of 'the problem of the Antipodes' in Isidore
at this point, but it would take us too far from out purpose to follow this (cf. Betten 1918;
Wittkower 1942; Flint 1984; Carey 1989). 14 The related questions of the presence of (1)
sketch-maps in Isidore's works (absent in modern editions) and (2) which map should
accompany which text, will be examined elsewhere (O'Loughlin forthcoming). These questions have been surveyed in O'Loughlin 1993a. 15 Contrary to popular conceptions about
medieval geography, the earth was *not* thought of as flat but as a sphere: the favourite
demonstration of this fact was the curved shadow it cast upon the moon (Betten 1923; for
a guide to more recent writing on this topic see O'Loughlin 1993b, 50, n 17).

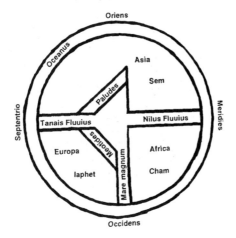

Mentioned by Isidore, but not shown in MSS:
Columnae Herculis
and

Totius ... terrae mensuram 180,000 stadiorum aestimauerunt

Figure 2 T-O map relating to the *De Natura Rerum*.

by Isidore to be 360,000 *stadia* for he said that the distance from one edge of the land to the other was 180,000 *stadia* (*De Natura Rerum* xlviii. 3). While imagining how someone dwelling on Iona would have located Britain and Ireland, and their own island, on such a world-map may seem to be going an inference too far, it is worth noting that just such maps, in the sense that they rely on the same basic information, actually exist from a later period, the St Sever world-map (mid-11th century) being a good example.[16] Moreover, with this figure in mind many of the references to places beyond Iona in the *Vita Columbae* can more easily be understood.[17]

So when a monk stood on Iona facing south-east, he would have imagined that – once he had crossed two short areas of water (from Iona to Britain, and from Britain to Gaul, both trips frequently and easily made) – ahead of him was a vast land-mass stretching on to Jerusalem and then out to the Asiatic coast of the same Ocean he was looking at. While to his back the Ocean stretched an equal distance: an impassable body of water heaving and tossing without interruption.

This picture explicitly laid out in Isidore would have been confirmed in

16 The part of this map which shows Britain, Ireland and the northern coast of France is reproduced by Hill (1981, 1). 17 See the discussion, below, of *Vita Columbae* i. 48, 48a; ii. 42, 95a; ii. 46, 102b-103a; iii. 23, 123b; iii. 23, 135b.

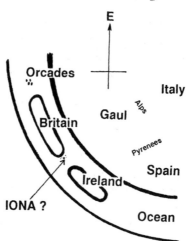

Figure 3 Mental map of how someone on Iona would have though of their position, based on information in the *Vita Columbae*.

other writings available on Iona which mentioned the Ocean incidentally. For example there are several references to the nature of the Ocean in Cassiodorus's *Expositio Psalmorum* (O'Loughlin 1994a). He says that the reader should understand the 'sea' mentioned in Ps 71.8 as referring to the Ocean which circles the edge of the earth (*PL* 70. 510). The 'abyss' in Ps 103.6 is identified with the Ocean, and the Ocean is described as surrounding the earth and as its margin (*PL* 70. 730). Similar descriptions of the Ocean – which neither add to, nor subtract from, what we have already mentioned – can be found in other places in the same work.[18] Even more interesting as a confirmation of this general picture would be the references to the Ocean in Jerome's commentaries on Isaiah and Amos, as they both mention the *Oceanus Brittanicus* as the extremity of the earth in the West, and the *Oceanus Indicus* as the opposite extremity in the East – but unfortunately for our purposes we have, despite the speculations of the late Denis Meehan, no evidence of the presence of these works on Iona (O'Loughlin 1994a).[19]

18 For example on Ps 106.3 he mentions that the cardinal points are indicated by the phrase *a solis ortu* (East) *et occasu* (West), *ab aquilone* (North) *et mari* (South, for the fourth point is in the Ocean which encircles the land) (*PL* 70. 768). A similar point to that already cited in the text is made about the reference to the 'abyss' in Ps 134. 6 (*PL* 70. 963). There are, of course, references to the Ocean in other works by Cassiodorus, of which several may merit further study, as that to islands in the Ocean which are rich in honey (*Variarum* v. 2: *PL* 69. 896), but since, at present, we have no evidence of their presence on Iona, I am leaving them out of consideration here. 19 The references in Jerome are *In Esaiam* xi. 40. 21-6 (*CCSL* 73. 463) and *In Amos* iii. 8. 11-14 (*CCSL* 76. 333). Despite references to these works in the apparatus to the 1958 edition of *De Locis Sanctis*, we have no evidence that they were part of the Iona library (O'Loughlin 1994a). Jerome's *In Ezechielem* was present on Iona and there is a reference to the Ocean in it (Introduction 14, line 10: *CCSL* 75.

When we come to Adomnán's own writings we immediately think of *De Locis Sanctis* as the place to look for geographical information. However, neither Iona nor the Ocean are mentioned; Arculf's journeys by sea are all within the Mediterranean, and the tale of his wandering ends with his arrival at Rome: *postea exinde Romam appetens enauigauit* (iii. 5.10). We can infer only one thing about the position of Iona from it. The most important contribution of *DLS* to how the Latin world saw itself is that in that work Jerusalem's location at the centre of the terrestrial world was first explicitly established as a *geographical fact*. It is as a result of the experiment described in *DLS* (i. 11) that this became a fact, in turn, on medieval maps.[20] We can conclude that if Jerusalem is at the centre of the land, and the Ocean at its periphery, then since Iona is situated far out in the Ocean – to the west of Britain – then it is about as far from Jerusalem as one could possibly be. I argue elsewhere (O'Loughlin forthcoming) that the geographical schema of Luke/Acts (the gospel is to be preached first in Jerusalem, then in the surrounding areas, and then out to the ends of the earth) is operative in the arrangement of material in *DLS*; if that is the case then in the gospel being proclaimed on Iona – at the very end of the earth – one of the prophesies of Christ before the Ascension (Acts 1.8) was being fulfilled. If this was the perception on Iona, then this is a continuity in theological understanding between Adomnán's community and Patrick.

In contrast, when we turn to the *Vita Columbae* for information on how the monks on Iona viewed their island home we have an embarrassment of riches.

The most obvious feature of the *VC* is the abundance of details about navigation: the sea is mentioned in almost every chapter. We hear about sailing to and from Ireland (i. 12, 20b; i. 18, 23b, 24b; i. 30, 32a), to Skye (i. 33, 34b) and, with full sails (*plenis uelis*), to the *Orcades* (ii. 42, 95a).[21] We hear of trips from Derry to Britain and Iona (i. 2, 11b and ii. 39, 90a, 91b); from Gaul to Iona (i. 28, 30b); and from Gaul to Britain (ii. 34, 81b). We hear also of shorter trips around the neighbouring islands which went to make up the monastery. We hear of journeys made under sail (i. 30, 32a; ii. 29, 90a) and of similar travels where the sailors had to row (i. 2, 11b; ii. 45, 100b). Under those means of propulsion we know that getting to and from Iona was a laborious business (i. 2, 12b).

677), but here it is simply used as a simile: Scripture is like an ocean. **20** See, for example, the world-map in BL Cotton Tiberius B.V. folio 56v (reproduced in Hill 1981, 2-3) and the Hereford *mappa mundi* (cf. Jancey 1994). The question of the significance of the *DLS* with regard to the location of Jerusalem is a large and important topic in its own right and one I hope to take up in detail in the near future. **21** This classical name is taken to be the Orkneys, but could it also refer to the Shetlands?

The sea was something that the community of Iona had to come to grips with: there are many descriptions of storms around the island, the heaving of the waves and swelling of the Ocean (i. 4, 16ab; ii. 12-13, 62a-63b). Likewise, they knew and feared the dangers of shipwreck (e.g. i. 5, 17a). When we consider how their lives depended on the sea it is not surprising that there is evidence for their detailed knowledge of the sea around them – one of the dangerous whirlpools was named (i. 5, 17a) – and of the forces of nature: Adomnán shows a keen awareness of the various winds (e.g. i. 18, 23b) and, relying on Isidore,[22] of their classical names in Latin (ii. 45, 100b-101a).

The *VC* provides information about how the community saw their island home in relation to the larger world. The monastery is spread over several islands, referred to as 'our islands' (i. 2, 13b); of these Iona is their principal home (*insula ... primaria*: i.1, 6b) and the Ocean comes right up to its shore (ii. 22, 70a). Iona and the nearby islands are considered to be a province[23] of Britain (second Preface 4a; possibly i. 2, 11b and ii. 39, 90a-91b). From Iona one can be blown north[24] over the limitless Ocean to a region – further north than the *Orcades* – beyond where it is possible to navigate. Anyone who sails into this northern region finds himself in a place from which there is no return (ii. 42, 96a; the point is repeated at 96b). From this incident we learn that beyond Iona is Britain, and beyond Britain is the *Orcades*. From two other incidents we learn that Adomnán considered Ireland to lie to the west of Iona. One of the monks is to look to the west for a visitor coming from the northern region of Ireland (i. 48, 48b), and when Columba dies Ernéne in Donegal knows of it by seeing a great pillar of fire (rising up from Iona) when he looks towards the east (iii. 23, 132b). These directions have been taken into account in constructing the mental map of how someone on Iona envisaged their location (Fig 3). We are not told from which direction the Gallic ship came (i. 28, 30b), but presumably it was from the south.

Iona, Ireland and Britain are the islands in the Ocean (*ociani insulae*) (second Preface 3a; ii. 46, 103a), and as such they are situated at the remotest ends of the earth (iii. 23, 135b; note that Mochta's prophesy about Columba's fame uses the *topos* – used by Patrick in his *Confessio* – of linking the last times to the last places: second Preface 3a). Britain is the largest of the Ocean

---

22 Adomnán mentions *Fauonius* (*Zephyrus*) and *Vulturnus* and the source of his information appears to be *De Natura Rerum* xxxvii. This same chapter about the winds is also used in the *De Locis Sanctis* i. 2. 5 (O'Loughlin 1994a, 49). 23 This notion of islands as the provinces of the Ocean is found in the second Preface 3a and at ii. 46, 102b-103a. 24 We should bear in mind that North, South, East and West are not simply directions in pre-modern geography, but specific regions of the earth.

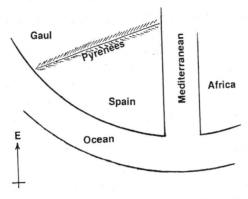

Figure 4 'Three-cornered Spain'.

islands, while Iona is a very small island and even more remote (iii. 23, 135b).
Moreover, this Ocean surrounds the whole circular land-mass of the earth
(*totum totius terrae orbem, cum ambitu ociani et caeli ... speculentur*: i. 43, 44b-
45a). In two passages we see how Adomnán images the larger world again.
These islands are in the part of the Ocean that is known as the Brittanic
Ocean and it laps the edge of the continent of Europe (iii. 23, 135b). Along
that shore of the European mainland lies Gaul and 'three-cornered' Spain
(Fig. 4)[25] separated by the Pyrenees; these are what Adomnán refers to as 'the
wider regions of Europe' (ii. 46, 102b). Beyond Gaul lies Italy – separated by
the Alps[26] – and in Italy is located the city of Rome (ii. 46, 102b) which is the
head of all the cities (*caput ... omnium ciuitatum*: iii. 23, 135b). From these
two references, where in each case Rome is mentioned with a sense of reverence, and the fact that Arculf's journey ends abruptly there, we get some idea
of the respect and awe with which Adomnán viewed Rome. Europe is clearly
the great land and the islands are just outlying scraps in the Ocean. Everything of significance in the world – not just religion or books or wine, but the
great plague described in ii. 46 – comes through Europe, and finally to Iona
as the least place of all. But from it also spreads out the fame of Columba,
first to Ireland, then to the largest island in the Ocean, and then to Europe:
to Spain, Gaul, Italy and then Rome itself (iii. 23,135b). There seems to be
a juxtaposition of Iona and Rome in Adomnán's mind: one is the largest city

25 At iii. 23, 135b Adomnán refers to 'three cornered Spain' (*ad trigonam usque Hispaniam*).
I understand this to be based on a passage in the *Etymologiae*: *Hispania ... sita est autem
inter Africam et Galliam, a septentrione Pyrenaeis montibus clausa, a reliquis partibus undique
mare conclusa* (xiv. 4. 28). We can envisage this on a T-O map (Fig 2): the first side is
from Gibraltar to the Pyrenees (a straight line running parallel to Africa); the second
side is the arc from Gibraltar to the Pyrenees; and the third side is the Pyrenees running
in a straight line (roughly NW-SE) from the Ocean to the Mediterranean. Thus Spain
is 'three cornered' and wedge-shaped (Fig 4). 26 The Alps are also referred to at iii. 23,
135b.

and the most central of places (after Jerusalem), the other is the smallest and
most remote of places. We might add that this same route of fame – Ireland,
Britain, then every corner of Europe – awaited Adomnán himself (O'Loughlin
1995a).

Lastly, we can get some notion of the attitude of the Iona community to
the sea by the way miracles are recorded in the *Vita Columbae*. In several
incidents Columba's prayers calm the sea's swell and ensure safe sailing (i. 1,
6b; i. 4, 16ab; i. 5, 17a; ii. 12-13, 62a-63b; ii. 42, 97b). In all these miracles
the sea in all its might and power (see i. 4, 16ab especially) is under the
divine command: it is something created, and nothing happens there without
the divine permission. The saint has access to God, and thereby can bring
about the control of this element. In this Adomnán makes clear that Columba
is modelling himself upon Christ who calmed the sea (Matt 8. 24-7, echoed
at i. 1, 6b), and is drawing upon that power, for 'even winds and sea obey
him' (Matt 8.27, echoed at ii. 42, 87b except that the detail is accurately
changed by Adomnán from 'winds and sea' – Christ's miracle was performed
on a 'sea' – to 'winds and Ocean' – the location of the event in the *VC*). The
Ocean also has that forbidding aspect which it has in Scripture. Hence the
great sea monster (*cetus magnus*)[27] which rises threateningly from the depths
of the Ocean to attack the monk Berach (i. 19, 24b-25b). Here there is a clear
allusion to the great sea monsters (*cete grandia*) mentioned in Gen 1.21 which
God has created in the depths of the sea. But both monks and the monster
are creatures and so both are in God's power (*Ego et illa bilua* [*belua*] *sub dei
potestate sumus*), and through faith in Christ the danger can be avoided. A
similar case can be found at ii. 34, 81b.

The Ocean is also a fitting place for monks to wage warfare against the
evil spirits in the manner of Antony in the desert. We are told of Cormac
who on three occasions set out 'on the limitless sea' in search of 'a desert in
the Ocean' (*desertum marinum* and *in ociano desertum*: i. 20, 25b). This 'desert'
is described elsewhere as *herimum in ociano*, which better describes what he
was looking for: a hermitage (i. 6, 17a). On one of his later searches for this
place he encounters evil monstrous creatures, but is delivered from them (ii.
42, 94b-96b). The sea is a brooding place; in it are the trials and temptations
of the saints, but in its depths the Lord's wonders and power can be seen.

---

27 This is translated restrictively, and overly rationally, by the Andersons as 'whale.' That
it should not be 'whale' is confirmed by the subsequent use of *belua* to designate the
creature. The translation 'great sea monster' is based on it being an echo of Gen 1. 21 (cf.
Speiser 1964, 4).

VERIFYING THE RECONSTRUCTION

The weakness in any reconstruction of how an individual or group in the pre-modern period viewed their world is in verifying that it does represent what they thought in some way. One possible way of controlling the reconstruction is to examine if it fits consistently with what some comparable figure said about their world. We have already noted how the reconstruction proposed here fits with several extant maps from a slightly later period, but clearly a known individual or group from closer to the end of the 7th century is preferable. Here the obvious choice is Bede: he was not only close in time, knew members of the Iona community, and was familiar with Adomnán's writings, but addressed himself explicitly to the question of the location of his island, Britain, with regard to the wider world. However, Bede's view is a topic in itself; here we can do no more than glance at one or two texts.

The most important Bedan text on the location of these islands is the opening chapter of the first book of the *Historia Ecclesiastica Gentis Anglorum* (*HE*).[28] This accords perfectly with what we have found in Adomnán: Britain is an 'island in the Ocean', off the north-western coast of Europe, and is far north in latitude towards the pole. To the south, on the mainland of Europe, the closest land is Belgic Gaul, while – on the opposite side – presumably as one faces north, lies the limitless Ocean. The *Orcades* are located in the Ocean off that side of Britain. Ireland, apart from being described as an Ocean island rich in milk, honey and vines, has a more favourable latitude – Bede's evidence is that it has a more clement climate where snow does not lie for more than three days – and so is presumably further south than Britain.[29] Bede's *De Natura Rerum* (*CCSL* 123A, 174-234), unlike Isidore's, does not have a chapter devoted to the Ocean.[30] However, in the chapter on the division of the lands (ch li) he states that the three continents are bounded by the Ocean (*Oceano cinctus*). Any number of other examples could be supplied. For instance in his commentary on the Song of Songs he states the need to explain things about Arabia and India to those like himself brought up far from that world on 'an island in the Ocean.' More locally, he states in the *Historia Abbatum* that Abbot Benedict 'crossed the Ocean' when he travelled to Gaul.[31] The evidence seems to indicate that our understanding of the mental geography of the monks on Iona may not be too wide of the mark.

28 The *HE* is referred to in the edition and translation of Colgrave and Mynors (1969). 29 These details not only accord with Adomnán, but are consistent with our hypothetical map (Fig 3). 30 *De Natura Rerum* xxxix does not deal with the Ocean *per se*, but with the disputed question *De aestu oceani* which Isidore dodged by saying that only God really knew. 31 These last two examples are taken from Jones (1969, 120-21), who gives a brief treatment of Bede's views of the seas.

Adomnán's Monastery of Iona

Aidan MacDonald

I confine myself here to a discussion of the monastery of Iona as it is reflected in Adomnán's life of Columba (*VC*).[1] So I am resisting the temptation to attempt a more inclusive survey by taking advantage of the important work that has been carried out there and published in recent times. There are, I suggest, two advantages inherent in this decision. The first is that it provides clearly defined and manageable limits to a topic that could otherwise too easily become both involved and diffuse. The second is that concentration more or less exclusively on the evidence of the life should highlight what Adomnán does and does not tell us. This might help to clarify matters where any attempt is being made to construct a picture of the Columban monastery based on information supplied by all categories of evidence, documentary, archaeological and toponymic.

These two advantages perhaps need to be stressed, because the evidence afforded by Adomnán is, inevitably, incomplete – indeed fragmentary. Adomnán is not concerned to describe explicitly details of the monastery and monastic life that would be entirely familiar to, probably, the majority of his readers: he takes much for granted – far more than we would wish. On the other hand, the monastery and monastic round provide the mundane background to the miraculous element that bulks so large in the life as a whole. As hagiographer, Adomnán must have been aware that his claims on behalf of Columba as miracle-worker – so as saint – might provoke resistance, as much, perhaps, from political as from strictly religious motives. His settings, therefore, had to be real and recognisable in order to ground the miraculous in shared everyday experience. So it is more often than not in incidental detail – the contextual detail of the stories and episodes that are his paramount concern – that he is most informative, certainly for the archaeologist, probably for the historian also. It is, of course, a service that he himself would not have envisaged.

---

1 The *VC* is referred to in the edition and translation of Anderson and Anderson (1961; rev edn Anderson 1991). Individual references are by book and chapter numbers – occasionally also by the section number of the Latin text, for more specific location in a long chapter. I have also consulted with advantage the translation of Sharpe (1995).

Even within this limited scope, however, there are two further considerations that pose at least potential problems. The first is that any picture of the monastery and monastic life derived from Adomnán must be a composite and so probably somewhat artificial one. Though doubtless many aspects remained unchanged from the mid-6th to the late 7th century, we cannot be sure, whenever and wherever the question may arise, whether we are being shown Columba's monastery or Adomnán's. As I say, there were probably many areas of essential continuity. But, where change may reasonably be expected to have occurred, or where there may be doubt of any kind for any reason, it seems safer in principle to assume that Adomnán reflects the situation that is familiar to him and his contemporaries of the second half of the 7th century (cf. Sharpe 1995, 74). The second potential problem is that, just as Adomnán is to a significant extent portraying his ideal abbot in St Columba, so too, to some extent at least, he may be portraying Iona as his ideal monastic community. In view of what I have said already, any such idealization would probably not affect fundamentally the nature and value of the information he affords on the workaday world of the monastery, its life and its physical environment. But it might have some bearing on his portrayal of the community precisely as religious community; and this possibility should be kept in mind.

One or two other preliminary considerations need to be aired at the outset, if only because some common assumptions about the nature of early Irish monastic settlements need, I think, to be revised. In the first place, I believe that Columba's and Adomnán's Iona, like many contemporary Irish foundations inside and outside the life, was a proper monastery. By that I mean something significantly different from the probably larger and more complex, increasingly secularized and multifunctional ecclesiastical settlements, approaching urban status, of which we seem to be increasingly aware in Ireland from (perhaps) the second half of the 8th century (cf. Sharpe 1995, 81-2). On the one hand, I suggest that 6th- to 7th-century Iona, and many other Irish monastic churches of the time, were originally regular cenobitic monasteries of a kind or kinds that would have been familiar enough in the late Roman world, East and West, or in contemporary Europe and (from the 7th century) Anglo-Saxon England. In other words, they were more or less enclosed and integrated religious communities living a common life under a common discipline and authority – whether or not such communal organization was articulated explicitly in a written rule. While they acknowledged an interdependent relationship with the lay world around them, they lived secluded lives as detached as possible from that world for the sake of their proper spiritual goal – the contemplative search for God. On the other hand, I suggest that there may have been qualitative as well as quantitative changes at work during the 8th century that led eventually not only to a dilution and diminution, perhaps isolation, of the strictly monastic element in the more materially successful churches (at least); but also to centrifugal tendencies within communities that resulted in fragmentation and consequently the individualism, impatient to a degree of centralized authority, that is so often regarded as characteristic of the early Irish Church – indeed of 'Celtic' Christianity at large. Such changes may have been facilitated, if not actually produced, by the progressive accommodation of the Irish Church to secular society; and by the growth of 'monastic' confederations partly at the expense of originally non-monastic churches.

It seems reasonable to suppose that the character – in terms of its structure, discipline and observance – of the particular group or community that built and occupied a particular settlement, will be reflected, just as much as its numerical size, in the character of the buildings and ground-plan of that settlement. Thus, the greater the emphasis on the common life, the more the main buildings of the monastery, their internal arrangements and their disposition within the enclosure, should reflect that emphasis. Conversely, the greater the emphasis on individual responsibility and activity, in eremitic or semi-eremitic groups, the more the buildings and ground-plans of the settlements of such groups are likely to reflect such basically centrifugal tendencies. Since an important part of my discussion of, especially, the principal domestic buildings of 6th- to 7th-century Iona is based on the premise that we are dealing with a fully cenobitic monastery, with all that that probably entails, I must now try to establish a convincing case that such an argument is tenable – not, of course, mathematically demonstrable – on the basis of the evidence that Adomnán provides.

Adomnán establishes Columba at the beginning of the life as 'father and founder of monasteries' (second Preface 2a). His essential role, then, is in the context of community. His community of monasteries might, admittedly, have been one of small eremitic or semi-eremitic groups, but there is no hint that this was so. Indeed, Adomnán's Columba is really only conventionally an ascetic (I believe – without detraction) and in no sense a solitary: he does not practise formal periodic private retreat. Yet such periodic retreat was practised by seniors of Columban communities, at any rate not long after Columba's day, if we may legitimately infer that Áedán's frequent withdrawals to Farne Island, mentioned by Bede (*HE* iii. 16),[2] reflect a discipline that he had originally learned as a monk of Iona (*HE* iii. 3, 5). (I will return to the anchoritic element in Columban monasticism later.) Adomnán's vignette of Columba at the end of the second Preface (4ab – 5a) portrays, I suggest, his ideal monk, enclosed and contemplative. But, while it may be readily interpreted as an ideal held up to a cenobitic community, there is nothing here

2 The *HE* is referred to in the edition and translation of Colgrave and Mynors (1969).

that points incontrovertibly to a predominant element of individualist asceticism – let alone to an avowedly eremitic ideal. It is also, surely, a noteworthy reflection of the kind of community over which Adomnán has Columba preside that he accords his exemplary abbot no explicitly pastoral role outwith the monastery; and only a very limited missionary one.

Around Columba and under his paternal authority is gathered the community. I will discuss the structure of the community briefly later: here I am concerned with its overall character. The very beginnings of Iona reflect cenobitic community symbolically, since Adomnán has Columba accompanied on his original journey to Britain by twelve companions (iii. 3, but 107a in the Latin text), whose number is that both of Christ's apostles and of the tribes of Israel (cf. Holzherr 1994, 10 and n 76). In fact, community is explicitly mentioned: 'his (Columba's) community of monks' (i. 1, 6b – *cenubialem coetum*: Iona is *cenubium* in iii. 23, 128a, Clonmacnoise likewise in i. 3, 14a, 15b); 'the monks of his congregation' (iii. 23, 125a – *monaci familiares*); 'my family of monks' (iii. 23, 126a – *meis familiaribus monacis*); 'only my family of monks' (iii. 23, 133b – *mei soli familiares monaci*). In iii. 8, the monastery of *Campus Lunge* under Baíthíne is described both as *eclesiae collectio* 'community of the church' and as *congregatio* (111a). Columba's paternal solicitude for his monks is shown (i. 29, 37; ii. 28; iii. 8, 23, 124b – 125a (cf. ii. 28), 126ab, 129ab). He gives orders to the assembled brothers, or to such of them as are present (i. 4, 32; ii, 3; iii, 12, 16; cf. iii. 23, 129ab). In i. 29 Laisrén at Durrow and in i. 37 Baíthíne in Iona direct collective work as Columba's lieutenants. Indeed, collective work is mentioned several more times: i. 3 (by implication, Clonmacnoise); ii. 28, 29; iii. 12 (by implication); iii. 15, 23 (124b; cf. ii. 28) – including instances in Adomnán's own time and experience (ii. 45, first and second occasions). The community's fundamental separation from the world is underlined by the account of Columba's funeral (iii. 23, 133b – 134a). As we shall see, though the principle of individual initiative in the matter of private devotion, both in the church and elsewhere, was apparently accepted (cf. second Preface 4b; ii. 26; iii. 8, 16, 18, 19, 20, 21 – of Columba himself), the church was the focus of communal worship and prayer, for both ordinary and extraordinary occasions. Perhaps these are merely random considerations – straws in the wind: but a similar case cannot be made for a high degree of individualism.

Obedience, furthermore, is a constantly recurring theme. And it is only in this context that we see brothers acting individually. In i. 22, 31, 32, 34, 41, 48; ii. 27, 33 (80b); iii. 11 and 12, we meet brothers, singly, in pairs, or collectively, including his attendant Diarmait, obeying Columba's various commands. Individual monks sail to Ireland in obedience to his instructions as Columba's emissaries on various missions (i. 18; ii. 4, 5, 38). But all members of the monastic hierarchy are under obedience. In i. 37, a *senior* makes known his inner experience at Baíthíne's behest. And in iii. 17, Columba celebrates Sunday mass in obedience to the unanimous decision of the four monastic founders who are visiting him on *Hinba*. Moreover, the virtue of obedience is also inculcated by its opposite: disobedience always produces admonitory results. In i. 6, Columba explicitly attributes Cormac's impending failure in his quest for a desert place in the ocean to the fact that one of his companions on the voyage, 'being the monk of a religious abbot, has departed without the abbot's consent'. In i. 19, the whale seems to threaten the disobedient Berach; while a little later Baíthíne's faith causes it to disappear at once. And in iii. 16, a brother who has deliberately transgressed Columba's express command is compelled – by a guilty conscience rather than by fear of what he has seen – to confess his fault publicly.

According to the *Rule of St Benedict*, there are four types of monk, of which 'the first is that of the cenobites, who serve under Rule and abbot in the monastery' (Holzherr 1994, 41-2). Bede, at any rate, clearly believed that this was the category to which the community of Iona belonged. Columba was, for him, 'a true monk in life no less than habit', *habitu et uita monachi insignis*; and 'he left successors distinguished for their great abstinence, their love of God, and their observance of the Rule', *successores ... regularique institutione insignes* (*HE* iii. 4). Áedán, then, founder and first bishop of Lindisfarne (635-51), brought the (monastic) discipline of Iona, in which he had been formed, to Northumbria: up to the time when Bede wrote his life of Cuthbert (c 721?), the abbot of Lindisfarne ruled the monastery, and all clerical grades, including the bishop, 'keep the monastic rule in all things', *monachicam per omnia ... regulam seruent* (*LC* 208-9).

Monks could be in priest's orders and in Columba's community there were clearly several priests. There were Columba himself (i. 44; ii. 39, 87a-88b; iii. 11, 12, 17, 23, 125ab: his diaconate as a young man in Ireland is also mentioned, in ii. 1 (i. 1) and 25); Baíthíne (ii. 15, chapter heading); and Columba's uncle Ernán (i. 45). Máel Odráin mocu-Curin, Adomnán's informant for i. 20, appears to have been a priest of Derry. Elsewhere, Findchán, founder of the monastery of *Artchain* in Tiree, is a priest (i. 36: there is nothing to indicate that *Artchain* was a Columban monastery). In i. 2, Adomnán tells a story of the young St Fintan mocu-Moie (Munnu of Taghmon, Co. Wexford), giving as his informant an elderly priest and monk of Fintan's. On the other hand, some monastic communities, perhaps usually small ones, may not have had a resident priest: this seems to be a possible interpretation of the background to an episode (i. 40) at Trevet, Co. Meath, which Adomnán describes as a *monasteriolum* (Sharpe 1995, 142-3, 301-2, nn 176-7).

Adomnán does not seem to have envisaged a resident bishop in Columba's community. In i. 44, the saint defers at Sunday mass to a visiting bishop from Munster, travelling apparently *incognito*. In i. 36, a bishop is summoned by Findchán to his monastery of *Artchain* to participate in an irregular priestly ordination. So it is interesting to note that there was in all probability a resident bishop at Iona during at least the later years of Adomnán's own abbacy. *Ceti epscop*, who is named in the list of guarantors of the decisions of the Synod of Birr (697), is to be identified with Coeddi, bishop of Iona, who died in 712 (Ní Dhonnchadha 1982, 180, 191 (no 21); Anderson 1922 I, 213; cf. Anderson & Anderson 1961, 101-2; Anderson 1991, xliv-xlv). It seems likely enough, from his presence at Birr, that he was already associated with Iona (or at least with the Columban community) at that date.

It seems theoretically reasonable to assume (I have already done so in practice) the existence of common features shared by different monasteries of apparently the same basic kind. It is hardly likely that Adomnán would mention, without qualification, a feature of some monastery that was not also present at Iona or a dependency and so perfectly familiar to his domestic readership. It seems quite legitimate, therefore, to illustrate an aspect of the monastic settlement at Iona, if necessary, by reference to another Irish site that certainly or probably represents a monastic community of the same type. This assumption seems safe enough in general terms: it does not imply a uniform or even standardized architecture and ground-plan, such as the claustral arrangement of later medieval times (the Benedictine abbey of Iona, for example). There is no evidence, that I am aware of, for any significant tendencies towards such standardization in pre-12th-century Ireland or Gaelic Scotland. On the other hand, I doubt that the layout at sites such as 6th- to 7th-century Iona was as haphazard as is usually assumed – as I hope to show.

The buildings of Iona in Columba's and Adomnán's days were wooden and probably normally thatched (cf. Sharpe 1995, 318, n 213).

The church

The church (there was apparently only one) was the focal point of the community's religious life. Not surprisingly, therefore, Adomnán mentions it fairly often: i. 8, 22, 32, 37 (probably Iona); ii. 14, 40, 42 (on the first occasion, certainly Iona; on the second, probably so), 45 (twice certainly, 'third occasion'); iii. 12 (probably Iona), 13 (not explicitly named, but clearly implied), 19, 20 (probably Iona), 23 (125b – 126a, 128b, 129b – 130b, 133a (Columba's death)). Adomnán usually calls it *eclesia* or *oratorium* (interchangeably it seems), once *sacra domus* (iii. 19). Doubtless it was not unlike Bishop Fínán's church at Lindisfarne (after 651), built 'after the Irish method, *more Scottorum*, not of stone but of hewn oak' and thatched 'with reeds' (*HE* iii. 25). The framework of the building was presumably provided by vertical (and also horizontal?) squared timbers, set directly in the ground or into horizontal beams laid in shallow trenches. The walls of this important building may have been of planks rather than of interwoven wattle panels coated with clay (cf. Sharpe 1995, 67-8). The roof was probably open (the problematic word *parasticia*, 126a, 'roof-courses' (Andersons), 'roof' (Sharpe), is discussed by Anderson and Anderson (1961, 112, 588 (Index of Latin words)); and by Sharpe (1995, 372, n 401)). The main floorspace was large enough to accommodate the entire monastic community, or such of it as was present at any given time (singing in choir is explicitly referred to in i. 37 and iii. 12). There may have been only one window, in the centre of the east wall above the altar. If the building were of any size, however, more light might well have been required. Extra windows along the south wall might have been preferred: in that case, the *exedra* (below) might have been attached to the north wall. The church was apparently lit at night only by the lamps of the brothers assembled for the office (iii. 23, 130a). It is implied, I think, that it had only one main door (iii. 23, 129b – 130a), probably in the west gable and possibly protected by a porch (in iii. 20, Colcu stands praying for a while one night beside the church door). Indeed, if the gospel really were read in the open air at Sunday mass (cf. iii. 17), then one would have thought that a porch would have been a practical necessity. The altar is mentioned in passing a number of times (i. 44; ii. 1, 39, 88ab, 42, 97a, 45, 100a; iii. 13, 17, 23, 129b), but without further elaboration. The floor might have been of wooden planks: perhaps it was as likely to have been of earth. There is no mention of seating of any kind; or indeed of any furniture.

The ground-plan overall, however, was apparently not a simple rectangle. It was complicated by the existence of a feature that Adomnán calls the *exedra* (iii. 19). This *exedra* has been discussed recently by Anderson and Anderson (1961, 112), MacDonald (1984, 283-4), Anderson (1991, xlvi – xlvii) and Sharpe (1995, 370, n 390). It seems impossible to be certain what precisely is envisaged; and Adomnán's lavish use of terminology is perhaps not altogether helpful. I offer the following tentatively: it is basically an elaboration of the Andersons' alternative suggestion (1961). The *exedra* was an annexe adjoining the church wall on either the north or the south side; and it did not intrude upon the main floorspace. It was entered from the church proper: it has been pointed out that an outside door to the *exedra* is not involved in the story. If Columba prayed before the altar (cf. ii. 42, 97a; iii. 13, 23, 129b), then the connecting doorway through which the heavenly light accompanying him must have streamed was presumably towards the eastern end of the church. It has been suggested that the *exedra* served as a sacristy or as a side-chapel: since Fergna (Virgno) entered it to pray, a function as a chapel certainly seems appropriate. But I suggest that it was actually partitioned and may have served both purposes. The outer compartment was a chapel entered directly from the church. The inner compartment, serving as a sacristy, is what Adomnán calls *illius exedriolae separatum conclave*, 'the separate lockable room of the *exedra*', entered through the 'inner door' –

interior janua – that could, as the word *conclave* implies (Anderson & Anderson 1961, 506, n 2), be locked. Fergna, then, tried to conceal himself from the heavenly light about Columba by retreating through the inner door into the inner compartment or sacristy, leaving the door partly open. It may be objected that, in such case, the door could not have been locked. But Fergna had entered the church alone; and church doors could be locked (ii. 36 – Terryglass). Either Fergna, an aspiring youth and future abbot, was entrusted with keys that could open both locks; or there were occasions, especially when visitors were few or absent (this was winter), when security was relaxed. *Cubiculum* in this context (cf. the chapter heading, discussed later) may refer to the inner *conclave*, or to the whole *exedra*, since the 'inner door' could be said to belong to either: perhaps reference to the *conclave* is more likely (cf. Anderson 1991, xlvii). The implied outer doorway, in this interpretation that communicating between the chapel and the church proper, may not have been closed with a solid door: it might have been left open (*janua* can mean simply 'entrance'), or perhaps curtained. The *exedra*, as an annexe, may have been covered by a lean-to roof at a lower level than that of the church roof proper. Whether or not it had its own windows, any windows lighting the church on that side would then have had to be placed above the roofline of the *exedra*.

Post-holes – all that may survive on excavation – leave everything to the imagination. Such churches could in fact have been quite ornate, both inside and out. Their woodwork could have been carved and painted; and their interiors adorned with paintings, tapestries and ornamental metalwork, the last especially on the altar. Carved gable finials – the crossed ends of the gable rafters – could have risen above the roof ridge (Leask 1955, 43-7). And, if the roof were shingled rather than thatched, the wooden shingles could have been variously shaped and coloured and laid so as to produce decorative patterns (cf. perhaps the 'Temple Page' in the Book of Kells, folio 202 v: Henry 1974, pl 68).

Communal prayer in the church consisted primarily in the celebration of the eucharist and the performance of the divine office. The eucharist was celebrated on Sundays and on feast-days; not, it seems, on ordinary weekdays. The canonical hours would have been recited at set intervals, the details of the timetable varying somewhat according to the time of year. The daily and to some extent also the nightly discipline of a religious community such as Iona was thus a highly structured one. There was, presumably, variation in the actual details of observance, with respect to the number of hours, their times and the intervals between them, from one monastery or monastic confederation to another. It does not seem possible to reconstruct in its entirety the practice of Iona at this period; and in any case, I am not qualified to make the attempt. (Discussion will be found in Anderson & Anderson 1961, 119-

24; Anderson 1991, lii-liii; and Sharpe 1995, 71-2, 311, n 202, 323-4, n 238, 348, n 344, 366-7, nn 378-9, 368-9, n 387, with references.) The liturgical language, as in western Christendom generally, was Latin.

The community could also be assembled in the church on extraordinary occasions (i. 8, 22; ii. 42, 96b-97b, 45 ('first occasion' – by implication); iii. 13). Usually, it seems, these were occasions of intercessory or petitionary prayer. At such times, as for the regular services, the brothers were summoned by bell (i. 8; ii. 42, 96b; iii. 13, 23, 129b: cf. Sharpe 1995, 269, n 82).

The church was also used for private prayer, both by day (ii. 14, 40) and by night (iii. 19, 20).

The cemetery

It would seem reasonable to suppose that the monastic cemetery lay adjacent to the church. It was, presumably, within the enclosure at any rate. The position at Derry in i. 20 might have thrown some light on that at Iona, if only in terms of broad comparableness, if one could be sure that *eclesia* there meant 'church as building' rather than 'church as community'. Sharpe thinks it more likely (1995, 281, n 112) that the local people sought refuge within the enclosure generally, under ecclesiastical protection. I also think that this is the more probable interpretation in the context. Indeed Adomnán uses *eclesia* in the sense of the 'ecclesial community' on several occasions: i. 2 (11a, 'among all the churches of the Irish' – *per universas Scotorum eclesias*); i. 3 (15b, 'the churches of Ireland' – *Scotiae eclesias* – twice); i. 5 (Iona is Columba's 'mother church' – *matrix eclesia*); i. 17 (Colcu, Áed Draigniche's son, is 'head of a church' – *primarius ... eclesiae*); ii. 24 (71b-72a, persecutor(s) of churches – *eclesiarum persec(qu)utor(es)*); ii. 45 (101b, Iona as *eclesia* contrasted with *plebei*, 'lay people'); iii. 8 (111a, *Campus Lunge* is Baíthíne's *eclesia* at the time); iii. 19 (chapter heading, Fergna abbot of the *eclesia* of Iona); iii. 22 (124a, 'the prayers of many churches' – *multarum ... eclesiarum ... orationes*); iii 23 (128a, 'saints ... of other churches' – *aliarum eclesiarum*, 131a, 'Saint Columba, the pillar of many churches' – *sanctus Columba multarum columna eclesiarum*). (For more detailed discussion, see MacDonald 1984, 278-80.)

The matter is complicated by the fact that lay people could be buried in Iona, whether by concession (therefore males only?), or by right we are not told (i. 16 – Ernán will eventually be buried 'on this island' – *in hac insula*). It does not seem to be the case that Iona supported a resident lay population in Columba's time. A timely windstorm cut off the island from the outside world for the duration of Columba's funeral ceremonies, so that only his family of monks (*mei soli familiares monaci*) was allowed to perform the obsequies (iii. 23, 133b-134a). The favour is pointless if, in Adomnán's knowledge, a lay population had been in fact already present and so able to attend also. Adomnán's attitude to monastic burial is, however, both exclusive and also markedly eschatological in outlook. A monk is buried with his fellow-monks and in expectation of the bodily resurrection (cf. Sharpe 1995, 340, n 318). Columba prophesies of Librán (ii. 39, 92ab), 'You will die in one of my monasteries; and your part in the kingdom will be with my elect monks, and with them you will awake from the sleep of death into the resurrection of life.' This is fulfilled at the end of the chapter: 'And he was buried among the elect monks of Saint Columba [at Durrow] ... to rise again into eternal life.' Similarly, of Ernéne mocu Fir-roide (iii. 23, 132a): 'He (himself a holy monk) lies buried among the remains of other monks of Saint Columba, and awaits the resurrection with the saints, in the ridge of Tóimm' (Drumhome, Co. Donegal). And of Columba himself, 'the venerable body ... was wrapped in clean fine cloths, and laid in the appointed burial-place that had been made ready, and was interred with fitting veneration, to rise again in bright and eternal light': the windstorm, meanwhile, maintaining the privacy of the community for the entire three days and nights of the funeral ceremonies (iii. 23, 133a-134a). Adomnán seems sure, indeed, that a monk's heavenly life also is lived with his community: monastic profession has explicitly an eternal dimension. These considerations make it most unlikely, to my mind, that he would have envisaged or tolerated a mixed monastic-lay cemetery on Iona (or elsewhere), either in theory or in practice. I think it may be maintained confidently that there were at least two cemeteries here – the monastic within, the lay outwith the enclosure.

His reference to Columba's burial in expectation of the bodily resurrection suggests to me that the saint's mortal remains had not been translated and enshrined when Adomnán wrote (cf. Sharpe 1995, 374-5, n 411). The other relevant passages are perhaps not altogether conclusive in this regard: the posthumous function of his pillow-stone (iii. 23, 129a); divine light about and angelic visits to 'the place in which his holy bones repose' (iii. 23, 135ab). It is, admittedly, unwise to base positive arguments on Adomnán's silences; but, if Columba's primary relics *had* been enshrined by this time, it is at least surprising that he makes no mention of the fact. There is, moreover, no explicit reference to pious recourse to the saint's tomb or shrine to solicit his intercession, especially for miraculous cures for bodily or mental ills (though it was visited, presumably for purposes of prayer (135ab): cf. Sharpe 1995, 377-8, n 421). Indeed, the cult of relics plays a noticeably inconspicuous part in the life as a whole; and involves the use of secondary relics only. In ii. 44, Columba's white tunic and books in his own handwriting are deployed by Adomnán to help end a drought. In ii. 45 ('first occasion'), Adomnán lays garments and books of Columba on the altar, 'with psalms and fasting, and invocation of his name', to obtain favourable winds through his intercession for bringing building timbers by sea to Iona. In ii. 8 and 9, again, leaves or books in Columba's handwriting seem to be well on the way to acquiring the veneration accorded to relics (ii. 8 is explicitly posthumous; 9 is probably so also). But that is about all.

The 'great house'

What is pretty clearly, to my mind, the principal domestic building of the enclosure is called by Adomnán both *magna domus*, 'great house', and *monasterium*. In iii. 15, a brother falls from the top of what is called in the chapter heading the *monasterium rotundum*, in the text the *magna domus*, then being built at Durrow. It is clearly a building whose height was potentially dangerous. It is not clear, however, that it is the same building which is referred to in i. 29, where Laisrén is driving Columba's monks 'in the construction of a large building' – *in alicujus majoris domus fabrica* (cf. Sharpe 1995, 292, n 138; Anderson & Anderson 1961, 265, n 9; Anderson 1991, 56, n 61). In ii. 45 ('first occasion') timbers are being brought by sea to Iona, for, amongst other things, the *magna domus*; on the 'second occasion', similarly, oak timbers are being brought from the mainland 'for the restoration of our monastery' – *ad nostrum renovandum ... monasterium*. But here the monastery as a whole may be meant. In i. 24, the first reference to the *monasterium* is clearly to a domestic building; the second *might* be to the monastery as a whole, but is perhaps more likely to be to the same building. In i. 4 Columba, 'sitting in the house' – *sedens in domu* – issues orders to the brothers (cf. perhaps iii. 12): the *magna domus* may be meant.

The 'great house' presumably functioned as a building suitable for daytime indoor activities; for assembly; and for recreation. Studies – reading, writing (including copying – cf. Sharpe 1995, 284-5, n 125) and teaching – were probably an important, if possibly specialized, part of such activities (cf. i. 23, 24, 43, 43b; ii. 40 (though Columba may be in his *tegoriolum*); iii. 18 and 23, 128b). Books were probably stored here, in a *scrini(ol)um* (ii. 8, 9: 'coffer' – Andersons; 'book case' – Sharpe: the same two chapters also mention skin book satchels – *pellicius sacculus*), or *scrini(ol)a.* These facilities may have been available to visiting students (such as Columba certainly taught), as well as to members of the community. In the days of Bishops Fínán and Colmán of Lindisfarne, many English people of all sorts repaired to Ireland, either for the sake of religious studies or to pursue a more ascetic life. Some settled into the monastic life, while others moved as peripatetic students from one teacher to another. 'The Irish welcomed them all gladly' says Bede (*HE* iii. 27), 'gave them their daily food, and also provided them with books to read and with instruction, without asking for any payment.' Many Irish (and eventually also Pictish) students may well have availed themselves of any such generosity on the part of Iona during the later 6th and 7th centuries.

The 'great house' may also have contained the refectory and kitchen. The

Andersons made this inference on the basis of the reference to a hearth and a vessel containing water in the *monasterium* in i. 24 (1961, 113; 1991, xlviii). This is possible, though the evidence is scarcely conclusive. One or more cooking and heating hearths might have sufficed for a small community such as Iona may have been originally. But a larger community, such as that over which Adomnán very likely presided, would probably have required the more formal arrangement of a proper kitchen. In fact, there is no explicit reference to a kitchen as such. And the only explicit reference to the refectory, *refectorium*, is to that at Aghaboe (ii. 13).

The main meal of the day was taken probably after nones (3 pm: cf. ii. 13). On Wednesdays (i. 26) and doubtless on Fridays, during most of the year, the community fasted until then. Ordinarily, there was presumably a (second) meal before this hour; and on Sundays and solemn feast-days there was an additional small meal (iii. 12). (See Anderson & Anderson 1961, 122; Anderson 1991, liii; Sharpe 1995, 324, n 239.) In i. 29, furthermore, it is implied that working monks might be provided with extra food and rest to sustain them against heavy labour in bad weather.

A word must be said about the monastic diet. In actual fact, Adomnán mentions explicitly as foods only bread, fish, fruit and milk. Bread seems to have been the staple (iii. 23, 126ab; cf. ii. 13 and Sharpe 1995, 319-20, n 219). Indeed, a baker is actually baking in iii. 10 (*pistor, opus pistorium exercens*), as Columba experiences a vision. Fishing on a small scale is the subject of ii. 19; but in iii. 23 (132a) the operation seems to be a larger one – perhaps geared to supplying a community. Sea-fishing, however, is apparently not mentioned. The garden (a gardener – *hortulanus* – is named in the chapter heading of i. 18) may have supplied fruit and vegetables; and herbs for culinary as well as for medicinal purposes (cf. Sharpe 1995, 279, n 106, 288, n 132 (referring to i. 27)). If the *monasterium* of Durrow, on the south side of which grew the fruit tree of ii. 2, is the 'great house' rather than the monastery as a whole, then monastic gardens may have contained fruit trees; or orchards may have been cultivated separately within the enclosure. Milk was clearly important (ii. 16; iii. 23, 127ab) – to the extent that it was apparently taken on voyages (in a milk-skin, ii. 38). Was meat eaten? The community owned a seal rookery, though we are not told what its function was in the monastic economy (i. 41: cf. Sharpe 1995, 302-3, n 181). The same chapter describes Columba ordering the killing of wethers, *berbices*, for the frustrated thief; and the despatch of a 'fat beast', *pingue pecus*, and six measures of grain from *Campus Lunge* to the same thief as last gifts before his (foreseen) death. In ii. 29, the monastic slaughter of cattle is envisaged, though the story requires that the attempted killing in this case be unsuccessful: the specific purpose of the attempt is not mentioned. Cattle and sheep could represent meat, milk, hides and wool. Meat was probably offered in the guest-house;

perhaps also to the sick. Hides would have been needed for, among other things, books, boats and boots; and wool would have been needed for clothing at the least. On the basis of the evidence provided by Adomnán, we may not take it for granted that the community of Iona ate meat in this period (cf. Sharpe 1995, 331–2, n 280). There is no mention of beer or a brewhouse; and wine (ii. 1 (i. 1); cf. i. 50, 52a) which might have formed part of a cargo in the Gaulish ship that puts in at a port in Argyll in i. 28: Anderson & Anderson 1961, 124; Sharpe 1995, 290–91, nn 135–6) may have been reserved for liturgical use. Writing of the immediate aftermath of the Synod of Whitby (664), Bede refers to the frugality and austerity of Bishop Colmán and his predecessors; and to the 'simple daily fare' of the brothers (*HE* iii. 26). Assuming, once more, that Irish practice at Lindisfarne followed that of the mother-house, Bede's words likewise do not support any notion that the 6th- to 7th-century community of Iona lived off the fat of the land (cf. McCormick this vol).

The refectory and kitchen, on the other hand, and the bakehouse perhaps implied in iii. 10, might eventually have been located separately, in view of the ever-present risk of fire.

It is normally assumed that Irish monks lived (or at least slept) singly or in twos and threes, in small cells scattered individually about the enclosure. This may have been true of eremitic and semi-eremitic settlements; and of all or most sites at a later date. I have argued before (MacDonald 1984, 285–9) that the night-quarters of Columban monks formed for all practical purposes a dormitory. This dormitory may have been in the 'great house' also and need not have been strictly an open one. On the basis of such evidence, admittedly, as Adomnán affords, a case can be made for either arrangement equally convincingly or unconvincingly. So my appeal here is largely to my belief in the essentially cenobitic character of the monastery of Iona (as I discussed earlier) and to common sense. The task of regulating communal discipline must have been immeasurably more difficult for the abbot and his assistants if the brothers were accommodated alone or in small groups in isolated cells. In other words, if the buildings and ground-plan of the settlement reflect the character of the community or group that built and occupied it, a cenobitic monastery accordingly should reflect basically centripetal, not centrifugal, tendencies.

In iii. 6, Columba visits a dying monk. The building in which the monk lies is *domus* and it is to be noted that the possessive pronoun does not accompany it: *ocius domum egreditur* – 'he quickly left the house'; *post sancti de domu secessum viri* – 'after the holy man had gone away from the house'. The monk's bed is *lectulus*. It appears that the *domus* was near or adjacent to the *plateola monasterii* – 'the court of the monastery'. In iii. 12, as 'the brothers were putting on their shoes in the morning, preparing to go the various labours of the monastery' – *dum fratres se calciantes mane ad diversa monasterii opera ire praepararent* – Columba changes an ordinary weekday into a feast-day. In arguing that a natural interpretation of this passage is that the monks have just risen and are still in or near their (collective) sleeping-quarters, when Columba addresses them collectively, I am aware that this explanation seems to exclude the possibility of a canonical hour of prime. But Adomnán is not giving us a systematic and detailed account of the initial daily routine. His attention is focused on the radical change of that routine as a necessary preliminary to the revelation of Columba's prophetic vision that is the primary interest of the chapter. Admittedly, a possible compression of the usual sequence of events here makes the significance of the passage uncertain for present purposes. *Monasterium* in this context almost certainly means the monastery as a whole. In iii. 20, the brother Colcu, disturbed by his nocturnal experience of heavenly light about Columba in the church, 'returned to his dwelling' – *domum revertitur* – where *domum* could mean 'to (the – his) *domus*' or simply 'home', I take it.

The individual sleeping-quarters of the brothers are described in the chapter heading of iii. 19, as *cubicula*, primarily 'resting- or sleeping-chamber(s), bedchamber(s)' (cf. *cubare*, 'to lie down, recline, sleep'). As we have already seen, *cubiculum* is also used in this chapter, with reference to the church, either of the *exedra* or an inner *conclave*: in either case apparently a compartment opening off a larger space. In i. 39, Columba foretells of an impenitent and stiff-necked sinner that he will eventually be caught and killed by his enemies 'lying in the same bed-chamber with a harlot' – *in eodem cum meritrice cubantem cubiculo*. The context here is presumably secular: compare, in the case of the partly related prophecy in i. 38, *cum meritrice in eodem lectulo cubanti* – 'as he reclines on the same couch with a harlot'. Monastic *cubicula* are, I suggest, individual bedchamber compartments opening, probably without doors, onto an inner area (in a circular building), or a corridor (in a rectangular one).

Writing of St Cuthbert's priorate of Lindisfarne during the period immediately following the Synod of Whitby and the departure of the Irish community (664-76), Bede, describing his nocturnal devotions and activities, says: 'Moreover he was so zealous in watchings and prayer that he is believed many times to have spent three or four nights on end in watching; since during that length of time he did not go to his own bed *(lectum)*, nor had he any place outside the dormitory of the brethren to rest in' – *neque extra dormitorium fratrum locum aliquem in quo pausare posset haberet* (*LC* 210-11). Bede is not, of course, a firsthand authority here. But he seems to be reflecting local tradition; and he was writing for and at the request of the bishop and community of Lindisfarne, who vetted his work (ibid., Prologue). Some foreshortening of perspective may, however, have occurred inevitably in his retrospective view. And it is possible that already at this time – certainly by 699 to 705 – Lindisfarne had been visibly influenced by the rule of St Benedict (cf. the anonymous *Life of St Cuthbert* (*LC* 94-7, 324, n; Holzherr 1994, 154-5), in which unfortunately, there seems to be no equivalent passage). I suggest, therefore, that for present purposes it is relevant to note the existence of a dormitory at Lindisfarne by probably c 700 at latest. But there seems to be no means of determining whether this reflects arrangements modelled earlier on those of Iona; or whether the daughter-house is here showing effects of influences on Northumbria from elsewhere (see Colgrave 1940, 7, 13, 94-7, 206-13, 142-7). Bede seems to imply an open dormitory.

Bede's words also seem to indicate that someone of Cuthbert's monastic rank might be expected to have his own more private quarters. Adomnán's vocabulary points, I think, in the same direction in Columba's case. In iii. 21, Columba's quarters are *hospitiolum* three times and *domus* once – specifically his *hospitiolum* and his *domus* it seems: (*ad*) *domum beati viri, beati viri illud hospitiolum* – 'the house, the lodging of the blessed man'; *ad mei hostium hospitioli* – 'to the door of my lodging'; *ad meum hospitiolum*. In iii. 23 (129a), his *lectulus* in his *hospitiolum* is said to be the bare rock, with a stone for pillow; and in 133a his body is brought back from the church where he has died to his *hospitium*. The combination of *domus* and the more usual diminutive *hospitiolum* indicates to me that Columba's (and his successors'?) quarters were a separate cell and not part of the 'great house' (cf. Sharpe 1995, 334, n 288).

The 'great house' could have been either rectilinear or curvilinear in plan. Compartmentalization could have been achieved in either case. In a circular building, partitions could have been arranged around the perimeter, leaving the central inner space as common ground. It might, however, have been found easier to subdivide the floor-space of a rectangular building on its long axis. The very fact, moreover, that Adomnán describes the *monasterium* of Durrow as *rotundum* in the chapter heading of iii. 15 suggests that that was not the usual outline: if it was, why say so? I believe that we must be prepared for the possible discovery, in whole or in part, of large rectangular common buildings on some monastic sites during future excavations. A secular timber hall tradition is attested on British Celtic as well as on Anglo-Saxon aristocratic sites of this period: a tradition that could be ultimately of Roman origin. (For further general discussion of the *monasterium*, see Anderson & Anderson 1961, 113; MacDonald 1984, 284-9; Anderson 1991, xlviii.)

The guest-house

The guest-house, *hospitium*, is mentioned several times. In i. 4, Columba orders the guest-house in Iona to be prepared against the foreseen arrival of St Cainnech of Aghaboe. In i. 31, Cailtán, prior of *Cella Diuni* beside Loch

Awe, summoned by Columba who has foreseen his impending death, dies in the guest-house at Iona. In i. 32, two pilgrim brothers, having taken the monastic vow at Columba's sudden and unexpected behest, die, one after the other in fulfilment of his prophecy, in the guest-house at Iona. In ii. 3, wattles are brought to Iona by ship for the building of a guest-house, having been taken apparently as of right from a layman's land. At the beginning of ii. 39, Columba receives the penitent Librán in the guest-house at Iona; and at the end, the now aged Librán dies in the guest-house at Durrow. The beginning of i. 50 may mention the guest-house at Coleraine.

The obligation of hospitality was considered a sacred duty among monastic communities. Columba condemns Vigenus in ii. 20 because he 'has spurned Christ in pilgrim guests' – *Christum in peregrinis hospitibus sprevit*: compare Matt 25. 31-46. Iona seems to have received many and various visitors: indeed, they were often a source of news of the outside world, especially Ireland. But the best illustration in the life of monastic hospitality in action is the episode concerning the exhausted crane from northern Ireland, related in i. 48. The bird is not, of course, accommodated in the guest-house proper: but the house, *domus*, in the western part of Iona where it is lodged for the three days and nights of its sojourn is its *hospitium*. The Andersons think (1961, 114; 1991, xlix) that three days and nights might have been the obligatory period for the maintenance of transitory guests.

Two other possible functions of the guest-house may be suggested tentatively. First, though the case of Fintan mocu-Moie in i. 2 is admittedly not a good example, I wonder if it was customary to receive postulants here initially. Under St Benedict, if the one seeking admission to the monastery passed the first test, he was then lodged in the 'room for guests', *cella hospitum*, for a few days. Cassian, earlier, seems to have advocated a similar arrangement as part of a process of probation. But in fact some such precautionary measure may go back further in the history of cenobitic monasticism (Holzherr 1994, 260-71). Second, the care of guests may often enough have necessitated an additional function of the building as an infirmary. On three separate occasions in the life, visitors sicken and die in the guest-house. No monastic infirmary is mentioned by Adomnán; and it seems that sick or dying brothers were looked after in their own quarters (cf. ii. 30; iii, 6). If these quarters were more or less communal, then isolation was apparently not part of medical practice at Iona at this time.

Unless ii. 3 implies it, there seems to be no indication that there was more than one guest-house. Since, therefore, both clerics and laity appear to have been lodged in the same building, it may have stood within rather than outwith the enclosure. The beds may have been in *cubicula*, as for the brothers. If the food offered to (some) guests was significantly different from that taken by the community, the guest-house may have had its own refectory.

The plate(ol)a

In i. 50 (51a), Columba is presented with the gifts of the local people assembled in his honour in the courtyard of the monastery of Coleraine. The phrase *xenia ... in platea monasterii strata* could mean both 'the gifts laid out in the courtyard of the monastery' and 'the gifts in the paved courtyard of the monastery': the Latin is ambiguous (Anderson & Anderson 1961, 320-21, n 3; Anderson 1991, 90-91, n 123). M Anderson draws attention in this connection (ibid., xlix) to a likely problem with surface water at Iona. But paving would, in any case, seem a sensible way of protecting an area that was in all probability much frequented. It is implied here that the *platea* could hold a large crowd. In iii. 6, Columba walks 'in the court of his monastery' (Iona) – *in plateola sui ... monasterii* – after visiting his dying monk.

The *plate(ol)a* was, I suggest, centrally placed among the principal buildings of the monastery. In this view, the church would have stood on the east side, its (west) door facing onto the courtyard. The 'great house' would have stood on the west side opposite: in iii. 23 (129b – 130a), a few of the brothers approaching the church for the midnight office see, as does Diarmait nearer at hand, angelic light about the dying Columba shining out through the open door of the church. These two pre-eminent buildings only may have bordered the *plate(ol)a*. A separate refectory with kitchen and bakehouse might, however, have delimited the third side. And the guest-house could have stood on or near the fourth (with its main doorway on the other side, facing outwards to the entrance to the enclosure?). If the *plate(ol)a* was rectilinear, it would seem easier so to arrange rectilinear buildings: but I am not thereby suggesting that this observation is in any sense a conclusive argument for the ground-plan of the main domestic buildings of monasteries like Iona. Nor do I suggest that the scheme outlined closely resembles the later medieval claustral plan: even if buildings lined all four sides of the *plate(ol)a*, it need not have been completely enclosed. And as I have indicated, it may have been open on one or two sides. Such a scheme would, on the other hand, point to a greater degree of formal planning, at least for the focal area of a 6th- to 7th-century Irish cenobitic monastery, than we have been prepared to accord conventionally to any pre-12th-century Irish ecclesiastical settlements. Indeed, the mere fact of Adomnán's *plate(ol)a* seems to me to be a pointer in this direction. I have discussed the *plate(ol)a* at greater length elsewhere (MacDonald 1984, 293-7, 301-2).

The enclosure

What else might have lain within the enclosure must have depended to a degree on the relative extent of the enclosure overall and the focal area of the main buildings and the *plate(ol)a*. It probably contained the monastic cemetery, the garden and perhaps an orchard. It may also have accommodated ancillary buildings, not necessarily disposed according to any ordered plan. Carpenters', wrights' and other workshops would have been needed (monks who are skilled metalworkers, for instance, are mentioned in ii. 29: altar vessels as well as tools and farm equipment may have been produced locally). The weaving of clothes, vestments, altar cloths and the like may also have been undertaken partly by the community; though some such articles may have been imported. Adomnán makes no direct reference to a mill, though its existence by his own day may be implied: the millstone into which a cross is fixed (iii. 23, 127a) could, by the late 7th century, have come from a water-powered mill rather than a hand-quern (cf. Sharpe 1995, 373, n 406). But the farm buildings proper seem to have stood outside the enclosure: i. 45, *canaba* (between the monastery and the harbour – 'shed', Anderson & Anderson 1961 and 115; Anderson 1991 and lii; 'corn-kiln', Sharpe 1995 and 308-9, n 195); iii. 23, 'the nearest barn' (*proximum ... horreum*, 126a – the nearest (of several) to the monastery, perhaps, but apparently outside it, 127a, but *proximum* could also mean 'nearby': Anderson 1991, xlix); and compare the *domus-hospitium* in the western part of the island in i. 48. So perhaps all such more mundane buildings lay outside the enclosure proper. It is noteworthy that all three crosses that Adomnán mentions also seem to have stood outside the enclosure. In i. 45, two, both believed to commemorate basically the same event, are situated a short distance apart, apparently on the way between the harbour and the monastery. In iii. 23 (127a), a cross marked the traditional spot in Adomnán's day where Columba rested on his way back from the barn to the monastery on the last day of his life. Again, it seems to have been regarded as essentially commemorative. All three were probably small wooden crosses or stone cross slabs: the last was the one fixed in a millstone (cf. Sharpe 1995, 309-10, n 196).

Columba's day- or writing-hut, his *tegori(ol)um*, was certainly within the enclosure. It is mentioned several times. In i. 25, Columba receives there a clumsy guest who upsets his ink-horn. In i. 35, Colcu Cellach's son is studying there beside the saint. In ii. 16, Columba, writing there, blesses a milk-vessel at a brother's request. (In ii. 29, similarly, while copying a book, he blesses a knife for a brother: the *tegori(ol)um* is clearly implied.) In iii. 15, while writing there, he sends an angel to rescue a brother falling from the roof of the new 'great house' at Durrow. In iii. 22, he has a vision from there (he is presumably writing or reading, but this is not said) of angels sent to escort his soul to heaven, standing on the shore of Mull. Finally, in iii. 23 (128ab), Columba copies a psalter in his *tegori(ol)um* on the last day of his life, the completion of which he bequeaths to his successor Baíthíne. In i. 25, ii. 29 and pretty certainly in iii. 23, the saint is attended by Diarmait; in iii. 15, by two brothers and an angel; and in iii. 22, by two brothers. These could be, if necessary, his agents or messengers. Most of these stories require that the door, or at least its upper half, be open. The hut faces east (i. 25; iii. 22).

The *tegori(ol)um* has been well discussed (Anderson & Anderson 1961, 109-12; Anderson 1991, xlvii-xlviii; Sharpe 1995, 285-6, n 127). So I am concerned here rather with its significance than with its structural details and form. Clearly, it was a visible and tangible symbol both of Columba's abbatial authority and of his scribal activity. Equally clearly, therefore, to my mind, it was so placed that the saint could oversee, as far as possible, both movement into and out of the enclosure and activity within it, while 'applying himself ... to reading, or to writing or some kind of work'. For these purposes, since it faced east, it must have stood at or near the western limits of the enclosure, possibly near an entrance (cf. i. 25; ii. 16, 29). It is not clear to me whether the building survived in Adomnán's day; or whether a traditional site only was known. It is likewise uncertain that it was used by any succeeding abbot, unless perhaps Baíthíne (iii. 23, 128ab). If it did survive more or less intact, then presumably Adomnán describes it as he knew it. But if it did not, I think it possible that his account, while based on local tradition, has been influenced also by his own scholarship – by, e.g., manuscript illustrations known to him of the inspired writer – prophet or saint – seen working in his study (through a window?). Adomnán's *tegori(ol)um*, in other words, may owe as much or more to outside literary sources as to local (oral and/or written) information.

The enclosure (*cenubii septa*, i. 3, 15b – Clonmacnoise) was delimited by the *valum* (sic) *monasterii*, the 'boundary-wall' or 'rampart of the monastery'. It is mentioned twice: i. 3 (14a, Clonmacnoise) and ii. 29 (Iona). While it had some protective function, the *vallum* was rather a spiritual and legal boundary: it was not, in any case, strictly a defensive one. We are used to thinking of one or more banks and ditches or stone walls – the archaeologically visible types of enclosing element. But wooden fences, palisades or hedges may also have been employed: St Wilfrid's monastery at Oundle, where he died in 709, was surrounded by 'a great hedge of thorn' – *sepes magna spinea* (*Life of Bishop Wilfrid* (written probably before 720): Colgrave 1927, x-xi, 146-7). Such barriers might leave little or no trace, even on excavation; and their course might be unidentifiable, especially where they were not accompanied originally by a bank or at least an external ditch. Some enclosures might even have been of mixed construction, depending on how and to what extent local topographical features might have been utilized: hedge or fence here, bank and ditch or wall there. Eventually, monastic or other ecclesiastical *valla* could contain several hectares; but we do not know the extent of the 6th- to 7th-century enclosure at Iona. We are also accustomed now to thinking that a curvilinear outline was normal in Irish (or, more generally, insular Celtic) contexts. There are indications, however, that the enclosure at Iona may have been rectilinear from the outset. (For the early medieval enclosure system here generally, see RCAHMS 1982, 31-3, 36-9. For possibly comparable evidence at Lindisfarne, see O'Sullivan 1989, 125-42, esp 136-40 and fig 11.)

Of the organization of the community reflected by these buildings and this layout we are told very little. Columba overshadows everybody else. He is the sole abbot, both in Scotland and in Ireland – a 'father and founder of monasteries' (second Preface 2a), 'predestined by God to be a leader of innumerable souls to the heavenly country' (iii. 1; cf. i. 2, 13ab – of Fintan mocu-Moie – and iii. 23, 129ab). The heads of Scottish dependencies are 'priors' – *praepossiti* (i. 30, 41; cf. iii. 8 – Baíthíne, of *Campus Lunge*; i. 31 – Cailtán, of *Cella Diuni* (but cf. Sharpe 1995, 293, n 143); i. 45 – Ernán, of *Hinba* (*praepossitura*); ii. 18 – Luigne mocu-Min, (later) of *Elena insula*). In the context of the one Irish church, the relationship of which with Columba seems clear – Durrow – Laisrén's formal office in i. 29 (if any) is not given (he is also a companion of Columba in Ardnamurchan in i. 12). Laisrén is in charge of building work at Durrow in i. 29; Baíthíne is in charge of harvest work in Iona in i. 37. Baíthíne, Columba's first cousin and 'foster-son' or 'disciple, pupil', *alumnus*, was his immediate successor as abbot (i. 2, 11b; iii. 23, 128b; cf. iii. 18); while Laisrén, also closely related to the saint in the next generation, succeeded Baíthíne (Anderson & Anderson 1961, 90, 208, n 9, 502-3, n 16; Anderson 1991, xxxviii, 20-21, n 20; Sharpe 1995, 256-7, n 55, 273-4, n 91). Otherwise, we hear of 'seniors' – *seniores* (i. 3 – *sanctus senior Columba*, *seniores* of Clonmacnoise (14b); i. 37 – a *senior* (38a) speaks for the harvest-workers, *noster senior Columba* (39a); ii. 4 – witness to a miracle of Columba before Abbot Séigíne and other *seniores* (57a); ii. 44 – some *seniores* (99a) act at Adomnán's behest to end a drought; iii. 9 – Columba reveals a vision to a few *seniores* with him; iii. 23 – some *seniores* (132a) as informants of Adomnán); and of 'youths' – *iuvenes* (i. 24 – youth at a task *in monasterio*; i. 28 – same youth hears a prophecy from Columba; ii. 16 – *iuvenis-iuvenculus* comes from the milking; ii. 18 – Columba cures youth of nose-bleed; ii. 31 – Columba cures *iuvenis-iuvenculus* of illness, one of his companions on a journey; ii. 38 – youth retrieves milk-skin; and the future abbot Fergna is a youth in iii. 19 (*iuvenis* specifically in chapter heading)). Simple reflection of age and seniority apart, the more frequently collective reference to seniors suggests that perhaps they were thought of as an abbatial 'council', their status and moral authority, while obviously acknowledged, being possibly not more explicitly defined in terms of specific duties or responsibilities (but cf. Sharpe 1995, 298-9, n 162). Juniors were presumably often more closely involved in the harder physical work of the monastery – though that is not emphasised by the direct references to them. Adomnán's ideal monastic community, setting off, as it were, his ideal abbot, may have always been thought of as small: they are an apostolic twelve who are said to have accompanied Columba on his original voyage to Britain (at the end of iii. 3). The reality of Adomnán's own time was probably quite different. The 'boy of the congregation' at Clonmacnoise (i. 3, 14b – *puer familiaris*), 'not yet approved by the elders', is not necessarily, I take it, evidence for child oblates in these monasteries.

There is no indication that anchorites were maintained in Iona itself in Columba's or in Adomnán's time. During Adomnán's time, Durrow supported the anchorite Fínán nearby (i. 49, 50ab). Possibly those whose solitary vocation was approved were sent to 'the place of the anchorites' – *locus anchoritarum* – at *Muirbolc-már* in *Hinba* (iii. 23, 131b). Indeed, *Hinba* might have trained and screened those who aspired to the solitary life. There is some evidence for a degree of specialization among the Scottish Columban houses (at least). Penitents likewise do not seem to have been accommodated in Iona, but were sent to *Hinba* (i. 21: cf. Sharpe 1995, 282, n 115), or to *Campus Lunge* in Tiree (i. 30: cf. ibid., 303, n 182; ii. 39). Those who sought the 'desert in the ocean', on the other hand, may have sailed from or returned to Iona: i. 20 (Báetán); ii. 42 (Cormac certainly returns to Iona at the end of his second voyage, though he may not have started from there; and at the end of his third voyage he returns to Columba, probably in Iona, which may have been his starting-point also). In ii. 42 it is clear that such voyaging was an activity for which the abbot had some overall concern, and in which the community shared a personal interest; i. 6 (Cormac's first voyage) makes it equally clear that it was also an activity subject to abbatial authority and discipline.

Text archaeology and hypothetical models must, of course, in the last analysis be disciplined by excavation and fieldwork. It is unlikely, however, that the latter methods can ever retrieve more than fragments of the 6th- to 7th-century monastery of Iona: so the former will probably always have their uses. The rich potential of Adomnán's life of Columba as a source of historical and archaeological information remains to be further explored.

Iona: the Archaeology of the Early Monastery

Finbar McCormick

A recent guide to Iona produced by Historic Scotland truthfully states that it is one of Scotland's best known but least understood monuments (Dunbar & Fisher 1995, back cover) (Fig 1). On the one hand, Adomnán's life of Columba (*VC*)[1] has left us a fuller knowledge about life in this early monastery than in any other Irish or Scottish ecclesiastical settlement. In contrast to this, material remains and the results of archaeological excavations have left a rather sparse and incoherent record. With the exception of a few centuries during the post-Reformation period the site has remained a centre of religious activity, and this has inevitably led to the removal of early structural and archaeological evidence. During the Benedictine period, for instance, intensive cultivation in the core of the monastic site, as evidenced by the development of a large depth of artificial garden soil (Shiel 1988, 207-8; McCormick 1993,107), must have destroyed much archaeological evidence for the earlier Columban monastery. In more recent times the demands of renovations in the Benedictine monastery, the digging of service trenches, and even the extension of the graveyard has led to continual removal of archaeological deposits, albeit under professional supervision. This chapter considers the evidence that has been derived from archaeological excavations concerning the early medieval monastery on Iona. Initially, I briefly examine the evidence for pre-Benedictine stone and mortar buildings.

STONE BUILDINGS

During its early centuries, the buildings of the Columban monastery at Iona would have been constructed almost exclusively of wood. Adomnán refers to the importation of oak for the monastic buildings from the mainland (*VC* ii. 45), while wattles are mentioned for the building of the guest-house (*VC* ii. 3). The fashion of building churches in stone seems generally to have been a

---

1 The *VC* is referred to in the translation of Sharpe (1995).

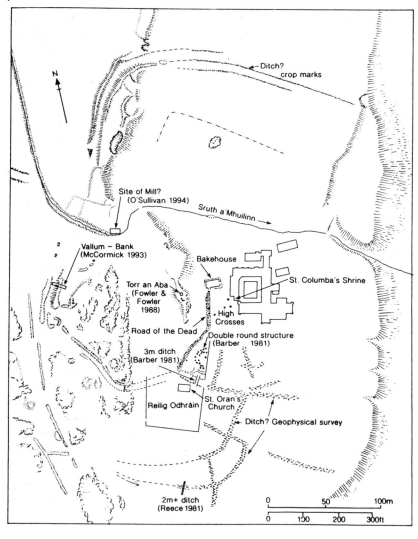

Figure 1 Iona: the monastery and excavated areas (after RCAHMS 1982).

late development in Ireland, the earliest annalistic reference being to the place-name *Dam Liac*, 'stone church' (Duleek), Co. Meath, in 725 *AU*. The literary evidence, however, suggests that the building of stone churches did not become widespread until the 11th and 12th centuries (Edwards 1990, 124). It is possible that stone churches and other monastic buildings were constructed in the Columban monastery during its latter years, but the huge demand for stone created by the erection of the Benedictine monastic complex from 1204 onwards would inevitably have led to the destruction and robbing of these earlier buildings.

The only pre-Benedictine stone buildings to have survived are St Oran's Church and 'St Columba's Shrine'. St Oran's is a small, Romanesque church dating to about the third quarter of the 12th century (RCAHMS 1982, 250). Its recent age would have precluded destruction and robbing by the Benedictine builders. Columba's 'Shrine' (Fig 2) is a small building with *antae*, measuring approximately 3.2 x 2.2 m. Its east-west alignment suggests that it was a church but its small size suggests a tomb-shrine such as St Ciarán's Church at Clonmacnoise, which measures 3.8 x 2.8 m and which also has *antae* (Manning 1994, 26). The identification of Columba's 'Shrine' as a tomb, however, is called into question by the fact that excavation in the vicinity has failed to produce any burial of demonstrably early medieval date, although later graves were found both within and beside the building. One would expect that a saint's tomb would have become an early focus of burial. The building is a likely candidate for being the church mentioned in the 13th-century Icelandic *Heimskringka* in the context of the visit of Magnus Barefoot to Iona in 1098. The church referred to in Snorri Sturluson's saga is described as 'the small church of Columcille' and it is said that 'the king did not go in, but closed the door again immediately, and immediately locked it, and said that none should be so daring thenceforward as to go into that church; and thenceforward it has been so done' (Anderson 1922 I, 107-8). Irrespective of whether Columba's 'Shrine' is the church described in the saga or, indeed, whether its identification as a tomb-shrine is valid, it is clear that it pre-dates the Benedictine buildings (Redknap 1977, 232) and that it was deemed to have been important enough for careful inclusion in the later monastic structure.

EXCAVATIONS

Renovation and building work has been occurring in the vicinity of the Benedictine remains at Iona since the latter part of the 19th century. This has often necessitated the disturbance of archaeological deposits and in recent years archaeological excavation has preceded building and other development. Occasional small-scale research excavations have also been undertaken.

Figure 2 Iona: 'St Columba's Shrine' (after restoration).

Some of these excavations remain unpublished, but those that are available provide insights into some aspects of the layout and economy of the Columban and later medieval monasteries at Iona.

The vallum

The surviving remains of the *vallum* have always been rather enigmatic as they suggest a rectangular rather than a circular shape as is the case in Irish monasteries. The surviving lines of the *vallum* are also difficult to follow. Only on the western side do substantial banks survive. On the northern and southern sides the evidence is in the form of crop-marks or the results of geophysical survey, while there is no surviving evidence of enclosures on the eastern side of the site and it is quite possible that this part of the *vallum* was never completed. A rectangular outline is, however, apparent and attempts have been made to find parallels in Ireland to account for its unusual shape. Thomas (1971, 29) produced a plan with a rectilinear earthwork for Clonmacnoise based on field-survey but neither subsequent aerial photography nor fieldwork have been able to substantiate such an enclosure (H King pers comm). Hamlin (1977) notes the presence of a rectilinear enclosure at Inch, Co. Down, but this could be associated with the Cistercian monastery rather than the early medieval monastery there. The existence of early medieval rectangular *valla* in Ireland has, therefore, yet to be proven.

Excavation of a section of the bank at Iona has provided a likely explanation for the unusual shape of the *vallum*. A layer of peat had already developed in the area when the bank was erected. As it was a living surface, the dating of the surface of the peat on which the bank was erected could, theoretically, indicate the date for the bank. Radiocarbon analysis suggests that the bank predated the Columban foundation. The dating provided a range of 5 BC–AD 125 at 66% probability or 40 BC–AD 220 at 95% probability (McCormick 1993, 80).[2] Although there are problems associated with dating old ground surfaces, thin-sectional analysis of the peat surface under the bank indicated that there was no evidence of truncation or inversion of the peat, and neither was there significant evidence of invertebrate burrowing, all factors which would have called the date into question (Carter 1993, 91-2). Independent evidence of activity during the first few centuries AD can be found in the recovery, within the area of the monastic *vallum*, of a sherd of Roman pottery from the south of England of approximately the 1st or 2nd century AD (Dore 1991).

It must, therefore, be concluded that when the Columban monks arrived at Iona they utilized an already existing section of bank and ditch to form the western part of the monastic *vallum*. No archaeological investigations of the

2 All the radiocarbon calibrations cited are those of Pearson et al (1986).

northern part of the *vallum* have been undertaken but two areas of the ditch along the southern part of the enclosure have been investigated. Two deep ditches were discovered lying about 100 m apart (Barber 1981a; Reece 1981). If one is to accept that the core of the original monastery lay in the vicinity of the extant Benedictine monastery and high crosses, it suggests that a double enclosure existed around the core. This conforms to the schematized layout indicated in the Book of Mulling and to the layout of some Irish sites such as Nendrum, Co. Down, where there is a triple enclosure (Lawlor 1925). However, it is also possible that the ditch excavated by Barber is not a *vallum* ditch as such, but instead an enclosure around the original burial area of the monastery (see below).

Both ditches in the southern sector were shown by excavation to have been substantial features. The southernmost was over 2 m deep and the top was 3 m wide but its excavation produced no dating evidence (Balaam 1981, 5). The other (Ditch 1 in Barber 1981a) was more rewarding because its lower layers were waterlogged and preserved organic material (Fig 3). The ditch was again about 2 m deep and 3 m wide. Twigs from peat at the bottom of the ditch yielded a radiocarbon date of AD 636–78 at 66% probability or AD 610–780 at 95% probability. This indicates that this major ditch was not made until after the death of Columba in 597. The implication is that the human resources necessary for major ditch construction were not available to the monastery until at least a generation after the saint's death.

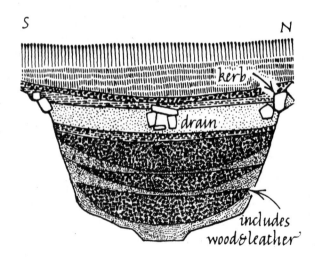

Figure 3 Iona: schematic section through Ditch 1 (after RCAHMS 1982).

Adomnán does, however, suggest (*VC* ii. 29) that some form of *vallum* bank existed during Columba's lifetime, mentioning that 'Molua went outside the boundary-bank of the monastery intending to kill a bullock'. Perhaps this refers to the pre-Columban banks already discussed or to originally smaller 'token' banks outlining the boundary of the monastery which were at a later stage replaced by the deep ditches. Excavation by Barber (1981a) uncovered a shallow ditch (Ditch 2) which predated the large ditch and, on the evidence of radiocarbon dates, could have been contemporary with the lifetime of Columba. However, because of its meandering shape, it is unlikely that this ditch is part of the early *vallum* and its function is unknown.

The creation of the two main ditches which were both about 2 m deep and 3 m wide must have produced a substantial amount of soil, but in both cases no evidence was found for associated banks. The implication is that these substantial banks must have been removed at a later period. Can it be assumed, however, that banks ever existed? The remains of surrounding earthen banks are strangely absent from early medieval Irish monasteries despite the general assumption that they were an inherent part of early *valla*. Can they all simply have been eroded away or levelled, despite the fact that the banks of thousands of ringforts survive from the same period? Excavations have, for the most part, failed to produce convincing evidence for these elusive features. The monastery at Tullylish, Co. Down, produced evidence for two substantial ditches, one in excess of 3 m deep, but no remains of a bank were found (Ivens 1987). Again, no evidence for a bank was found in areas excavated both immediately inside and outside the 2- to 3-m deep ditch at Armagh (Brown et al 1984). Admittedly, vestigial remains of a bank were found at Kilpatrick, Co. Westmeath (L Swan pers comm), and there are remains of a bank around part of the enclosure circuit at Kilmacoo, Co. Cork (Hurley 1982, 319). However, the extant evidence from excavations and aerial photography suggests that, in general, boundaries of early monasteries consisted of ditches rather than of banks and ditches. The main exception are in those instances where stone-walled *valla* are present, but in the few instances where these have been excavated, such as Reask, (Fanning 1981) and Nendrum (Lawlor 1925), no ditches were found.

The evidence from Iona indicates that the image of a monastery demarcated by a substantial, formal, banked boundary cannot be substantiated. The *idea* of the *vallum* was more important than its monumentality. The evidence from the excavation of Ditch 1 indicates that after it was dug it was left to fill with peat and silt, and there was no sign of it being cleared out or re-cut. On the contrary, the ditch was used as a dump for food and craft-working waste. The macro-plant remains suggest a soggy quagmire, its sides overgrown with bramble, nettles and ash (Bohncke 1981; Fairweather 1981).

Wooden buildings

The excavations at Iona have provided little evidence of the extent or the range of buildings that must have existed within the monastery during its earlier years. Adomnán mentions a church, which had a side-chapel (*VC* iii. 19), as well as a guest-house (*VC* ii. 3), a *domus*, which MacDonald (this vol) argues was a communal domestic building divided into cubicles for individual monks, and two buildings used by Columba. The first of these was Columba's lodging, *hospitiolum* (*VC* iii. 23), which contained his sleeping-quarters, the second, a raised wooden hut, *tegoriolum tabulis subfultum* (*VC* i. 25), which was used as his private *scriptorium*. A shed and barn are also mentioned, but these were probably located outside the monastery.

Of the early medieval Columban church, no remains have been discovered and, as we have seen, the small stone 'Shrine' is probably relatively late (see above). Excavation has confirmed the presence of wooden buildings within the area of the monastery but none can be closely dated. Reece (1981, 29-37) found a mass of post-holes beneath the stone-built bakehouse of the medieval Benedictine abbey. Unfortunately, these produced no coherent plan, although an analysis of the holes based on their depth suggested that the end of an oval building may have been present (Fig 1). These post-holes predated a burnt layer that produced calibrated radiocarbon dates of the 8th to the 11th century. It is likely, therefore, that the post-holes represent a succession of wooden buildings belonging to the early Columban monastery but the possibility that they pre-date its establishment cannot be dismissed. An incoherent group of nine post-holes were also present immediately south of Columba's 'Shrine' which stratigraphically pre-dated the Benedictine monastery (Redknap 1967, 230-32) but their actual date could not be ascertained.

A more rewarding set of post-holes was found to the north of the inner *vallum* ditch excavated by Barber (1981a, 299-303). It consisted of a central post-hole surrounded by post-holes in two concentric rings. The upper habitation layers of the structure had been truncated by later disturbance and its dating was consequently problematic. It appears to be later than a pit that produced a radiocarbon date of AD 595±55 (which calibrates to 600-780 at 95% probability) and lies beneath the base of some later medieval cultivation furrows (Barber 1981a, 303, 358). On the basis of these admittedly tenuous stratigraphical relationships the structure seems to date to the early medieval period. Only half of the structure was uncovered but enough survived to indicate that it had a diameter of 18 m. Round houses are a feature of early Irish monasteries and are almost invariably built of stone. Traces of a wooden example with a diameter of 4.8 m have recently been discovered at Illaunloughan, Co. Kerry (White-Marshall & Walshe 1994, 27).

The problem with the structure at Iona is its large size. If these post-holes are indeed the remains of a wooden building it is about three times

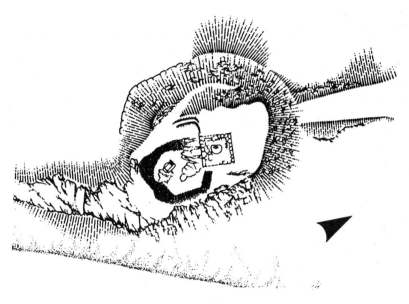

Figure 4 Iona: Plan of Tòrr an Aba (after RCAHMS 1982).

greater than the largest known from an early medieval context in either Ireland or Scotland, that at Moynagh crannóg, Co. Meath, which has a diameter of 6 m (Bradley 1993, 76). Why would a building of such a size be needed in an early monastery? Because of its shape it was clearly not a church, but might perhaps have been similar to the circular communal *domus* at Durrow which is mentioned by Adomnán (*VC* ii. 15). The architectural and engineering implications of erecting a round building of 18 m are considerable. It would have been much easier to produce the equivalent floor space in the form of a long rectangle. The post-pipes of the outer ring are only 15–25 cm in diameter. Wooden posts of this size would have been too small to have been structural, load-bearing supports in a building of this scale.[3] An alternative interpretation can be put forward in that the concentric rings of post-holes represent two superimposed round enclosures rather than a building. Binchy (1973, 82), for instance, notes that pigsties at this time were circular enclosures, no doubt to avoid the weak angular corners which would have been susceptible to the destructive habits of swine. On balance, identification of this arrangement of post-holes as a building is highly questionable.[4]

The centre of the monastic enclosure is dominated by a rock outcrop

3 The inner ring had been previously excavated and backfilled by Charles Thomas and the results are as yet unpublished (Barber 1981, 301). 4 John Smith, the late leader of the British Labour Party, now lies interred within this structure.

known as Tòrr an Aba (Fig 4). Excavation demonstrated artificial revetting of the outcrop and the presence of a 'structure' on its top (Fowler & Fowler 1988). Given the unsuitability of the site, it is not surprising that the structure is composite. It consists of the base of some stone walls, lines of stakeholes presumably representing the remains of post-and-wattle fences, some deliberately modified natural rock surfaces, and an arrangement of three split granite slabs which the excavators described as a 'fitting'. This conglomeration of features is most likely to have constituted a building of some sort and the excavators interpreted it as being one of the huts used by Columba. It is impossible to produce any archaeological evidence for a direct link between the building and the saint but circumstantial evidence at least supports the possibility of this conclusion.

Adomnán makes it clear that Columba had two 'private' buildings, a place where he wrote and a place where he slept. One of these was built on a high place, as it is recorded in one instance that 'there were two men standing by the door of his hut, which was built in an elevated position' (*VC* iii. 21). Tòrr an Aba is the most elevated area within the flat interior of the monastic enclosure and would be the most likely location for the hut described in this reference. Unfortunately, it is unclear whether his sleeping- or his writing-hut is referred to. The hut that Columba wrote in is described elsewhere as 'his raised wooden hut' (*VC* i. 25). As Sharpe (1995, 285, n 127) notes, the Latin description of this hut (*in tegoriolo tabulis subfulto*, 'in the hut supported on planks') is open to more than one interpretation. Sharpe is of the opinion that this indicates a hut supported on joists, but there is no evidence for the use of joists in any buildings at this time in either Ireland or Scotland. Fowler and Fowler (1988, 199), in tentatively accepting that the structure on Tòrr an Aba is one of Columba's two huts, propose an interesting solution to the disparity between the archaeological and written evidence. They identify the entrance as being on the east side of the building. A door in this position would lead to a steep and inconvenient incline for anyone leaving or entering. They postulate that access would therefore have necessitated a stepped arrangement of some sort. Such a series of wooden steps and platform at the entrance may have given an impression of 'a hut supported on planks'. Further speculation seems futile and perhaps we should be satisfied with the fact that at Iona we have archaeological evidence for one hut, in conjunction with documentary evidence for a saint and two huts, a situation that exists for no other monastery of the period.

Agriculture and diet

While the excavations at Iona have produced limited structural evidence, considerable information concerning the diet and agricultural practices of the Columban monastery has been accumulated. Dumps of animal bone representing discarded food refuse have been found in several areas within the monastery, while pollen from the *vallum* ditch provides evidence concerning early monastic agriculture.

It has already been noted that *vallum* Ditch 1 was dug after the first generation of the monastic settlement. Pollen from the lowest levels indicate that oak and ash cover was fairly extensive on the island when the ditch was initially in use (Bohncke 1981, 346-8). Soon after this, the trees were for the most part cleared and arable agriculture with cereal growing began to be established nearby. Although the species of cereal could not be identified it is most likely to have been barley, as this is the most suitable crop for the climate of the island. Barley produced by the monastery is also referred to by Adomnán (*VC* ii. 3). The tree pollen from the ditch bottom implies that the monastic community were still 'colonizing' the landscape in the century after the death of Columba and that the effect on the landscape of the initial settlement must have been relatively limited. The evidence of cereals in the ditch declines, implying that as time passed the arable lands of the monastic 'estate' were located elsewhere on the island. Adomnán mentions the monks building a stone wall around the sandy machair plain on the west of the island (*VC* ii. 28) and elsewhere implies that crops were grown on the same machair (*VC* i. 37). Perhaps this agricultural geography refers more to the situation during the lifetime of Adomnán than during that of Columba, when cultivation was for the most part confined to the environs of the *vallum*.

There is much secondary evidence, in the form of millstones, for the processing of cereals at Iona. Adomnán refers to a cross being held in position by a millstone (*VC* iii. 23). It is extremely unlikely that the small, hand-turned querns of the early medieval period would have been capable of producing a stable footing for a cross of any significant size, and it can be assumed that Adomnán is referring to the millstone of a watermill. Millstones that were used as cross-supports still survive on Iona, one used as a cross-base on the side of the medieval Road of the Dead (Barber 1981a, 308), another unfinished specimen forming part of the cist-like support for St John's cross, which dates to the late 8th or early 9th century. If the base is contemporary with the cross, and there is no reason to doubt this, it indicates that a watermill was used by the Columban community. The earliest Irish watermills date to the second quarter of the 7th century (Rynne 1992, 23) so perhaps the technology was introduced to Iona in the generations after Columba. It is not known where the mill associated with the monastery was located but Sruth a'Mhuilinn, the 'mill stream', which runs through the monastic enclosure, seems the best candidate. Excavation by O'Sullivan (1994) uncovered a large, sub-rectangular pool-basin on the side of the river that may have formed the undercroft of a horizontal watermill but no dating evidence was recovered.

The remains of discarded food refuse provide much information about the meat diet of the Columban and later Benedictine monastery (McCormick 1981; 1993; Noddle 1981). The majority of the animal bones found in these kitchen dumps were of the main domesticated species. The minimum number of individuals[5] distribution of the species present is shown in Table 1.

Animal	Vallum	'Guest-house'	Benedictine midden
Cattle	9	22	13
Sheep	5	8	14
Goat	-	3	-
Pig	2	10	3
Horse	2	2	1
Dog	-	-	1
Cat	-	1	-
Red deer	4	20	1
Roe deer	1	4	-
Badger	-	1	-
Fox	-	1	-
Otter	1	-	-
Seal	2*	6	-
Cetacean	1	1	-

Table 1
Distribution of minimum numbers of individuals from different bone assemblages from Iona (based on McCormick 1981; 1993; Noddle 1981).
* Grey seal.

The animal bone remains display a mixed livestock economy. In the Columban monastery cattle were the dominant species with sheep becoming more important during Benedictine times. The rise in importance of sheep reflects a general increase in sheep numbers in Ireland and Scotland at this time, presumably as a consequence of the development of the wool trade. Adomnán indicates that cattle were kept for dairying (*VC* ii. 16; iii. 23) which reflects the situation in Ireland in his day (McCormick 1992). Both sheep and goat are mentioned in passing. The goat was generally regarded as a low-status

5 This (the MNI) is an estimate of the minimum number of individuals of each species that would have to have been killed to account for the animal bone assemblage present in a given context.

animal, being essentially the 'poor man's cow'. It is not, therefore, surprising that goats are absent on high-status sites such as Lagore crannóg, Co. Meath (Hencken 1950), and at Iona, where some of the rougher land would have been quite suitable for them, only a few animals were present. The main disadvantage of goats is that they are extremely difficult to control and will create havoc with crops and in cultivated areas. One of the goats present in the Columban middens suffered 'capped elbow', a pathology caused by having been tethered on stony ground or confined with insufficient bedding (Noddle 1981, 42). Whichever the cause, the injury indicates that the goat was restrained from roaming freely. Pigs thrive best where there is available forest for foraging. After the clearance of the woodland by the monastic community, Iona would have been quite unsuitable for pig rearing, so the possibility must be considered that many of the pigs present were derived from off the island, perhaps being given to the monastery as tribute.

The impression given of the horse in Adomnán's text is that of a valued farm animal: 'as the saint was sitting there for a few minutes' rest ... a white horse came to him, the loyal work-horse which used to carry the milk-pails' (*VC* iii. 23). The inclusion of their bones with other discarded food refuse, however, implies that the animal was occasionally eaten by the monks, a situation emphasised by the presence of butchering marks on some of the horse bones from the *vallum* ditch (McCormick 1981, 315). The eating of horse was generally frowned upon by the Church, as indicated by some 9th-century Irish penitentials (Bieler 1963, 161), and for Adomnán the eating of horse meat was a culinary habit fit only for thieves (*VC* i. 21). Bannerman has suggested that the pagan practice of eating a mare's flesh at royal inaugurations was the reason for Adomnán's disapproval (1989, 129). Perhaps the presence of butchered horse bone in the monastic midden should be interpreted either as 'emergency rations' in time of severe food shortage or within the context of someone passing off horse flesh as beef to the monastic community. It should be noted, however, that in the secular *Bretha Crólige*, a legal text concerning sick-maintenance, the eating of horse meat is not completely forbidden but simply deemed unsuitable for invalids, as it tended to 'stir up sickness in the stomach' (Binchy 1938, 21).

The high incidence of wild game in the diet in the Columban middens of Iona is extremely unusual. The large numbers of red deer, roe deer and seal are quite unprecedented on a site of this period. Adomnán mentions (*VC* i. 41) a breeding colony of seals on a small island off Mull. It is implied that the breeding animals belonged to the monastery and that the hunting of the seals by outsiders was regarded as poaching. Some of the seal bones found were of young or new-born animals that could have been easily taken from the rookery. Old seals were, however, also present at Iona and one individual displayed a hunting wound in its pelvis (Noddle 1981, 42). The high incidence

of seals may represent the systematic exploitation of coastal resources by the
monks, given the limited amount of grazing on the island. It is also possible
that seal flesh was regarded as a special food in the monastery. Martin Martin
noted (1703, 136) that Catholics on the Hebrides ate seal flesh on fast-days
on the basis that they believed it was the equivalent of fish. An early Irish
penitential attributed to Adomnán, the *Canones Adomnani* (Bieler 1963, 177),
notes that the eating of dead 'marine animals' washed up on the shore was
permitted by the early Church on the grounds that they were unlike terrestrial animals, where the carcass had to be bled immediately after death or the
flesh was regarded as unclean. The interest of the monastery in the seal
rookery near Mull may therefore have been due to the fact that seal meat was
a food that could be consumed during periods of fasting.

A high incidence of deer in the diet is highly unusual on Irish or Scottish
sites of the period but has been noted on a few Iron Age Hebridean sites such
as Cnip on Lewis (McCormick forthcoming) and Dun Mor Vaul, Tiree
(Noddle 1974). The evidence from these sites suggests that deer were exploited in an extremely ordered fashion to ensure conservation of the herd.
One gets the impression that the deer were considered almost as a domesticated breed, emphasised by the fact that in some cases they were present in
higher numbers than cattle in the middens. Lewis and Tiree, however, are
relatively large islands and it is difficult to see how herds of deer could have
co-existed with a monastic community on Iona which is only 5.5 km long and
at its maximum 2.5 km wide. Being present in such a confined area the deer
would have constituted a danger to the crops and gardens of the monastery.
It seems much more likely that the red and roe deer were derived from
nearby Mull. The fact that deer are present in such large numbers may
suggest that the monastery had estate lands on that island.

It is possible that the efforts to acquire venison, as in the case of seal
meat, may have been for special, ecclesiastical, dietary reasons. The 9th-
century *Céli Dé* document known as *The Monastery of Tallaght* indicates that
the eating of venison was associated with monastic holiness (Gwynn & Purton
1912, 129). As additional support for this hypothesis it can be noted that the
only Irish early medieval site to have produced an unusually high incidence
of red deer was the monastic site of Moyne, Co. Mayo (McCormick 1987,
67). Doherty (1982, 301) suggests that the Iona community were 'living off
the fat of the land', implying gastronomic indulgence; it seems more likely,
however, that their diet was determined by the environment and ecclesiastical practice.

Badgers and foxes are no longer present on Iona and it again seems likely
that these were brought from elsewhere, presumably Mull. It is unlikely that
these animals, along with otter, were eaten and their presence in the middens
may reflect hunting for skins.

Adomnán's few references to fishing refer to freshwater fishing, although these do not relate to Iona. There are no suitable lakes or rivers on Iona for this and the archaeological evidence makes it clear that the early monastery was involved exclusively in sea fishing. The range of fish, along with birds, found on the site of the monastery is shown in Table 2.

Species	'Guest-house' and Ditch *1*	*Abbey Medieval*
Fowl/chicken	+	+
Goose	+	+
Shag	+	+
Cormorant	+	
White-tailed eagle		+
Golden eagle	+	
Raven	+	
Manx shearwater	+	
Curlew		+
Jack snipe		+
Fulmar		
Gull spec.	+	
Ray		+
Herring		+
Gurnard	+	+
Cod	+	+
Hake	+	
Ling		+
Whiting		+
Gadidae		+
Saithe	+	
Red sea bream	+	
Flatfish		+

Table 2 Occurrence of excavated fish and bird bones on Iona
(based on Bramwell 1981; Coy & Hamilton-Dyer 1993;
McCormick 1981; Wheeler 1981).

With so many sea journeys mentioned by Adomnán it is not surprising that there is evidence for deep-sea as well as inshore fishing. Some of the cod present were in excess of 10 kg in weight and such fish would rarely be found in shallow inshore waters (Wheeler 1981, 47). The large saithe, along with

hake and grey gurnard are all generally deep-water fish. As some of these are bottom fish it implies that they were caught by baited hook rather than by net. The birds included a small number of domesticated fowl, seabirds and some scavengers and raptors, the latter probably deliberately killed because they were a nuisance rather than as a source of food.

Crafts

As centres of large populations early monasteries were also centres of craft activity. In addition to producing mundane objects for everyday use, monasteries were also a focus for specialized crafts ranging from manuscript illumination to fine metalworking. The former leaves little in the archaeological record, but the probability that the Book of Kells was at least partly produced at Iona, along with the surviving stone sculpture, emphasises the importance of the monastery as a centre of artistic and craft activity.

Iona, like any other monastery, would for the most part have been self-sufficient for most of its general necessities and many of the monks would have been skilled craftsmen. Adomnán refers specifically to 'the monks who knew the blacksmith's craft' (*VC* ii. 29). Several pieces of slag were found by Barber (1981a) but it was not established if these represented ironworking. They do, however, provide clear evidence for working in metal.

Archaeological excavation indicates that fine metalworking in bronze is confined to monastic and high-status secular sites during the early medieval period (Ryan 1988). At Iona one would expect the emphasis to be on the production of metalwork of an ecclesiastical nature; while no surviving finished objects of this type are attributable with certainty to a workshop at Iona, Fisher has suggested an Iona origin for certain high-quality pieces found elsewhere (1994, 45). Excavation, however, has provided evidence for such a workshop. Barber (1981a, 349) retrieved several mould fragments that would have been used for casting bronze, although most came from re-deposited contexts. Small fragments of early medieval crucibles that underwent x-ray fluorescence analysis provided evidence for copper and tin, indicative of bronzeworking (McCormick 1992).

Excavation also produced evidence for glassworking. A tiny blue/green glass rod with an applied, yellow glass spiral helix constituted raw material (Barber 1981a, 439) and could have been used for making beads or *millefiori* (Fig 5b). The Iona example was unstratified but similar rods have been found in early medieval contexts in Armagh (Youngs 1989, no 205 a-d). A 7th- or 8th-century clay mould for making glass studs from the site is described by Graham-Campbell (1981, 23-4) (Fig. 5a). The only other known mould of similar size is from the royal site at Lagore, Co. Meath. Graham-Campbell notes that the pattern on the Iona mould is closely paralleled by a roundel in the Book of Kells.

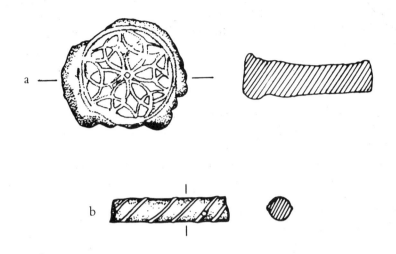

Figure 5   Iona: (a) mould for glass stud (diameter 2.9 cms);
(b) glass rods (length 1.3 cms).

The organic deposits within the *vallum* ditch produced evidence of craftworking in materials which are generally absent from archaeological sites. It was clear that there was a wood-turning workshop near the ditch during the 7th and 8th centuries (Barber 1981a, 328-46). The ditch produced the remains of three wooden bowls but also some thirty cone-shaped objects which were a by-product of bowl production by turning on a pole lathe. Virtually all the bowls were made of alder, and pollen evidence indicated that this could have been derived from the island. The few exceptions were made of willow. The shapes of some of the bowls from the ditch were based on imported E-ware pottery prototypes (Earwood 1993, 94-7).

In addition to turned vessels, a stave from the ditch indicates the use of stave-built vessels, possibly similar to the type referred to by Adomnán when he describes milk being carried back to the monastery in a 'wooden pail' (*VC* ii. 16). The workshop near the ditch also undertook general carpentry and much of the wood in the ditch consists of offcuts from such activity. Adomnán makes several references to wood being imported to the island. He describes (*VC* ii. 45) how 'pine trees and oaks had been felled and dragged overland. Some were to be used in the making of a longship, and besides ships' timbers there were also beams for a great house to be brought here to Iona.' In the same chapter he refers to 'oak trees ... being towed by a group of twelve curraghs from the mouth of the River Shiel to be used here in repairs to the monastery.' This would have necessitated a sea journey of some 60-70 km, implying that suitable wood for major building purposes was not available on the island or even on the neighbouring island of Mull. Even the withies used in post-and-wattle building were brought by boat, indicating an off-island source (*VC* ii. 3). The ditch material indicates the exploitation of a wide range of woods in the monastic workshop including oak, hazel, alder, birch, pine, poplar, ash, willow and fir (Barber 1981a, 338-9).

The remains from the ditch indicate a sophisticated level of carpentry that accords better with the description of the elaborate wooden church in Cogitosus's life of St Brigid (*PL* 72. 789; de Paor 1993, 222) than with the small wooden wattle churches of the popular imagination. There is evidence for mortise-and-tenon and dowelled jointing. There is a fragment that appears to be a sill beam, while a squared section of oak with grooves cut along opposite sides could have been used to hold wall panelling in place. At Iona few, if any, of the buildings would have been of stone and a carpentry workshop would have been in continual used throughout the duration of the life of the monastery. It should be noted that only the lower parts of the waterlogged levels within the ditch contained woodworking material, implying that the workshop moved to another location during the late 7th or early 8th century. One may postulate that by this time all the raw materials on the island were exhausted and it was found to be more convenient to relocate the workshop on the shore at the point where imported wood was landed.

'Likewise, one day, when the brethren were putting on their shoes ... to go out to their various tasks about the monastery, St Columba ... gave orders that there should be no work that day' (*VC* iii. 12). On the basis of the leather remains from Ditch 1 we now know that the monastery at Iona had its own leather workshop occupied primarily with making shoes (Groenman-van Waateringe 1981). The hides used consisted of cattle, horse, red deer, seal and goat/hairy sheep. It is quite clear that the hides were derived from the animals that were slaughtered for food. Although it was not possible to ascertain the age of the cattle killed, because of the small sample size, evidence from contemporary rural Irish sites shows a recurring pattern of very few calves, a majority of semi-mature animals and a lesser number of mature animals (McCormick 1992). It is possible to ascertain roughly the age of an animal on the basis of the pores on the leather. Of the cattle leather in the ditch, 6% was of calf hide, 56% from semi-mature individuals and 38% from mature cattle, indicating that the availability of hide was simply a product of the normal slaughter cycle. There was no evidence in the remains from the ditch of the specialist preparation of calf hides that would have been necessary to produce vellum for books.

The collection of shoes from Iona is the only closely dated group from early medieval Ireland or Scotland. Groenman-van Waateringe (1981, 320) noted that some features, such as heel stiffeners, indicate clear parallels with Roman shoes while other features are general in shoes of later periods. Some features, however, such as the tongues rising at the back of the heels, and their decoration, have no counterparts. Barber has noted (1981b, 103) the correspondence between the shoes from Iona and those worn by the symbol of Matthew in the Book of Durrow.

Pottery making seems also to have been undertaken at the site while imported pottery types reflect overseas contacts (Lane & Campbell 1988, 208-12). Predictably, some of the pottery appears to be imported 'souterrain ware' from the north-east of Ireland, a type that dates to the later half of the early medieval period. There are also pieces of pottery that superficially look like souterrain ware but with geological inclusions that indicate a local origin. The presence of E-ware (Reece 1981, 19) indicates contact with Gaul within the 6th or 7th century, perhaps as a result of the trade in wine necessary for liturgical purposes. A sherd of north African red slip ware indicates contact with the Mediterranean during the early years of the Columban settlement. This is the northernmost incidence of this pottery in Britain, the only other examples being confined to the south coast of Ireland and Wales and the south-western coast of England (Edwards 1990, 71).

Some Gaulish 2nd-century AD Samian ware may reflect activity on the island before the foundation of the monastery. Occasional pieces of such pottery, however, are commonly found in later archaeological contexts and it has been suggested that the pottery was 'powdered' for medicinal purposes (Bradley 1982).

The dead

Christian burial was an integral aspect of early monasticism but Adomnán's life is unclear about the nature of the early burial ground at Iona. The only references in the text to a burial is in the context of a former pagan who died immediately after being baptized. The man was subsequently interred at the place of his baptism and a cairn raised over his grave (*VC* i. 33). The fact that he was not buried in a communal cemetery clearly reflects a continuation of pagan usage rather than a Christian burial rite.

The antiquity and location of the original Christian burial ground at Iona is not known. None of the many excavations have produced direct evidence for the location of the primary monastic graveyard. A small number of burials were discovered by Redknap (1977, 247) immediately south of Columba's 'Shrine', but he concluded that they dated between the building of the 'Shrine' and the 15th century, and it is unlikely that any are earlier than the later medieval period. It seems much more likely that the original graveyard was located in the present graveyard, Reilig Odhráin, as the presence of late medieval monuments indicates that burial here extends back several hundred years. Christian burial was based on the belief that one should be buried with one's forefathers, as stipulated in Gen 47. 30: 'but I shall lie with my fathers, and thou shall carry me out of Egypt, and bury me in their burying place.' Once a burial tradition has been established it would be extremely difficult, if not impossible, to re-locate a burial area, and it is not easy to see how Reilig Odhráin could have become a secondary site with the original graveyard being abandoned. Documentary sources indicate that most Scottish kings between the mid-9th and the end of the 11th century were buried at Iona (Sharpe 1995, 277, n 100). Therefore the abandonment of a graveyard with such an important burial tradition for a new site at Reilig Odhráin would seem unthinkable. It is difficult to avoid the conclusion that the original graveyard at Iona must have been located at Reilig Odhráin.

If this hypothesis is accepted it implies that the monastic graveyard was separated from the core of the monastic area by a 3-m deep ditch (Ditch 1). If the high crosses mark the spiritual focus of the monastery, the graveyard must have been regarded as an area that had to be clearly separated from it. It is interesting to note that at Reask, Co. Kerry, the lintel grave cemetery was physically separated from the remainder of the monastic enclosure by a wall (Fanning 1981). The excavator (ibid., 150) quotes several other early monastic enclosures where there is an internal boundary dividing the sacred areas of church and burial ground from the habitation sector, i.e. the separation of the sacred from the worldly. At Reask, the sacred area contained the lintel grave cemetery as well as two cells and an oratory, but where stratigraphical relationships could be demonstrated, these building were clearly later than the lintel graves. Is it possible that in the earlier phases of monastic sites the dead were clearly separated from the activities of the living but that this separateness became blurred with the passing of time?

As stated above, the deep Ditch 1 at Iona clearly suggests the physical separation of the dead from the living, in many ways reminiscent of the Roman practice of locating cemeteries outside the boundaries of towns. Indeed, writing in the late 7th century, Adomnán implies that at Iona there was a certain degree of taboo relating to contact with the dead. It was as if the dead or, more specifically, the corpse was shunned. In a life that is characterized by demonstrations of the kindness of the saint one incident concerning the death of the monk Brito seems a little unusual:

> Once when St Columba was living in Iona, one of his monks, a Briton, dedicated to good works, was taken ill with a bodily affliction and came close to death. The holy man came to visit him in his last hour, standing for a time beside his bed and blessing him. But he soon left the monk, for he wished not to see the man die. The end came as soon as the saint had left the house (*VC* iii. 6).

The idea that it was the dead who were shunned, as opposed to the dying, has been considered by Paxton (1990, 84-7), who notes that this attitude is demonstrated more forcibly in the 9th-century *Monastery of Tallaght* (c AD 840), a text associated with the *Céli Dé*. This latter reference is particularly important because it demonstrates that the shunning of the dead was endorsed, if not dictated, by Diarmait, an abbot of Iona appointed in 814 *AU*:

> Now, to eat a meal with a dead man (though saintly) in the house is forbidden; but instead there are to be prayers and psalm-singing on such occasions. Even one in orders who brings the sacrament to a sick man is obliged to go out of the house at once thereafter, that the sick man die not in his presence; for if he be present in the house at the death, it would not be allowable for him to perform the sacrifice until a bishop should consecrate him. It happened once on a time to Diarmait and to Blathmac mac Flaind that it was in their hands that Curui expired. When he died, they were about to perform the sacrifice thereafter, without being reconsecrated, till Colchu hindered them from doing so. The authority is Leviticus; and Diarmait also, the Abbot of Iona, was with him on that occasion (Gwynn & Purton 1912, 153).

The dead, therefore, were regarded as unclean by clerics, and as Paxton (1990, 86) explains: 'the reference to the Old Testament book of Leviticus is the key to understanding the *Céli Dé* attitude, for it recorded the injunction of the Lord to Moses that the sons of Aaron – that is, the priests – should not defile themselves by contact with the dead.' In the *Vita Columbae* and the documentary evidence relating to Tallaght we have powerful evidence to show that clerics living in 7th- to 9th-century Iona regarded the dead as unclean. Is it not likely that this theological attitude was reflected spatially in the monastic layout by the separation of the area of the dead from the area of the living? It is perhaps within such a context that the deep ditch between Reilig Odhráin and the remainder of the monastery should be interpreted.

The idea of the graveyard being separate from the monastic core is also suggested at Eileach an Naoimh, to the north of Jura. Here, the presumed early medieval burial ground is set apart from the churches and cells of the monastic complex (RCAHMS 1984, 170-79) and there are no ecclesiastical buildings within the burial enclosure. This settlement has been identified by some as the Columban settlement of *Hinba* (ibid., 171), although this is unproven.

Ecclesiastical remains outside the monastic enclosure

Burial grounds and ecclesiastical buildings are not confined to within the Columban monastic enclosure and some of those which are outside may be of early medieval date. The Augustinian nunnery, located some 400 m south of the Benedictine monastery, appears to have been founded at the beginning of the 13th century. The site was used as a burial place of 'laywomen of noble birth' during the later middle ages and several fine medieval burial slabs survive (RCAHMS 1982, 178). Immediately north of the nunnery is St Ronan's Church, a parish church of 12th- or early 13th-century date.

Excavations of the interior of St Ronan's uncovered part of a clay-bonded rectangular building which was rendered with white lime plaster on its interior and exterior walls. This was interpreted by the excavator as the remains of an earlier church (O'Sullivan 1994). This building in turn overlay a series of burials. Unfortunately neither the building nor the burials could be closely dated but the stratigraphical evidence suggests that they are early medieval. The presence of an early burial ground would imply that ecclesiastical activity of that date was not confined to the area within the *vallum*. A series of later medieval burials within St Ronan's Church were all of women, infants and young children (Home Lorimer 1994, 347-53). If this is a continuation of the earlier burial tradition it would imply that there were segregated burial places during the early medieval period. O'Sullivan (1994) considered the Irish evidence for segregated women's burials and quoted the examples of Reilig na mBan at Carrickmore, Co. Tyrone, and Inishmurray, Co. Sligo. In both cases, however, the antiquity of the practice cannot be demonstrated.

It is a great pity that the poorly preserved remains from the early burials at St Ronan's did not produce enough material for radiocarbon dating. Interpretation of a second excavated burial ground, at Martyrs' Bay (Port nam Mairtír), immediately south of the modern pier at Iona, was also encumbered with problems of dating. Tradition of uncertain antiquity held that this bay was the site of a slaughter of monks by the Norse (Reece & Wells 1981, 63). The most famous massacre was in 806 *AU* when sixty-eight of the community were killed, an occasion which led to the transfer of leadership of the Columban *familia* to Kells. Reeves (1874, cxxxvi-cxxxvii) noted an 18th-century report of human bones being found in a mound on the side of the modern public road adjacent to Martyrs' Bay, a find that must have strengthened the tradition of a massacre there.

In 1961 the laying of a water main beside the road at Martyrs' Bay uncovered two burials. Subsequent excavation revealed the remains of at least thirty-eight individuals (Reece & Wells 1981, 63-102). What could be more appropriate? – a mound of burials on the edge of Martyrs' Bay, at a site traditionally associated with the slaughter of the Columban community by Norse raiders. Alas, the evidence was soon to show that this was not the case.

Firstly, there was considerable disturbance within the burials, indicating that they represented inhumation over a long period of time rather than a single event. Secondly, none of the skeletons displayed evidence of violent death and, finally, the great majority were of adult females. The burials then are clearly not those of a group of slaughtered monks and what they do represent is extremely difficult to ascertain

The mound in which the burials were found consisted of wind-blown beach sand that accumulated around a rock outcrop. The burials were inserted into this natural mound with the later burials usually disturbing the earlier. It is important to note, however, that three of the stratigraphically earliest burials, along with the two discovered during the laying of the water main, were in crude stone cists. There was one single youth present, and of the skeletal elements that allowed determination of sex, 73% were female or probable female and the remainder male or probable male. Expressed in another way, of the thirty-eight individuals present, only six were male. With the exception of one unclassifiable youth the remainder were definitely or probably females (Reece & Wells 1981, 86). The males and females were all adults and most were middle-aged, or old, at death. Analysis of the female pelvises that survived in good condition indicated that none displayed the changes indicative of pregnancy. The bone specialist concluded, somewhat subjectively: 'It is not for the anthropologist either to impute virginity or to deny wedlock to these ladies but, at least as far as it goes, the evidence suggests that, for reasons best known to themselves, their wombs died barren and unfruitful' (ibid., 91).

Two burials were radiocarbon dated. The stratigraphically lowest burial provided a date of ad 1359±75 (UB-604) which provided a calibrated date of 1270-1440 at 95% probability. The highest stratified burial, however, provided a date of ad 695±65 which calibrates to 650-900 with 95% probability. The implications of these inverted dates is either that the stratigraphy is wrong, that the radiocarbon dates are wrong, or that the samples were at some stage confused. The fact that the stratigraphically lowest skeleton was in a cist grave strongly suggests that the samples submitted for radiocarbon dating may have become confused. In both Scotland and Ireland cist burials are confined to the earliest medieval period and do not extend into the later middle ages.

If it is assumed that this burial site had its origin during the early medieval period how should it be interpreted? The burials in the mound, with their virtual absence of children and high incidence of females is certainly atypical for a normal population. The disturbance on the site does not allow us to determine if the sex ratio of the occupants remained consistent during its period of use. All that can be said is that of the three early cist burials two were female and one possibly male. Martyrs' Bay was the original landing bay for the island prior to the erection of the pier (Reece & Wells 1981, 63). The location of a burial mound at this site suggests that the bodies might be of those who came from outside the island. Perhaps the whole island was regarded as a holy area, a hypothesis that could be supported by the fact that the *vallum* seems never to have been completed. We know that Iona was regarded as an important place of burial by the kings of Scotland, but there is no reason to suppose that persons of lesser status did not also consider Iona a desirable burial place. There may have been a series of burial places for outsiders, of which the present Martyrs' Bay mound was only one. Reeves (1874, cxxxv-cxxxvii), for instance, identified nine burial grounds on Iona, so the proposed idea that the island served as some form of necropolis should be considered. A quatrain in some versions of the 12th-century Irish life of Columba refers to 'Iona with its many burial-places', *I co n-ilar a martra* (*ILCC* § 63, n 5).

Archaeological excavations at Iona have been a focus of research since Smith undertook an investigation of the animal bones from later medieval kitchen middens in 1878. In most instances, however, they have been on a small scale and this, coupled with the longevity of ecclesiastical activity, has led to somewhat piecemeal results. Our understanding of the physical layout of the Columban monastery is still extremely limited and many of the archaeological discoveries, such as the separation of the monastic core from the presumed burial area, and the probable existence of early medieval churches outside the *vallum*, are unusual to say the least. The fact that part of the *vallum* is of pre-Columban date is also surprising. On the other hand, the waterlogged deposits from Ditch 1 provide information on aspects of 7th-century monastic life that is unparalleled on any similar site of the period in Britain or Ireland. As stated at the outset, it is certainly true that Iona is a difficult site to understand, but the combined historical and archaeological evidence provides us with a body of data that is central to early monastic studies.

ACKNOWLEDGEMENTS

The writer would like to thank Historic Scotland for financing the excavations on Iona with which he was involved, Maura Pringle for her help with the illustrations and Rilla Bray for her help and hospitality during the 1988 season of excavation.

Columba the Scribe

Timothy O'Neill

Among the finest achievements of Columban civilization are the great manuscripts associated with the monasteries of Iona, Kells and Durrow. For centuries the Book of Kells, the Book of Durrow and the *Cathach* were regarded as personal relics of Columba, and to a large extent it was this status which ensured their survival.

Adomnán's life of Columba (*VC*)[1] records that the saint could not pass even the space of a single hour without applying himself to prayer, reading or some kind of work (*VC* second Preface), so did he write many books? He could scarcely have managed more than two major manuscripts per year as a full-time scribe and, given his duties later as head of a large monastic federation, it is likely that his output would have been much less. But he wrote psalters, as the legend of the *Cathach* bears out, and he was working on a psalter the day he died (*VC* iii. 23). He is said to have written gospel books: a story in the life of St Berach relates that when Columba visited that saint he left with him the gospel, which he had written with his own hand, as a sign of the agreement between them (Plummer 1922 I, 39; II, 39, §77). Books written by Columba were treasured as relics on Iona in Adomnán's time, and were on one occasion used to cure a drought on the island when, along with the saint's white tunic, they were carried in procession around the ploughed fields and later opened and read on the Hill of the Angels (*VC* ii. 44).

The first books would have arrived in Ireland with the earliest Christians and the spread of the faith in the 5th century must have created a huge demand for more, a need which increased in the following century with the proliferation of monasteries. Book production was a most important activity in any sizeable monastery – providing texts for use in services, for private devotions and for study, teaching and schoolwork. The life of Columba by Adomnán and the lives of other early Irish saints have numerous references to books and writing which may illustrate some practical aspects of scribal activity. The question of scribal terminology has recently been reviewed by Lambert (1991).

---

1 The *VC* is referred to in the edition and translation of Anderson and Anderson (1961; rev edn Anderson 1991).

It seems likely that a pupil's first attempts at writing and letter formation would have been with chalk on slate, if such materials were available. Numerous fragments of incised slates were found during the excavations at the early monastery of Nendrum, Co. Down (Lawlor 1925; O'Meadhra 1979). Some have samples of ornament, and one (now lost) had part of the alphabet in insular style (Ó Cróinín 1995, 182). It seems likely that such slates would have served as permanent exemplars for young scribes to copy, initially perhaps with chalk, but later with a metal stylus in wax; iron styli were also found at Nendrum. A traditional early Christian horror story from Italy tells how school-master Cassian of Imola was martyred by his students, who killed him by stabbing him with their styli during the persecution of Diocletian in the early 4th century (*CE* 362a).

According to a story in the life of Ruadán, Columba had a special set of tablets which he used for his pupils' writing (perhaps to teach them) (Plummer 1922 I, 328; II, 319, §56). These writing-tablets are referred to as a 'gold manual', *manuail órdha*, and also, in the same story, as a book, suggesting that several panels were linked. It is possible that the name 'gold manual' came from the fact that the panels had gilt-bronze corner pieces strengthening the wood, although one could speculate about letters engraved or incised on metal plates and presented, perhaps, in the manner of the finely drawn square letters below the decorated rim of the Ardagh chalice which are set off by a stippled background.

Waxed tablets were used for writing all over the Roman empire and beyond. Flat wooden panels were hollowed out and filled with wax, providing a surface which could be easily inscribed with a pointed stylus. These must have come in all sizes, singly, in pairs or in groups, hollowed front and back and strung together on leather thongs. Most were plain, but it seems that some, like those attributed to Columba, had corner pieces or were decorated with carving. The enigmatic 7th-century *Hisperica Famina* has a poetic description of what must have been one of the commonest items in a school of the time:

> This wooden tablet was made from choice pieces;
> it contains rubbing wax from another region;
> a wooden median joins the little divided columns,
> on which lovely carving has played.
> The other side has a somewhat larger area of wood;
> it is fashioned with various painted designs
> and has decorated borders.
> This once grew among the leafy oaks of a green field;
> the artisan cut off a growing branch with his iron axe,
> hewed the square product out of the fibre of the wood,

carved a small border with his knife,
and finished the embellished tablet,
which is carried in the right hand of the scholars
and contains the mysteries of rhetoric in waxen spheres
(Herren 1974, 106-7).

Wax writing-tablets were used by pupils learning to read and write and by all
literate people for letter-writing and note-taking. Cainnech, Columba's friend,
although he had withdrawn temporarily to a quiet place in the woods, kept
instructing a boy in writing. The saint, we are told, wrote for him in wax.
The brethren discovered the master and pupil because the fingers of Cainnech's
left hand shone like candles, enabling the lesson to continue in the dark
(Plummer 1910 I, 165, §35). The script on a set of wax writing-tablets (six
small boards of yew, each 21 x 7.5 cm) discovered in Springmount Bog, Co.
Antrim (Webster & Backhouse 1991, no 64), is not that of a student learning
to write, but of a trained cleric writing around AD 600 (Ó Cróinín 1995, 182).
The inscribed text consists of verses from Pss 30 and 31 and is a reminder
that the psalms were used in monastic schools as a primer for learning to
write, to read, to pray and, presumably, to chant. Hence the expression 'to
learn one's psalms' meant to receive an education. It seems that boys like the
young Déclán of Ardmore began to learn their psalms about the age of seven
(Plummer 1910 II, 37, §5). Bairre of Cork is described reading his psalms,
which clearly means doing his lesson with his tutor (Plummer 1922 I, 12;
II,13, §12). Later (§13) he rewards the tutor for teaching him and some time
afterwards goes to Bishop Mac Cuirb for instruction (§17). With the bishop
he 'read the book of Matthew and the book of the Apostles' (§20), which
suggests that having learned the psalms the student graduated to the gospels
and the next stage of schooling. By this time, presumably, the youth would
have progressed to writing with quills and copying texts on vellum, although
he would make daily use of the wax tablets for taking notes and sending
messages. Needless to say some students had difficulty with writing, like the
boy in Comgall's monastery whom nobody could teach to write and whose
writing nobody could decipher, because it looked like the work of a bird's
claw (Plummer 1910 II, 13, §29). St Comgall, however, blessed his eyes and
hand and the novice went on to be a great calligrapher.

Vellum must have been reserved for copying, being far too valuable for
anything other than book production. Vellum and parchment are interchangeable terms meaning animal skin made ready for writing. Vellum, from Latin
vitulus, 'calf', is strictly speaking prepared calf skin and forms the pages of
almost all insular manuscripts. The method of preparation of skins has probably changed little over the centuries and involved soaking the skins in a
solution of lime and water or burying them with excrement, until the hair on

one side and the fatty tissue on the other could easily be removed by careful scraping. After repeated washing, smoothing, stretching and drying selected skins were measured, cut, folded and ruled for the formal writing of texts.

The only other writing done on vellum was the addition of annotations by scholars and teachers in the margins of books. It is the marginal notes and glosses on the meaning of words in such manuscripts that provide the earliest written examples of Old Irish. The compressed angular scripts used by the scribes for such annotations became the standard script for writing Irish in later centuries. In order to write like this the scribe altered the angle of his edged pen to about forty-five degrees, and the resulting compression of the letter forms meant that more words could be fitted in a space than if the writing was done with the same pen held at a flat angle. A good example of the two scripts may be seen in the Psalter of St Caimín where the scribe, using a broad pen, wrote the text of Ps 118 in Latin using insular majuscule in the centre of the page and surrounded it with a commentary written with a smaller nib held at a sharper angle (O'Neill 1984, 23). A few other examples of specially designed text-and-commentary manuscripts written in insular majuscule have survived from the early Irish Church. In the elegantly produced 12th-century manuscript Rawlinson B 502, for the text of the *Amra Coluim Cille*, an Irish hymn in praise of the saint, the scribe began writing the hymn using majuscule letters and the appropriate pen-angle, but after a few verses changed to a sharper angle to write the minuscule forms with the same pen. It is strangely appropriate that one of the latest surviving written examples of insular majuscule should be connected with Columba, who had done much to establish the script six centuries earlier.

In a monastery great importance was attached to accurate copying. At the end of his life of Columba, Adomnán, mindful of the vagaries of scribes, concluded thus: 'I beseech all those that may wish to copy these books, nay more I adjure them through Christ, the judge of the ages, that after carefully copying they compare them with the exemplar from which they have written, and emend them with the utmost care; and also that they append this adjuration in this place' (*VC* iii. 23).

It is a significant pointer to the importance of writing and manuscript production that Baíthíne, Columba's confidant and successor, is presented as a meticulous scribe. According to Adomnán (*VC* i. 23), he went to the saint one day and asked that one of the brothers should run through a psalter he had just written and check it with him. The saint replied that it was hardly necessary since the copying was so accurate that nothing would be found wanting except a letter -*i*-, which proved true. That Baíthíne was also an expert at writing from dictation can be deduced from the fact that Adomnán records Columba's regret (which was no doubt his own) that Baíthíne was not present on a certain occasion to record important revelations of Columba

(*VC* iii. 18). Finally, Baíthíne was commissioned by Columba to finish the psalter which he was copying the day he died, which merited the comment from Adomnán that it was fitting that Baíthíne 'succeeded him not in teaching only, but in writing also' (*VC* iii. 23).

Writing on vellum was done with quills. Most likely the wing feathers of geese and swans were used, as they have always been the choice of calligraphers. Other birds may have provided pens occasionally. St Molaisse of Devenish, according to his Latin life, was in a remote place without a pen when he needed to copy a book belonging to a cleric he had met. He raised his hands and immediately one of the birds flying overhead dropped a feather with which he could write (Plummer 1910 II, 135, §18). It is difficult to use uncured quills for writing as they are generally too soft and pliable. Traditionally quills are tempered with heat, which fuses and hardens the barrel and enables a clean, sharp nib to be cut to suit the writing style.

The basic scripts of insular manuscripts in the tradition established and practised in Columban monasteries required the pens to have a chisel edge rather than a point. A pen with a chisel edge can produce both a broad and a thin line depending on the angle at which it is held rather than pressure. The pen-angle of the script of the *Cathach*, the Book of Durrow and the Book of Kells is basically the same, the chisel-edge nib being held practically parallel to the ruled guide lines. The letters were formed more by a sequence of strokes than by a continuous flowing movement. Thus the letter -*o*- was formed from two semicircles in two strokes from the top downwards, first to the right and then to the left. This vital calligraphic point is well illustrated by an incident in the life of Cainnech of Aghaboe, Columba's contemporary. It appears that one day when Cainnech was writing he heard the sound of the bell summoning the monks, and so obedient was he that he left one half of the letter -*o*- unfinished (Plummer 1910 I, 153, §3).

In the design and layout of a manuscript the most important unit was the width of the nib, which determined the '*o*-height' of the letters. This was generally about four and a half or five times the width of the nib, and since formal bookhands are written between two lines, it was the space between the lines within which the letters were formed. These lines created the grids which determined the page lay-outs and regulated the design of the entire book, even the illuminated pages, including such complex examples as the opening words of the gospels in the Book of Kells.

In manuscript illustrations scribes (and evangelists) are sometimes shown holding pen and knife as, for example, St John in MacDurnan's Gospels or St Matthew in St Gall codex 1395 (Alexander 1978, ills 328, 281). The pen, with all the flights or barbs removed, is shown curving snugly into one hand while the other holds the 'penknife'. The knife was used for cutting the quill initially and later for trimming as it got worn. Modern scribes who use quills trim them frequently, but so little needs to be removed that master calligrapher Donald Jackson estimates that he wrote seventy-two vellum documents of sixteen lines each with 4 cm of a good goose quill (Child 1985, 33). The scribe's knife was also used for correcting mistakes by scraping the ink from the vellum surface, and the rounded end of the knife-handle would have been useful for burnishing the scraped surface to make it smooth again for writing. The point of the knife was sometimes used for ruling, and some manuscripts have the writing-lines scored to give a furrow on one side of the folio and a ridge on the other. Sharp penknives may have cut more than pens and vellum on occasion, as notes written under blood-stains in later Irish manuscripts prove (Plummer 1926, 2).

There were two types of ink used in the scriptorium, a black carbon ink (basically lamp black or soot) and iron gall ink made from crushed oak galls and iron sulphate. The latter with its characteristic dark brown tint was the one most commonly used. It appears that ink was sometimes made from thorn wood: the 'ink of the green-skinned holly', *dub in chuilinn chnesglais*, is mentioned in a 12th-century poem attributed to Columba (Murphy 1956, 70-71). The earliest formula for thorn ink is given by the monk Theophilus, writing in the 11th century (*DDA* i. 38). Like the pigments for illumination, ink was stored as powder and reconstituted with water as required. It is possible that the two narrow-necked vessels in the right foreground of the portrait of Ezra as scribe in the early 8th-century *Codex Amiatinus* (Alexander 1978, ill 27) were used for sprinkling water on to powdered ink or pigment; clay replicas (c 8 cm high) made recently by the author functioned perfectly as water-droppers.

The scribe kept the liquid ink in his ink-horn. The type of ink-horn used in the insular monasteries had a long spike attached to the well or horn tip, as can be seen in the illustrations of St Matthew in the Book of Mulling and St John in MacDurnan's Gospels (Alexander 1978, ills 210, 328).This was a very practical design enabling the ink-horn to be fitted into a desk or chair or into a wall bracket, as appears in St Luke's portrait in MacRegol's Gospels (ibid., ill 263; cf. ills 176-8). It could also be stuck into the floor of a cell or into the ground if one was working outside. Such an ink-well is fixed in the ground beside the chair of St John in the Book of Kells (folio 291v), and Columba probably had a similar device in his writing-hut on Iona. Adomnán tells how one day the saint foresaw that his ink would be spilt by an awkward visitor (*VC* i. 25). The accident happened as the guest, in his eagerness to greet Columba, knocked over the ink-horn with the hem of his garment. Traditional, 20th-century Ethiopian scribes, copying manuscripts on vellum with reed pens, use an ink-horn which they fix in the ground while working. These are identical in design to those depicted in the insular manuscripts. The scribes use carbon ink which they dissolve in the horn, and when the horn is full there is enough ink for eight to ten days' writing (Selassie 1981, 17).

There is a natural capillary action in a quill which affects the ink flow. This is further controlled by the scribe writing on a tilted surface as frequently shown in miniatures. It is not known whether the early scribes used some kind or reservoir, such as the little strip of thin metal which contemporary calligraphers fit beneath their quills, or whether, like Islamic scribes, they put thread or a cloth pad in the bottom of their ink-horns to control the amount of ink taken at each dip of the pen. Consequently it is not clear what the scribe of the Book of Armagh meant when he wrote: *tri tuimthea gléso in letraim didenach*, 'three pen dips did that last column' (Plummer 1926, 12, n 2).

The production of manuscripts involved many tasks such as the calculation of page sizes, the measuring and cutting of vellum and pens as well as the ruling and scoring of lines, but by far the most difficult and tedious part was the actual writing by hand. *Is scíth mo chrob ón scríbainn*, 'my hand is weary with writing' (Murphy 1956, 70-71), was a common complaint of scribes in all ages, and often much more than the hand was affected. The laborious nature of writing is well described in a note in an 8th-century German manuscript, which exorts readers to take care to wash their hands, to turn the pages slowly and to keep fingers away from the lettering, because writing is such hard work and causes the eyes to be weary, the kidneys to be crushed, and all bodily parts to be saddened. It concludes: *tria digita scribunt, totus corpus laborat*, 'three fingers write but the whole body labours' (Trost 1991, cover). Little appears to have changed through the ages. An Italian treatise on occupational illness published in 1700 states, concerning the diseases of scribes and stenographers: 'what really crucifies these workers is their intense and incessant attention, for in this work the whole brain, the nerves and their fibres have to be under great strain' (Zanchin et al 1996, 82).

Cold and damp working conditions also militated against scribes, as illustrated by complaints penned in the margins of texts, and such conditions would have made fine writing very difficult. Columba's writing-house on Iona was wooden or had a wooden floor (*VC* i. 25), which was surely more comfortable than the clay or rush-strewn floors of other cells. Its doorway faced east, away from the prevailing wind, and the saint (presuming he was right-handed) sat inside writing where the light from the left fell on to his page.

Questions are often asked about the length of time it takes to write manuscripts, and it is possible to make suggestions based on the experience of modern scribes and some marginal notes left by medieval penmen. These estimates are useful only when considering the main text of a book, as the time taken over complex illuminations and initials depends very much on the abilities of the artist-designer and the amount of creative work involved. A proficient scribe, writing a script similar to that of, say, the Book of Durrow, would average perhaps 180 to 200 words per hour. It would be difficult to write such a formal hand for more than six hours a day even in ideal conditions. On the basis of these figures it is possible to estimate that the 485 text pages of the Book of Durrow could have been written in about sixty working days (O'Neill 1989, 99). The painted pages could in all probability have been completed within the same period (Van Stone 1994, 241). If the same scribe did the whole the book could have been finished well within a year.

This time-frame is consistent with that of Ethiopian scribes whose practices appear similar to those of early Irish scribes. A copy of the four gospels in the Bibliothèque Nationale de France (no 35), consisting of 202 folios (335 x 230 mm) was, according to its colophon, begun in 1482 and completed the following year. A 16th-century copy of 304 folios in the Vatican Library was also written within a year. As recently as 1919, a committee of the Minister of Pen in the Ethiopian government issued a regulation determining the time-limit for writing various books of the Bible and other liturgical works. In this list five months were allotted for a psalter and eight months for the four gospels (Selassie 1981, 32). Accordingly the miracle story in the life of St Crónán of Roscrea, which tells how the scribe Dímma wrote the four gospels for him in forty days and forty nights seems quite possible timewise. However, to accept that he thought he had been working for only one day (Plummer 1910 II, 24, §9) – because 'the favour of Crónán and the power of God' caused the sun to remain in the same place – perhaps requires greater faith.

The scribe of the *Leabhar Breac*, writing in the early 15th century, left marginal notes from which it is possible to estimate roughly his writing speed (O'Neill 1984, 42, using Ó Concheanainn 1973). He was affected by the legibility of the exemplar and says so in places; he was also hindered by the cold: *is am fuar toirsech and, cen tine, cen tugaid*, 'I am cold, weary without fire or covering', he jotted on page 235 (Plummer 1926, 4, n 3). Still he wrote thirty-five pages (141-75) in six weeks, approximately a page a day (excluding Sundays). An average of 900 words per page indicates five hours' writing at 180 words per hour.

Normal scribal practice required the main text of a manuscript to be written first; afterwards colour and decoration would be added according to the status and use of the book. The illumination of a manuscript would begin with initial letters for which space would be left during the writing, as can sometimes be seen in unfinished works such as the late medieval Book of Lismore. The making of any kind of elaborate initial involves drawing the letter with a pointed rather than an edged quill and gradually building up and filling in the form (see the incomplete letter -*c*- in Henry 1970, pl C). It is easy to see how zoomorphic elements fit naturally on to drawn letters, but, since few scribes would have risked experimenting with initials on the written page, such letters must have been worked out separately and then transferred. As with later scribes and illuminators, there is every reason to suppose that these designs would have been kept for reference and future use in the same way as metalworkers kept their bone trial- or motif-pieces.

Obviously a work like the Book of Kells was as highly regarded for the intricacy of its decoration and illumination as for its text, but there were probably very few books completely devoid of colour or decoration. The *Cathach*, clearly a psalter for personal use, has very simple decoration in the form of large initials, some with spirals, simple crosses and animal heads, others surrounded by red dots and filled with a yellow colour. As one of the oldest surviving Irish manuscripts its simple decorative scheme can be considered a prototype of insular manuscript decoration: a large initial followed by some letters getting gradually smaller until the opening words merge with the main text; the use of a dotted surround to highlight certain words; the filling of letters with colour, the addition of simple dot and dash patterns as space-fillers to extend text lines, and the use of red for writing introductory material. In the Book of Durrow this basic scheme is also followed, though more elaborately: large initials with spirals and interlace introduce the gospels; gradually the opening words get smaller until the ordinary writing size is reached; letters surrounded by dots are set on a field of dots; many letters are filled with colour and the space-fillers at the ends of lines become more elaborate spring-like devices. In addition, because it is a gospel book, evangelist symbols and carpet pages are included. A century later the Book of Kells, the 'great gospel of Colum Cille', follows the same scheme essentially, but infinitely more elaborately, with the opening words of the gospels taking full pages, with many portrait pages in addition to those of the evangelists, with more than two thousand decorated smaller initials and hundreds of drawings of animals, birds and people as space-fillers.

Colours, whether for panel painting or manuscript decoration, were essentially natural pigments. The principal colours used in the insular monasteries were red, which was produced from red lead, a bright yellow from orpiment (arsenic sulphide), green from 'rust' of copper (copper acetate) and white from white lead and chalk. These were mineral pigments and were more durable than many of the organic colours which were also used (for a comprehensive discussion of colours and painting techniques in the Book of Kells see Fuchs & Oltrogge 1994). Colours were stored in the form of fine powder and had to be mixed with water and a binding medium, usually egg-white or yolk, to form paint. References to pigments and illumination are scarce in early Irish sources, but there are a few later examples. In the early 15th century Mac Fhirbhisigh wrote a note about the vermilion and yellow in the Book of Lecan: *anocht aidchi domnaig 7 tairnig dath do chur ariu lebar sa uili*, 'it is the eve of Sunday tonight and I have finished putting colour on the whole of this book' (Plummer 1926, 14, n 13), and a note in the roughly contemporary manuscript, Laud 610, also records colouring being done on a Saturday night (ibid., 15, n 9).

Completed books were bound. Jonas, who wrote his life of Columbanus in the early 7th century, says that in the monastery of Bobbio Abbot Athala made books firm by bindings, *libros ligaminibus firmat* (Krusch 1902, 117, §5; Ryan 1931, 291, n 10). Depending on size, the sections or gatherings of pages were sewn onto thongs laced into wooden boards which were flush with the edges of the vellum leaves. The spines were neither glued up nor covered, and this enabled even the thickest books to open flat, as can be seen in the only manuscript from the period of the early monasteries which survives complete with its wooden binding and satchel. The Corpus Christi Missal has 212 vellum folios, but little is known about its provenance other than that it appears to have been written in Ireland about 1130 (Henry 1970, 61, pl 1).

Covers were decorated according to the importance of a book. The original boards of the Book of Armagh (written in 807) survive and, like the representations of books shown in paintings in the contemporary Book of Kells, they were once covered with pink goatskin and decorated with blind tooling. The boards of the Stowe Missal, a manuscript of the same period written for private use, were also leather-covered.

The bound books were stored in leather bags or satchels which had long carrying straps. The satchel called *tiag* in medieval Irish and *scetha* in Hiberno Latin was, to judge by surviving examples, a carefully crafted piece of leatherwork, its manufacture and tooling reflecting skills on a par with those of the scribes (Waterer 1968, 70). The *Hisperica Famina* gives a poetic description:

> This white satchel gleams,
> it has thick bristles that provide a rather small cover;
> the aforesaid container is sewn in the shape of a square;
> the upper rim surrounds a single opening,
> which is closed by a tight covering with many-angled turning knobs,
> then is bound by twelve cords,
> and the curved load is born[e] on the necks of the scholars.
> I shall describe the excellent construction of this book satchel:
> not long ago it protected the fattened flesh of a sheep;
> a butcher flayed the hairy hide with a sharp knife;
> it was stretched on the wall between thick stakes
> and dried with fiery smoke.
> A proud craftsman cut out the aforesaid container,

drew taut the skin covering with tight laces,
fashioned the four angles,
and finished the leather container with a choice strap
                                        (Herren 1974, 104-7).

A satchel was practical for keeping and carrying manuscripts safe from rodents and free from damp but was not waterproof. Adomnán relates in one story (*VC* ii. 8) how a man, while carrying books in a skin satchel, fell from a horse into the Boyne, and, in another (*VC* ii. 9), how a book of hymns in a satchel fell from the shoulder of a boy as he was crossing a bridge. In both instances, of course, the handiwork of Columba survived intact. In the monasteries the satchels hung from pegs on the walls, as the *Hisperica Famina* describes:

> Hang your white booksacks on the wall,
> set your lovely satchels in a straight line,
> so that they will be deemed a grand sight by the rustics
> (Herren 1974, 84-5).

Vellum books with wooden covers kept in satchels have a long history in Ethiopia, and it was from the Ethiopians that the Arabs adopted the use of the codex with wooden covers in the 7th century (Selassie 1981, 22). The drawing of the interior of a library of Ethiopian monks in Egypt seen by Robert Curzon in 1837 gives an impression of what a scholar's cell may have been like in early Ireland (O'Neill 1989, 100). It may even resemble Columba's own cell on Iona, because, according to a note in the *Félire Óengusso*, he too had a 'hanging library':

> *In tan ba marb Lon tuitid na tiaga lebar ro batar isin aracul i raibe Colum cille. Sochtaid uili frisin tair[m]crith sin na lebar. Is ann isbert Colum cille: Longarad, ar se, sui cach dana i n-Osraigi, atbath indossa.*

When Lon was dead the book-satchels that were in the cell where Colum cille dwelt fall. All are silent at that noisy shaking of the books. Then said Colum cille: 'Longarad' saith he, 'the master of every art in Ossory, has just now died' (Stokes 1905, 198-9).

Reading the Scriptures in the
Life of Columba

Jennifer O'Reilly

While commentators have acknowledged the importance of the monastic life of Iona to the *Vita Columbae* (*VC*),[1] the book has also been discussed in the context of dynastic and ecclesiastical politics at the time of its composition shortly before 700 (Herbert 1988; Sharpe 1995). It has been seen, in part, as 'Adomnán's answer to Northumbrian attacks on Columba' which had been made during the Easter controversy and as a response to the pressure on Iona exerted by the Roman party in Ireland and the primatial claims of Armagh (Picard 1982, 174; 1984). Important work has been done on the work's sources and literary character. It features vivid circumstantial details drawing on oral and written testimonies of Columba as well as examples of his continuing power from beyond the grave, as experienced by Adomnán, the ninth abbot of Iona (679-704), and other named eyewitnesses. Adomnán's tripartite account of the saint's gift of prophecy, his miraculous powers and converse with angels also testifies to Columba's holiness according to universally respected literary models (Herbert 1988). Gertrud Brüning long ago identified passages which echo Evagrius's translation of Athanasius's *Life of Antony*, the *Life of St Martin* by Sulpicius Severus and the *Dialogues* of Gregory the Great (Brüning 1917); the structure of the *Vita Columbae* and the patterning of its miracle stories have since been compared with other 7th-century Irish saints' lives and with earlier continental hagiography (Picard 1985; Stancliffe 1989).

A good deal remains to be done, however, on the use of Scripture in the *VC*. This chapter examines some examples of scriptural passages which Adomnán actually quotes and biblical parallels he evokes; it suggests that Scripture provides not simply authenticating models for some episodes in his life of Columba, but an interpretation of them in the manner of the monastic tradition of *lectio divina*, which is often expounded through his narrative. The chapter concludes with a reading in this tradition of the sustained ac-

1 The *VC* is referred to in the edition and translation of Anderson and Anderson (1961; rev edn Anderson 1991).

count of the last days of Columba (*VC* iii. 23), which illustrates Adomnán's monastic objectives and inspiration but also reveals unexpected insights into aspects of the Easter controversy.

THE COVENANT

Bede and Adomnán, Constantine and Joshua (VC i. 1)
The book's opening story of Columba and the Saxon king Oswald has been seen as part of an aggrandizing claim for the role of Iona: Adomnán's manipulation of Old Testament models in his portrait of Columba as the champion of rightful kings reveals that Adomnán himself, as Columba's successor, 'was bidding for a role in their selection and in the determination of their policies. That was clearly his grand design' (Enright 1985, 100-2). Others have read the episode partly as a measured answer to the Northumbrians after Whitby or a counterpoise to the cult of Cuthbert at Lindisfarne (Picard 1982, 172-5).

A vision of Columba appeared to the exiled Saxon ruler Oswald before his battle against the British king Cadwalla and assured him: 'The Lord has granted to me that at this time your enemies shall be turned to flight' (*VC* i. 1). Though vastly outnumbered by the enemy, Oswald was victorious in the land of the Saxons which, until then, had been darkened by paganism. Adomnán's opening story thus demonstrates Columba's posthumous prophetic and intercessory power and presents Iona's founder as the heavenly patron of the evangelization of the land of the Saxons. Yet Adomnán does not use this episode as a partisan opportunity to vaunt or even mention the importance of the Columban monks of Iona, either in baptizing Oswald while he had been in exile 'among the Irish' or in evangelizing the English after Oswald's victory in 634. It was left to Bede to record Oswald's invitation of the Iona mission to Northumbria during the abbacy of Séigíne and the setting up of its base at Lindisfarne under the exemplary figure of Áedán (*HE* iii. 3, 5, 17).[2] Bede's account of Oswald does not include the vision of Columba and draws a parallel with Constantine (Stancliffe 1995, 50-51).

The two versions of the Oswald story perhaps bear further comment which may help clarify Adomnán's use of Scripture. Eusebius, in his *Ecclesiastical History* ix, had described Constantine's victory at the Milvian Bridge over the tyrannical Maxentius. Bede describes God's latter-day triumph in the victory of Oswald against 'the outrageous tyranny of the British king' at the brook called Deniseburn (*HE* iii. 1). In the *Life of Constantine* i. 26-9, Eusebius tells how Constantine had been commanded by Christ to make a

---

2 The *HE* is referred to in the edition and translation of Colgrave and Mynors (1969).

likeness of the trophy of a cross revealed to him in a vision and to use it as a safeguard in battle. Bede pictures Oswald setting up a newly-made cross as a standard or trophy and praying with his army for God's help in a just war against the enemy at a place called Heavenfield, a name which was 'an omen of future happenings; it signified that a heavenly sign (*caeleste tropaeum*) was to be erected there, a heavenly victory won' (*HE* iii. 2). Oswald, who was the first to introduce the cross into Bernicia, took the initiative in inviting Irish monks to evangelize the whole people whom he now ruled and gained from God 'greater earthly realms than any of his ancestors had possessed. In fact he held under his sway all the peoples of Britain, divided among the speakers of four different languages, British, Pictish, Irish and English' (*HE* iii. 6). The implied parallel is with the victory of Constantine by which the Church was established throughout the various peoples of the Roman empire.

In Adomnán's earlier account there is also a Constantinian element but it is related to the means by which Oswald was assured of divine favour. While he was sleeping in his tent in camp on the eve of battle, the vision of Columba appeared and promised him that his enemies would be turned to flight. Oswald himself described the vision to Séigíne, the reigning abbot of Iona, from whom it was handed down to Adomnán. Constantine told his biographer Eusebius how Christ had appeared to him in his sleep at night (Lactantius has the detail of its being on the very eve of the battle) with the sign which was to safeguard him from his enemies. Adomnán says that, following his victory, Oswald was 'ordained by God as emperor of the whole of Britain'; Oswald's rule is seen as the divinely-ordained context for the baptism of realms previously pagan. In recalling different aspects of the story of Constantine in their accounts of Oswald, Adomnán and Bede share a providential view of history and a belief in the universal nature of salvation.

There are details unique to Adomnán's account which give a further insight into his particular purpose in telling the story in the *Vita Columbae*. Quoting from Exodus 15, Eusebius had compared Constantine's victory over the tyrant Maxentius, whose troops were drowned in the River Tiber, with the victory of Moses and 'the God-fearing nation of the ancient Hebrews' when the 'villainous tyrant' Pharaoh and the Egyptians were drowned in the Red Sea. Bede does not explicitly retain the parallel but Adomnán interestingly makes the comparison instead with Moses' successor, Joshua. Unlike Bede, who says that Oswald's entire army prayed at the trophy cross before the battle, Adomnán says that when Oswald's followers heard of his vision of Columba, they promised to receive baptism after the prophesied victory; previously 'all that land of the English was shadowed by the darkness of heathenism and ignorance, excepting the king Oswald himself, and twelve men who had been baptized with him, while he was in exile among the Irish.' The apostolic number twelve is frequently specified in accounts of the founding of churches and missions by those seen as the successors of the apostles, including Columba's original foundation of Iona (*VC* iii. 3). Such an interpretation here may seem at first sight to be precluded because the twelve baptized men who are specified in Adomnán's account of Oswald's expedition are lay followers of a military leader. There is, however, a further guide to interpretation in Adomnán's text.

In Oswald's Constantinian vision on the eve of battle, Columba, 'radiant in angelic form', addressed him with words of encouragement which were 'the same that the Lord spoke to Joshua ben-Nun, before the crossing of the Jordan, after the death of Moses, saying: "Be strong, and act manfully; behold I will be with you" and so on'. The epic story thus begun in the Book of Joshua three times repeats this divine assurance that the promised land would be delivered into the hands of the children of Israel if they continued to observe God's law (Josh 1. 6-18; cf. Deut 31. 6-7, 23). They left their camp, led by the Levites carrying the Ark of the Covenant in which the written law was enshrined, and came to the River Jordan whose waters miraculously drew back for them to cross, signifying the living God in their midst. The Lord commanded Joshua to choose twelve men, one from each of the non-priestly tribes of the chosen people, to take twelve stones from the river bed where the priests stood with the Ark (Josh 3). They were to set up the stones in the camp they pitched at Gilgal on the far side of the Jordan as a perpetual monument of their divine deliverance and to mark the territory which they were to conquer from the enemy with numerically smaller forces. The Old Testament account itself shows that the crossing of the Jordan into the promised land recapitulated the Israelites' deliverance from the Egyptians in the crossing of the Red Sea at the beginning of their long exile and demonstrated God's continuing protection of a new generation of his people. God commanded that the meaning of the twelve stones was to be explained to future generations, 'that all the people of the earth may learn the most mighty hand of the Lord' (Josh 4.19-25). In *De Locis Sanctis* (*DLS*) Adomnán records that the pilgrim Arculf actually saw those same twelve stones preserved in the great church at Gilgal; it was 'built in the place where the sons of Israel first pitched their tent and dwelt in the land of Canaan when they had crossed the Jordan' (*DLS* ii. 14-15). Adomnán quotes in full the Lord's command to Joshua to have the twelve men set up the twelve stones (Josh 4. 2-3) and elaborates the point that the church containing those same stones was built on the very site where the tabernacle had been pitched after the Jordan crossing. The Christian site and church building at Gilgal in the Holy Land, 'honoured with wondrous cult and reverence by the folk of that region', thus at the literal level of understanding commemorated the historical entrance of the children of Israel and the Ark of the Covenant into the earthly promised land.

The Joshua story was interpreted in patristic exegesis as a prefiguring of Christ leading the new chosen people of the universal Church into the *heavenly* promised land. Joshua's victory over the enemy occupying the promised land could be read as a spiritual battle. Jesus, the Greek form of Joshua's name used in the Septuagint (and twice used by Adomnán in *DLS* ii. 13) helped establish the parallel. Jerome described Joshua as 'a type of the Lord in name as well as in deed, who crossed over the Jordan, subdued hostile kingdoms, divided the land among the conquering people and who, in every city, village, mountain, river, hill-torrent and boundary which he dealt with, marked out the spiritual realms of the heavenly Jerusalem, that is, of the Church' (*Ep* 53: Gibson 1894, 99-100). The works of Jerome were well known in Columban monasteries (Meehan 1958, 14); *Epistle* 53 is warmly commended in Cassiodorus's *Institutes* and this particular passage from the epistle is closely paraphrased by Isidore of Seville in his *Etymologiae* vi. 2.8. Hillgarth has noted (1984, 8) that the *Etymologiae* was used by at least ten Irish writers before the end of the 7th century. The patristic interpretation of the Joshua story was to be perpetuated in the tradition of Hiberno-Latin exegesis. The etymological discussion of the *nomina sacra* in Angers 55, for example, says:

> just as in the historical sense, Jesus/Joshua the son of Nun, led the children of Israel over into the promised land, similarly, Jesus himself whose name means Saviour or Salvation, led the children of Israel (that is, the souls of those who see God) into the new promised land (that is, into eternal life). Of this land the prophet says: 'I believe I will see the good things of the Lord in the land of the living' (Ps 26. 13; cf. Ps 114. 8-9; Ps 141.6; Latin text in *CCSL* 108B, 147).

Sacramentally, this divine deliverance is effected in baptism. In mystagogical exegesis Joshua's crossing of the Jordan was commonly a figure of Christ's sanctification of the baptismal water for believers, and the twelve stones set up in the Jordan were seen to prefigure the apostles whom Christ appointed as ministers of baptism (Matt 28. 19). The twelve stones of the Joshua story prefigure the twelve apostles in the *Laterculus Malalianus*, which has been ascribed to Adomnán's older contemporary, Theodore of Tarsus, archbishop of Canterbury 668-90: 'for each single tribe of Israel, there is one apostle in the New Testament, as if they brought back twelve living stones from the bed of the Jordan' (Stevenson 1995, 147, 213; cf. 1 Pet 2. 5; Gal 2. 9; Eph 2. 20; Rev 21. 12-14).

The image from the opening of the Book of Joshua had already been applied in the 6th century by the British historian Gildas to a still earlier stage of the history of the Church in Britain. During the Roman persecution, the River Thames had opened up at the prayer of the newly converted St Alban to provide him with a pathway which would lead him beyond death to the heavenly city, 'a route resembling the untrodden way made dry for the Israelites, when the ark of the testament stood for a while on gravel in the midstream of the Jordan'. Gildas notes that Joshua's military victory, by which the people of God were, historically, settled in the promised land, may be interpreted in its moral (or tropological) sense as the conquest of sin and the establishment of 'the spiritual Israel' (Winterbottom 1978, 19-20, 55-6).

The original biblical context of the Joshua episode, and the traditional interpretation of its various prophetic levels applying to Christ, to his body the Church, to the individual soul and to eternal life can, therefore, offer an insight into Adomnán's particular shaping of the Oswald story. His allusion to Joshua does not simply evoke a familiar type of the warrior leader who transmitted and observed God's law. The fulfilment of Columba's prophecy of Oswald's victorious entry from exile into his own promised land, which brought all his people to baptism, presents a latter-day image of Christ's deliverance of his new chosen people and of the continuing sacramental and eventual eschatological fulfilment of the Old Testament prophecy contained in the Joshua story. Adomnán succinctly presents Oswald's victory as part of the *continuing* fulfilment of this Old Testament prefiguring of the Church by combining the Joshua story with a reminiscence of the dream of Constantine, whose divinely-ordained military victory had earlier led to the historical establishment of the Church throughout the peoples of the Roman empire. Similarly, it is implied, the darkness of heathenism on the edge of that world in another generation was vanquished by the victory of Oswald who was 'ordained by God as emperor of the whole of Britain'. God speaks through Columba; like an Old Testament prophet he is sanctified from before birth (*VC* second Preface) and set over nations and kingdoms (cf. Jer 1. 5, 9-10), but his prophetic power transcends partisan claims. Adomnán's opening chapter shows the saint to be involved in Christ's universal work of redemption, and so announces a major theme of the book.

De Locis Sanctis and water from the rock (VC ii. 10)

Bede devoted a good deal of his exegesis to Jerusalem and its temple as an image of the Church on earth, of the individual soul and of the heavenly Jerusalem to which the Church is journeying (O'Reilly 1995). In his account of how the Church of the apostles was taken to the ends of the earth, however, Bede honoured Jerusalem as the historical starting-place of the Church by incorporating extracts from his *De Locis Sanctis*, based on Adomnán's earlier work of that title. The extracts describe in particular the great Constantinian churches which enshrined the hallowed Christian sites of the Nativity, Crucifixion, Resurrection and Ascension, and the Martyrium commemorating the finding of the True Cross (*HE* v. 16-17). Adomnán makes these stones speak.

In *De Locis Sanctis* (c 686-9) Adomnán repeatedly insists that the worthy pilgrim Arculf 'saw the things that we describe here with his own eyes' (i. 12). Arculf drew sketch plans of the Holy Sepulchre and of three other churches for Adomnán (i. 2, 18, 24); he described the physical features of the holy buildings and places, collected local stories and wonder-tales about them and their associated relics, and participated in liturgical ceremonies and devotions at the sites through which the sacred scriptural events they commemorated were made vivid in the lives of the pilgrims. Arculf often used to visit the sepulchre of Christ in the Anastasis 'and measured its features with his own hand' (i. 2); through an opening in the lid of a reliquary he touched the chalice used at the Last Supper (i. 7); he kissed the relic of Christ's shroud (i. 9); he swam to and fro across the Jordan at the site of Christ's baptism (ii. 16). He was 'a sedulous visitor' to the church on Mount Olivet which enshrined Christ's footprints in the place from which he had ascended and once Arculf 'was actually present ... at the very hour' to experience the force of the divine wind which filled the church, as it did every year, after the midday mass on the anniversary of the Lord's ascension. He related that the light from the eight lamps of this hill-top church at night pours into the hearts of the faithful 'greater eagerness for divine love and imbues them with a sense of awe coupled with great interior compunction' (i. 24).

In the *Vita Columbae* Adomnán also sketches a holy land, but at the northernmost edge of the Christian world where Christ's work of redemption, prophesied in the Old Testament, continued to be articulated through Columba. The veracity of the memorials to Columba enshrined within Adomnán's book is attested by venerable local eyewitnesses in stories full of graphic details of time and place, of coastal weather and Irish names and folklore; by the topography of the island monastery of Iona and places in its area of influence made sacred by the presence of Christ in Columba; by the continuing practice on Iona of the monastic office and the recurring cycle of the liturgical year, some of whose scriptural texts and feasts had been so illumined by the saint. Adomnán's two works are more complementary in objective and technique than has generally been recognised.

O'Loughlin has ably revealed a different aspect of *DLS*, namely how Adomnán used Arculf's testimony, supplemented by other historical written evidence, to help clarify details in the literal text of various passages in Scripture concerning the Holy Places, in the manner advocated in Augustine's guide to hermeneutics, *De Doctrina Christiana*. O'Loughlin also notes the importance of Jerusalem itself to the monastic life and imagination through its role in Scripture, exegesis and liturgy. He quotes Cassian's well-known use in *Collationes* xiv. 8 of Jerusalem as an example in a systematic demonstration of how Scripture can be understood both historically and at various spiritual levels – allegorical, anagogical and tropological (O'Loughlin 1992c). The critical resolution of any apparent discrepancies or ambiguities in the literal text and its historical meaning is not only compatible with a spiritual interpretation but is its essential preparation. Some topographical and other local features recorded in *De Locis Sanctis* prompted Adomnán to comment not only on the literal sense but on the spiritual interpretation of certain Old Testament texts, including Isa 33. 16-17 and Pss 44. 8; 73. 12; 77. 16. Like many commentators since Irenaeus and Origen, including Cassian in his demonstration of the fourfold meaning of Jerusalem, Adomnán quotes the example of St Paul in I Cor 10.4 as a standard authority for the exegetical method by which the inspired text of the Old Testament is read as a figure 'written for our correction'. It has been suggested that Adomnán's particular association of I Cor 10. 4 with Ps 77. 16 may be adapted from Cassiodorus's *Expositio Psalmorum* (O'Loughlin 1994b, 25), but its use within the narrative of *DLS* and the implications of this for reading the *VC* have not been explored.

Arculf reported that a stream miraculously created at the time of Christ's birth was still to be seen at Bethlehem, near the church built on the site of the Nativity; Adomnán then expounded the 'literal text' of the visible evidence and supposed history of the stream as a graphic sign of a theological truth. It originated in a miracle performed by Christ, 'of which the prophet sings: "Who brought forth water from the rock" [Ps 77. 16] and the apostle Paul: "Now the rock was Christ" [I Cor 10. 4] – he who, contrary to nature, brought forth a consoling flow for the thirsting people from the hardest rock in the desert' (*DLS* ii. 3). Adomnán here recalls St Paul's well-known interpretation of the incident of Moses striking water from the rock during the journey through the desert (Ex 17. 6) as a prefiguring of Christ's deliverance of his chosen people and of his continuing provision of the life-giving sacraments for the journey to the promised land. This divine assurance or 'consolation' to the faithful is embodied in the account in *DLS* ii. 3 that Christ had provided the stream at Bethlehem at his incarnation and 'from that very day up to our time through the cycles of many centuries ... without any failing or diminution'. Adomnán stresses both this continuity and Christ's divine identity by citing an additional text to show 'It is the same power [of God] and wisdom of God' (cf. I Cor 1. 24) which first brought forth water from the rock at Bethlehem and always keeps its channels full of water. Ps 77. 16 and I Cor 10. 4, texts directly quoted by Adomnán, are both from key scriptural reminiscences of incidents on the Exodus journey, including the crossing of the Red Sea, which Paul interprets as a prefiguring of Christian deliverance through baptism into Christ. The typology of the water from the rock is based not on the thirst of the chosen people of the Old Covenant but on

God's provision for their needs, so it could be read as a prefiguring of the eucharist, but Adomnán gives the common baptismal interpretation. He supplies the narrative detail that when the water used in washing the infant Christ had been poured away, it had flowed into a natural channel in the rock, and had miraculously continued to stream from the rock beside the church of the Nativity. The apocryphal story of the washing of the Christ Child was traditionally interpreted as an image of his baptism in which he blessed the sacramental cleansing water for believers; it is of interest that Adomnán records, not that the pilgrim Arculf drank from this 'purest water', but that he washed in it.

In the *VC* Adomnán describes the miraculous origins of another spring. 'At one time during the saint's life in pilgrimage, while he was making a journey', Columba prayed in a waterless place and blessed a rock from which water then flowed in an abundant cascade (ii. 10). How are we to read this? Gregory the Great's listener in the *Dialogues* ii. 8 readily recognised that the story of St Benedict's miraculous production of a water supply for three of his monasteries built on a mountain-top showed that 'like Moses he drew water from the rock'. Gregory corrected his listener's assumption, however, that this and other such biblically-patterned stories simply revealed that Benedict 'was filled with the spirit of all the saints'; rather, such stories revealed that Benedict 'had the spirit of him alone who by the grace of his redemption has filled the hearts of all his elect'. Similarly, the brief episode in *VC* ii. 10 does more than conventionally glorify Columba through his implied identification with Moses. Adomnán's narrative detail that the water from the rock was provided to enable Columba to baptize a child interprets the significance of the Old Testament story in accordance with St Paul's interpretation in I Cor 10. 4. Without directly quoting the scriptural texts used to expound the meaning of the miraculous spring at Bethlehem seen by Arculf, the circumstantial local details concerning the child baptized by Columba, such as his Irish name and parents' place of origin, and the fact that the holy spring, potent in the name of Columba, is still to be seen there 'even today', bring to life, here and now, the sacramental continuation of Christ's work of redemption and provision of spiritual refreshment for his pilgrim people which the Old Testament type prefigured.

Such a reading does not require that the incident in the *Vita Columbae* be regarded as a complete literary fabrication. Patristic commentators insisted that the historical or material truth of biblical texts was not invalidated by the fact that they have a spiritual significance. In the *City of God* xiii. 21 Augustine says it would be arbitrary, for example, to assume there was no material rock from which water flowed when Moses struck it, just because the passage in Ex 17. 6 can be interpreted spiritually, as St Paul did when he said 'Now the rock was Christ' (I Cor 10. 4).

The early development of the Pauline methodology and its application to the spiritual life passed into the monastic tradition particularly through Cassian and Cassiodorus. Expounding I Cor 10. 4, Irenaeus had shown that the divine law and institutions revealed to Moses on the mountain and the events experienced in the desert were prefigurings of things to come, written down for our instruction, so that the chosen people might learn how to persevere in serving God and be called 'from secondary to primary matters, that is through the figurative to the true, through the temporal to the eternal, through the carnal to the spiritual, through the earthly to the celestial' (Grant 1997, 148). This was expounded in detail in Origen's extensive series of homilies on the Pentateuch, in which the entire Exodus story of deliverance and the lifelong pilgrimage through the desert, with repeated experiences of temptation, hunger, thirst and weariness, and of divine consolation provided by resting-places and nourishment on the way, became an image of the spiritual life (Heine 1981; cf. Chadwick 1968, 83-4). MacDonald (1995) has discussed an example of such a parallel in *VC* ii. 2, which recalls Ex 15. 22-6, and there is an incident in *VC* i. 37 which, though it does not cite a specific Old Testament text, seems in the light of the tradition outlined here to be open to such an interpretation.

Food for the journey (VC i. 37)
Baíthíne, who is described as Columba's cousin, foster-son (*alumnus*) and one of the original twelve companions, was Columba's successor as abbot of Iona and shared his feast-day (Anderson 1991, 239; Herbert 1988, 37-9). The *VC* gives valuable glimpses of his formation and exercise of spiritual authority under Columba. One harvest time Baíthíne was in charge of a group of monks returning, heavily laden, from the fields to the monastery. At the halfway point of their homeward journey they were all revived by an extraordinary sensation of joy and sweetness. A senior among them described a fragrance 'as of all flowers combined into one', a miraculous lightening of their heavy load so that it seemed no burden, a heat like fire but not painful, and 'for several days they had this feeling, in the same place, and at the same vesper hour'. Baíthíne discerned that Columba ' "is much distressed when we are late in reaching him. And for the reason that he does not come in the body to meet us, his spirit meets us as we walk, and in this fashion refreshes and gladdens us". Hearing these words, they ... worshipped Christ in the holy and blessed man' (i. 37). In the monks' eventual recognition of Christ in the spiritual consolation mediated to them by Columba, the reader sees something of the disciples' delayed recognition of the risen Christ's sustaining presence with them on the Emmaus road at sunset: 'Did not our hearts burn within us?' (Luke 24. 32; cf. Ps 125).

The circumstantial details of time and place in Adomnán's account of the

monks' repeated experience – 'in the evening', 'at the vesper hour', on their
weary homeward journey to the monastery – is a vivid literal realization of
their daily and life-long spiritual journey to their heavenly home. It recalls
the Exodus story of how the Israelites were physically sustained by God on
their pilgrimage to the earthly promised land. The Israelites marvelled at the
miraculous manna; the very name means 'What is it?', *Quid est hoc?* (Ex 16.
15). Moses explained 'It is the bread God has given you.' When asked for a
sign, Christ interpreted the manna as referring to himself (John 6. 30-51);
the Old Testament incident prompts the faithful to continue asking the
meaning of this divinely provided consolation. Similarly, the Columban monks
had begged Baíthíne 'that he would endeavour to explain to them ... the
cause and origin' of their miraculous experience of spiritual refreshment.

The tableau in *VC* i. 37 enacts a central theme in monastic literature.
Those addressed in the *Rule of the Master*, for example, are pictured travelling the road of the pilgrimage of this life, tired, thirsty and burdened with
their sins. The divine voice draws them, 'Come to me, all you who labour
and are burdened and I will give you rest ... my yoke is easy and my burden
light' (Matt 11. 28-9), and they are refreshed from a spring of living water
(Isa 55. 1; Eberle 1977, 94-5). In answer to the question 'What is the holy art
that the abbot must teach his disciples in the monastery?', the Lord replies
through the master, outlining the scriptural precepts of the monastic life.
The spiritual consolation and sacramental refreshment enjoyed by those who
persevere in this life is but a foretaste of the paradisal fruits and flowing
rivers awaiting them in 'the heavenly homeland of the saints', heady with the
fragrance of flowers (Eberle 1977, 117, 138). Columbanus's *Regula Monachorum*
ix draws on Cassian to warn monks humbly to seek the spiritual counsel of
their elders: 'We are enjoined through Moses: "Ask thy father and he will
show thee, thy elders and they will tell thee" ' (Deut 32. 7). Through such
lowliness the monks may learn the lowliness of Christ in order to feel the
easiness of his yoke and the lightness of his burden: 'For lowliness of heart is
the repose of the soul when wearied with vices and toils and in so far as it is
wholly drawn to the meditation of this ... so far does it enjoy repose and
refreshment within, with the result that even bitter things are sweet to it, and
things before considered hard and toilsome it feels to be plain and easy'
(Walker 1957, 139-41).

Drought and relics (*VC* ii. 44)

Adomnán's account of one of Columba's posthumous blessings also takes up
this theme. He describes how the community ended a severe drought on Iona
by walking in procession around the lifeless fields with the saint's relics,
elevating the relic of his tunic three times and invoking Columba's name (ii.
44). This use of relics recalls a story in Gregory's *Dialogues* iii. 15 (Brüning

1917, 251; Herbert 1988, 137-8), but it is transformed in Adomnán's eyewitness account. He places the ceremony after the months of March and April (and therefore after Easter) yet still 'in the season of spring' shortly after ploughing and sowing, which might well indicate the period of rogationtide observed in Gallican practice during the three days before the feast of the Ascension. Rogationtide was traditionally a time of supplication characterized by penitential fasting and processions accompanied by the recitation of litanies. Such processions were originally concerned with securing the protection of God and his saints for the newly planted crops and their eventual good harvest, but they could include more general supplications, or be directed to local crises and needs in which the carrying of locally revered relics would have been particularly appropriate.

Adomnán's telling of the story however, does not simply record a memorable historical example of such a procession or reproduce a hagiographical *topos*. The occasion of the ritual is used to expound its continuing significance for the present community. The narrative focuses on the fulfilment of a prophetic scriptural text but also suggests that Scripture offered models for behaviour and reactions to events, not simply a lens through which the past was viewed. Adomnán says that the severe springtime drought 'about seventeen years ago' seemed to threaten the monastery with 'the Lord's curse laid upon transgressors, where he says, in the book of Leviticus: "I will give you a sky above like iron, and earth like bronze. Your labour shall be spent in vain. The earth shall yield no produce, nor shall the trees give fruit" and so forth' (Lev 26. 19-20; *VC* ii. 44). Adomnán specifically says that, 'Reading this, and in dread of the impending stroke, we formed a plan', namely to take the tunic worn by Columba at his death and books written by his own hand in solemn procession around the fields.

The original context of the scriptural quotation offers an insight into Adomnán's presentation of an incident which he stresses he personally witnessed. In Leviticus 26 God recalls his covenant made through Moses on Sinai (Exod 20) and renews both his promise and his warning to his people, summarized in solemn benedictions and maledictions: 'If you walk in my precepts and keep my commandments, and do them, I will give you rain in due seasons. And the ground shall bring forth its increase and the trees shall be filled with fruit ...' (Lev 26. 3-4); conversely, 'If you do not hear me, nor do all my commandments, if you despise my laws ... I will break the pride of your stubbornness: and I will make to you the heaven above as iron, and the earth as brass. Your labour shall be spent in vain; the ground shall not bring forth her increase; nor the trees yield their fruit ...' (Lev 26. 14-15, 19-20). The passage quoted by Adomnán also appears in the list of divine blessings and cursings which sanction the ten commandments in Deut 28. 23. Such sanctions are reiterated, in whole or in part, several times in the Pentateuch, ritually recapitulating as a rule of life for the present reader the Exodus deliverance and God's covenant with his chosen people. He promises them a fruitful land, 'a land of hills and plains, expecting rain from heaven'. If they obey God's commandments he will give to their land 'the early rain and the latter rain', that they may gather in their corn; however, if they depart from him, he will 'shut up heaven and the rain come not down nor the earth yield her fruit'. Repeatedly he exhorts them: 'Lay up these my words in your hearts and minds ... teach your children that they meditate on them' (Deut 11. 8-18). The renewal of the law, divinely inscribed on stone, was received by Moses on the mount and placed in the Ark of the Covenant, which had been made for the purpose at God's command (Deut 10. 3-5, 8, 11). This archetypal reliquary enshrining the written word of God was ceremonially carried by four Levites on the Hebrews' exile in the wilderness, leading the people of God on their journey through the desert to the promised land (Deut 27. 2-3).

Against such a biblical background, Adomnán's description of the relic procession around the parched fields of Iona may be seen as rather more than a rain-making ceremony. It is a ritual enactment by the monastic community of its renewed pledge to walk in the divine precepts in order to make the earthly promised land of the monastery itself spiritually fruitful, a foretaste of the heavenly paradise. On their symbolic pilgrimage, the Iona monks carried books written by Columba's own hand and the tunic worn by Columba 'in the hour of his departure from the flesh' (ii. 44), when he had crossed over 'to the heavenly country from this weary pilgrimage' (iii. 23). They exalted him, not only as their founder and intercessor, but as the embodiment of the monastic life they were pledged to live; carrying the relics of one so close to God reassured them of God's continuing presence with those who keep his commandments. Adomnán does not describe any reliquaries, though it seems reasonable to assume that, by the late 7th century, these relics would have been enshrined; the text suggests that the tunic and at least some of the books remained accessible and were exposed on occasion. There is a striking contemporary analogue for the concept underlying the Iona ceremony in the panegyric beginning *Benchuir bona regula*, 'Bangor of the good monastic rule', preserved in the 7th-century Antiphonary of Bangor, which pictures the monastic community of Bangor itself figured in the Old Testament image of the Ark of the Covenant, protected by cherubim and carried by four men. This is a monastic and local application of the patristic interpretation of the Ark as representing the Church, the place of the divine presence among the new chosen people on their pilgrimage through the desert exile of this life to the heavenly paradise and the new Jerusalem. The Old Testament Ark of the Covenant which, when not being carried, stood in the Holy of Holies in the desert tabernacle and later in the temple in Jerusalem, could represent both of these earthly sanctuaries and, like them, was a common figure of Christ's body, the Church, and of the individual Christian called to be like him. But the Ark was also a prefiguring of the heavenly sanctuary of the new Jerusalem on which the tabernacle and temple were patterned and which the pilgrim Church of the faithful on earth, and particularly the monastic life, seek to imitate.

Just as the good monastic life of Bangor could be pictured in the image of the Ark of the Covenant, so the portable reliquary of an individual saint in whom the spiritual life had been perfected could evoke the Ark. The later Irish reliquary of St Manchán still preserves its four carrying rings. The Old Testament Ark could only be carried by its guardian Levites. In describing how St Benedict had overcome the temptations of youth and become a mature spiritual guide for others, Gregory the Great noted in *Dialogues* ii. 2: 'The same principle was taught by Moses, when he ordained that the Levites ... should not have charge of the sacred vessels until they were fifty' (McCann 1980, 22). Similarly, Adomnán specifies it was decided that the relics of Columba should be carried by some of the monastic elders. The unworthy carrying of the Ark, and of reliquaries, could have dire consequences. In Northumbria in the 680s Ecgfrith's queen had brazenly stripped Bishop Wilfrid of a precious reliquary and worn it as an ornament while riding around in her chariot: 'But this brought nothing but evil upon her, as it did to the Philistines when, after routing the people of Israel, they captured the Ark of God and brought the holy of holies through their cities' (Colgrave 1927, 71).

Adomnán's narrative of the relic procession in *VC* ii. 44 describes associative rather than corporeal relics, but these tokens of Columba's earthly and heavenly life are used in a way peculiarly fitted to suggest the presence of the saint. It was decided that those who carried Columba's relics should 'three times raise and shake in the air' the white tunic in which the saint had died. The pilgrim Arculf testified that he had been present in Jerusalem when the shroud which had covered Christ's head (a relic whose authenticity had been miraculously demonstrated when it rose from a pyre and fluttered 'on high like a bird with outstretched wings') had one day been taken out of its reliquary, raised up and revered by the faithful (*DLS* i. 9). The raising and shaking in the air of the white tunic of the dove, Columba, may similarly have suggested his risen life.

Insular monastic writers were heirs to a rich exegetical tradition on the Pentateuch's descriptions of Moses going up into the mountain, or entering the tabernacle in which the Ark of the Covenant was housed, in order to speak with God. They became common images of the contemplative life and of monastic *lectio*, most memorably described in Cassian's *Conference* xiv.10 where he stresses it is impossible for the impure and worldly, however learned, to gain the gift of spiritual knowledge. As an heir to this tradition Gregory the Great in his *Pastoral Care* exhorted spiritual leaders constantly to meditate on God's word, to follow Moses' example and stand before the Ark and consult the Lord, seeking a solution to any particular problems they may have in the pages of the sacred word. Adomnán presents the elders' perambulation of the drought-stricken fields of Iona with Columba's relics as such a decision inspired by the reading of Scripture; he further notes that the ritual itself included reading from Columba's books (most probably from his transcriptions of Scripture), on the Hill of the Angels, exactly 'where at one time the citizens of the heavenly country were seen descending to confer with the holy man' (*VC* ii. 44). At this hallowed place of contact between heaven and earth, like Moses on the mount or before the Ark, Columba thus continued to speak to God on behalf of his people. In describing the exaltation of his relics (which in the next story are laid on the altar 'with psalms and fasting'), Adomnán also suggests the life of sanctity perfected in Columba which his community offered up in the penitential pilgrimage of their monastic life.

After the relic procession had been performed 'according to the adopted plan', Adomnán reports that the sky, which 'had been bare of clouds' for two months, 'was with marvellous rapidity instantly covered with clouds that rose from the sea; and there was great rain, falling by day and by night. And the earth, previously parched, was well watered, and produced its crop in season, and a very plentiful harvest in that same year.' The image of rain-filled clouds, frequently used in the Old Testament to describe God's mercies, in exegesis typified the raining down of God's spiritual blessings on the faithful. In Adomnán's story such blessings are mediated by Columba. Similarly, Cassian describes in *Conference* xiv. 16 how the word of salvation which a holy man with spiritual knowledge commits to his hearers, 'will be watered by the plentiful showers of the Holy Spirit ... [as] the prophet promised, "the rain will be given to your seed, wherever you sow in the land, and the bread of the corn of the land shall be most plentiful and fat" ' (Gibson 1894, 444).

THE LAST DAYS OF COLUMBA (*VC* iii. 23)

Final blessings

Gregory the Great had said of St Benedict of Nursia that he was 'rightly called Benedict since he was so much blessed by God'. The play on the monastic name highlights the role of Benedict as a vessel of divine grace. Similarly, Adomnán in his second Preface explains the appropriateness of Columba's name, which reveals his nature as a special dwelling-place of the Holy Spirit (O'Reilly 1994, 345-54), evokes images of Columba being caught up in contemplation and filled with the Spirit and shows him to be a particularly potent mediator of grace in the world, his blessing much sought. Columba's last days are filled with ritual blessings. In the final chapter Adomnán records in six scenes how the saint blessed the whole island from the periphery to the centre, its inhabitants and stock, the barn and grain, the draught-horse, the monastery, the company of monks. Columba's last action was to move his hand 'as much as he was able, in order that he might be seen to bless the brothers ... And after the holy benediction thus expressed he presently breathed out his spirit.'

Adomnán begins the final chapter with a story already told in *VC* ii. 28. Columba was drawn in a wagon to announce his coming death to the monks working on the western edge of the island and consoled them in their grief with his blessing. 'Raising both his holy hands he blessed all this island of ours and said: "From this moment of this hour, all poisons of snakes shall be powerless to harm men or cattle in the lands of this island, so long as the inhabitants of that dwelling-place shall observe the commandments of Christ"' (ii. 28). Underlying this and other hagiographic examples of the snake-poison motif, or variants such as the banishing of snakes from a certain sacred space, there are important scriptural texts which were interpreted as relating to the spiritual life. Christ's own promise to his faithful followers, 'Behold, I have given you authority to tread upon serpents and scorpions' (Luke 10. 19), for example, is directly expounded in the *Life of Antony*. The saint shows how the monk may be said to trample serpents underfoot and render the demonic forces of evil and temptation harmless when, in devotion to Christ, he perseveres in monastic discipline. Such spiritual combat is conducted through the ascetical practices of fasting and vigils, by prayer and good works and the cultivation of inner virtues, particularly humility.

Immediately before leaving his disciples Christ had prophesied that the ability to take up serpents or drink deadly poison and yet remain unharmed would be among the signs by which his faithful followers would be known (Mark 16. 18), a prophecy St Paul fulfilled on the island of Malta when he miraculously survived a venomous snake-bite (Acts 28. 3-6). Gregory the Great, however, explained that though the gospel prophecy was fulfilled literally in miraculous external signs in the earliest stages of the Church's growth, because miracles nourish nascent belief, Christ's words also apply to what the Church now does daily 'in a spiritual way what it then did materially through the apostles'. When, for example, believers 'remove malice from the hearts of others by their good works of exhortation, they are picking up snakes ... Surely these miracles are all the greater to the extent that they are spiritual?' (*Homily* 29: Hurst 1990, 229). Gregory stresses the even greater need of God's power to enable the faithful to perform such miracles of the spiritual life. Similarly, Columba's blessing, which was conditional on the

Iona community's observation of the commandments of Christ (ii. 28), is not a mere charm against snake-bites but summons divine aid for the future spiritual well-being of the island monastery. In bearing witness in the last chapter to the continuing fulfilment of Columba's prophecy about the powerlessness of snakes on the island of Iona, Adomnán thereby testifies to the health of the community's spiritual life in his own day and reminds the community of its calling (iii. 23).

Moses had interceded on behalf of his people when they were punished for their faithlessness in the desert by venomous snake-bites (Num 21. 4-9; cf. John 3. 14-15). The Pauline interpretation of the events of the Exodus deliverance from Egypt and journey to the promised land as a figure written down for the spiritual guidance of the new chosen people, the Church (I Cor 10. 1-11), was, as already discussed, a foundation document for patristic exegesis. St Paul cites the idolatrous transgressions and lapses of faith of the Hebrews of old during their long exile and quotes their divine punishment: 'Wherefore the Lord sent among the people fiery serpents, which bit them and killed many of them.' By this Old Testament example, St Paul warns the Christian reader to avoid spiritual evil and worldly preoccupations: 'Neither let us tempt Christ, as some of them tempted and perished by serpents' (Num 21. 5; I Cor 10. 9).

Bede described Ireland as a land of milk and honey, abounding in vines and creatures of earth, air and water; a place where serpents could not survive, where indeed 'almost everything that the island produces is efficacious against poison' (cf. Gen 1. 20-30; *HE* i. 1). By alluding to the earthly paradise and thus to the state of grace enjoyed by humanity before falling to the temptation of the serpent, Bede was not suggesting that Ireland was still in a pre-lapsarian condition but was picturing a spiritual landscape, a metaphor of the *heavenly* paradisal life of grace to which the Church on earth, and the monastic life in particular, aspires by abounding in spiritual fruits. Adomnán's account of Columba blessing the island of Iona and banishing from it the power of snakes 'from then to the present day' (iii. 23) symbolically makes present in the life of the monastic community Christ's work of redemption which fulfilled the Genesis prophecy of the serpent's defeat (Gen 3. 14-15). Columba does not kill or banish snakes but renders them harmless to all creatures on the island – men and beasts – evoking the paradisal peace of the new creation: the asp and basilisk 'shall not hurt, nor shall they kill in all my holy mountain' (Isa 11. 8-9).

Insular writers were also familiar with the patristic and monastic traditions of using the image of the venom of serpents to characterize in particular the deadly spiritual evils of contention and discord which result in heresy and pollute this paradisal life. In *De Excidio Britanniae* xii, Gildas had described Arianism as a savage snake vomiting poison and causing 'the fatal separation of brothers who had lived as one', and Bede, in describing Pelagius as spreading poison, quoted some couplets of Prosper of Aquitaine which denounced Pelagius as a serpent (Winterbottom 1978, 20; *HE* i. 10). It is possible that in the context of the unresolved issue of Easter dating in the late 7th century, Adomnán's testimony that Columba was still continuing to vanquish the power of the venom of serpents on Iona carried assurances of the spiritual harmony prevailing on the island and enjoined on the community by its founder. There is some parallel in the account of St Antony's announcement of his own imminent death: he had directly warned his monastic followers, both those far off in the outer mountain and his two attendants in the inner mountain, to avoid the corrupting influence of schism and heresy, spiritual evils threatening peace and fellowship which he had earlier denounced as being worse than the poison of serpents. Similarly, Columba's final blessing delivered to those on the outer plain of the island monastery was to save the community from the poison of vipers while Columba's final command, delivered in his lodging in the monastery and only in the hearing of his attendant, bound his followers to have among themselves 'mutual and unfeigned charity, with peace'.

Moreover, he identified the monastery with Jerusalem, whose standard etymology was 'vision of peace'. On the day before his death, Columba blessed the monastery from a small hill overlooking it and foretold its future greatness among all peoples and saints, kings of the Irish and rulers of barbarous and foreign nations alike. Thus, the monastery itself is described in terms reminiscent of Old Testament prophecies that the holy citadel of Jerusalem on Mount Zion, the site of the temple, would one day be revered by all and would draw peoples from far and near (Isa 2. 2-3). In the New Testament the image is in turn used of the eschatological city of the living God, the citadel of the heavenly Jerusalem (Gal 4. 26; Heb 12. 22).

Sabbath and octave

Columba gave the blessing against snakes to console his monks when he announced his imminent death: 'At the Easter festival recently held, in the month of April, I desired with desire to depart to Christ the Lord ... but I chose rather to put off a little longer the day of my departure from the world, so that the festival of joy should not be turned for you into sorrow.' The distinctive phrase *desiderio desideraui* is a reminiscence from Luke's account of Christ's words at the Last Supper which refer to his death but, unlike St Cuthbert in Bede's prose life, Columba in his last days was not called to follow the way of the cross in physical suffering and spiritual anguish. His imitation of Christ took a different form. Christ's words to his disciples at the Last Supper refer to the Jewish Passover which prefigured his own Passion and its sacramental commemoration, but also point beyond the Crucifixion to the promise of the messianic banquet at the end of time, that is, to the heavenly life of all the faithful which is anticipated in every celebration of the eucharist: 'With desire I have desired to eat this pasch with you, before I suffer. For I say to you that from this time I will not eat it, till it be fulfilled in the kingdom of God.' Columba's cryptic allusion to the beginning of this speech in Luke 22. 15-16 marks the beginning of the account of his own last days and death in *VC* iii. 23, an account which forms an exposition of the significance of Christ's words, rather than a parallel to the Passion.

The Lucan text was important in the complex exegetical debate which underlay the Easter controversy. The debate centred on the problems of the spiritual interpretation of the literal text of the Old Covenant prescriptions for the commemoration of the Passover in Exodus 12, and of showing how Christ fulfilled the law. Cummian, for example, in his letter *De Controversia Paschali* (?632), had cited Christ's words *Desiderio desideraui hoc pascha manducare vobiscum antequam patiar* (Luke 22.15), together with St Paul's acclamation, *Pascha nostrum immolatus est Christus* (1 Cor 5.7), in the identification of the Passion as the fulfilment of the Old Covenant pasch (Walsh & Ó Cróinín 1988, 60, 64). Cummian's editors have explained how he, and some at least of the southern Irish, following earlier authorities, had regarded the Last Supper and the Passion as 'equally important in the Easter celebration as the Resurrection'. Though the Last Supper and the Crucifixion had 'occurred on separate Julian days (Thursday and Friday), they were ... deemed to have taken place on the same lunar day, *luna xiiii*' (ibid., 24-9). The twice-blessed day (Good Friday which, historically, was the preparation day for the Jewish Sabbath) in this view marked the beginning of Easter. Walsh and Ó Cróinín speculate (ibid., 27) that Séigíne, fifth abbot of Iona, and Beccán, to whom Cummian's letter was addressed, had probably pointed out to him 'that Easter is the celebration of the Resurrrection, and that the lunar-limits of the cycles (whatever ones they might be) had reference to that day and not to the Passion.'

Adomnán does not mention Easter tables and lunar limits. He does not, directly, deal with the Old Covenant pasch. By transposing his spiritual interpretation of the Old Covenant from the temporal constraints of linear time, in which the Church annually commemorates Good Friday, Easter Saturday and Easter Day, and by locating it instead amidst events which took place *after* Easter one year, Adomnán freed himself to undertake through his narrative an exposition on the nature of the feast of the Resurrection.

The contrast between Columba's joy and the monks' sorrow at the prospect of his death is repeatedly marked in the final chapter. Still bound by lingering earthly preoccupations, they grieved to lose his physical presence. Columba, however, had already been fully living the monastic ideal of the *vita angelica* on earth, as the rest of the third book shows, frequently conversing with the angelic citizens of 'the heavenly country' which he longed to enter (*VC* iii. 16). A few days after consoling his monks he alone, in rapture, saw an angel in church during mass on the Lord's day, waiting to conduct him heavenwards soon. The eucharist instituted by Christ at the Last Supper was for Columba, therefore, truly the 'bread of angels' prefigured in the manna in the Old Testament (Ps 77. 25) and a sacramental foretaste of the eternal life which Christ invited him to enter just one week later.

The next recorded event is that Columba blessed the monastery's barn, rendering thanks that his family of monks would have enough bread for the year if he should depart from them. There are details in Adomnán's narrative which suggest that the story is not about an unusually early harvest on Iona and that Columba was not simply taking stock of his stewardship of the monastery's resources. The time is distinctively noted: it happened 'after an interval of six consecutive days' following the Sunday mass just described (that is, on the next Saturday which is repeatedly described as the Sabbath day). The saint blessed *two* piles of grain which were already stored in the barn. Each day for six consecutive days the Israelites had collected the bread which God rained from heaven; on the sixth day they were told, through Moses, to gather double the daily portion in preparation for the seventh day, the Sabbath, which was divinely ordained as a day of rest (Exod 16. 4-5, 22-30). Patristic exegetes noted that the manna which physically sustained the Israelites in the desert had first been given on a Sunday and that in this earthly life (the sixth day) it is necessary to store spiritual sustenance against the Sabbath to come (Heine 1981, 308-11). Christ had interpreted the manna as a sign, *signum*, of himself, the bread of life (John 6. 30-35, 48-52), and of 'every word that proceeds out of the mouth of God' (Matt 4. 4; Deut 8. 3). The implication is that, in imitating Christ, Columba's own spiritual life expounded God's word and was a means through which his monks received heavenly food on their journey to the promised land.

Columba used the scene of the grain, harvested and stored by the Sabbath day, to explain his imminent departure 'more plainly'. In 'a few secret words' which his attendant Diarmait was sworn not to disclose until after the saint's death, Columba explained: 'This day [Saturday] is called in the sacred books "Sabbath", which is interpreted "rest" (*quod interpraetatur requies*). And truly this day is for me a Sabbath, because it is my last day of this present laborious life. In it after my toilsome labours I keep [the] Sabbath'; he explained that Christ had revealed to him that the time of his death would be 'at midnight of this following venerated Lord's-day'. Liturgically speaking, this refers to the beginning of the next day, Sunday. Adomnán's account of the last week of Columba's life thus very precisely marks out an eight-day period beginning and ending with a Sunday and gives a rare example of a specific piece of exegesis attributed to Columba. What might this have meant for Adomnán's monastic contemporaries?

In the patristic exegetical tradition inherited by insular monasticism, the image of the octave could refer to the whole of salvation history, past, present and future. After the six days of creation God rested and sanctified the seventh day (Gen 2. 2-3), which was ritually prescribed as the Sabbath day of rest in the Old Covenant during the Exodus (Exod 20. 8-10). In the New Covenant Christ himself fulfilled what the Jewish Sabbath rest had prophesied: through his resurrection his followers entered not into temporal but into eternal rest. To mark this spiritual interpretation of the Old Covenant sign, the Sabbath was celebrated by the new chosen people, the Church, not on Saturday but on Sunday, the day of the Resurrection and human redemption, signifying a new creation. Sunday was therefore regarded as both the first day of creation in the cosmic week and as the eighth day, the true Sabbath of eternal heavenly rest and the figure of the resurrection in the world to come (Daniélou 1956, 319-32).

The image applied also to the individual Christian who interpreted the Old Testament institution of the Sabbath spiritually rather than by the letter of the law, and therefore sought to abstain not simply from physical work one day a week but from worldly preoccupations and sin throughout this earthly life. The Christian consecrated to keeping a lifelong interior Sabbath would at death enter into the heavenly life of the eternal Sabbath rest. Speaking on Saturday, the seventh day within the octave marked out in Adomnán's narrative, Columba expounded the Sabbath rest of the Old Covenant as a figure of the eternal Sabbath rest of the eighth day which he was about to enter on the Sunday.

The theme of the Sabbath rest is related to other aspects of the Exodus story. The Israelites who had faltered in their belief and obedience during the lifelong desert pilgrimage (Num 14. 26-38) were not allowed to enter the promised land, which is described as God's 'rest' in the reminiscence of the story in Ps 94. 11: 'These men have not known my ways so I sware in my wrath that they shall not enter into my rest (*in requiem meam*).' The desert incident, described in Num 14 and recalled in Ps 94, is quoted in the New Testament as a warning and a spiritual guide for Christians (Heb 3. 7 – 4.11). The entry into the earthly promised land is already seen here as an image of the faithful Christian's entry into eternal rest. Adomnán describes the transition from Columba's last day on the literal Sabbath to his death, early on the eighth day, as a 'crossing over to the heavenly country from this weary pilgrimage'.

The Vulgate version of Heb 4. 11 expresses urgency in its exhortation of the faithful: 'Let us hasten (*festinemus*) to enter into that rest.' Ps 94 is the daily invitatory psalm in the *Rule of the Master* and the *Rule of St Benedict*

(Fry 1981, 159) and the image of Ps 94. 11, as understood in Heb 4. 11, is appropriated in monastic literature, including the final chapter of the *Rule of St Benedict* which urges those who would hasten toward their heavenly home to keep the monastic rule (cf. Heb 11. 16). The Prologue of the rule cites God's summons to the faithful through the words of Ps 94 and, like the *Rule of the Master*, uses other scriptural texts to characterize the monastic life as a hastening to the Lord: 'It is now the hour for us to arise from sleep' (Rom 13. 11); 'Run while you have the light of life, that the darkness of death may not overtake you' (John 12. 35; Eberle 1977, 101; Fry 1981, 159). The tradition illumines details in Adomnán's narrative. At the beginning of the final chapter he stresses that because Columba was 'an old man, weary with age', he had to be carried out in a wagon to visit his monks. Diarmait even had to raise the saint's right hand to enable him to give the final blessing as he died. Nevertheless when, sometime after the evening vesper office on Saturday, the monastery bell sounded for the first office of the Lord's day and the prophesied hour of his death, Columba 'rose in haste and went to the church and, running, entered in advance of the others' to pray. As he entered the completely dark church at midnight (and so into the everlasting Sabbath day) the church was filled with heavenly light, just briefly glimpsed by Diarmait as he approached and by a few brothers 'when they too were a little way off'. The rest of the company of monks then arrived bringing lights into the darkness of the church. Seeing by this light only that Columba was dying, they lamented even though he, 'with wonderful joy and gladness of countenance', could see the holy angels who had come to take him to the promised rest of the eternal Sabbath.

The image of the octave which, as has been seen, applies both to the passage of time through the whole of salvation history and to the lifelong interior journey of the individual, also refers to liturgical time. Literally meaning a festal period of eight consecutive days from one Sunday to the next, symbolically it denotes the Church's particular celebration of the Resurrection over the fifty-day period which spans eight Sundays, from Easter Sunday to Pentecost Sunday. Pentecost, the eighth 'day' in this symbolic octave, illumines the meaning of the Resurrection by showing its fruits for the faithful in the descent of the Holy Spirit (Daniélou 1956, 319-32).

As Easter is historically linked to the Old Testament Passover, and to the Jewish seasonal feast of unleavened bread associated with it (Lev 23. 5-7), so Pentecost is linked to the date of the giving of the law on Sinai fifty days after the Passover (Lev 23. 16) and to the seasonal feast of the first fruits of the grain harvest. The Pentateuch's various prescriptions for the celebration of these feasts are linked with its code for the observance of the Sabbath. The giving of the law on Sinai was fifty days after the slaying of the Passover lamb, but the descent of the Holy Spirit at Pentecost was fifty days after

Christ's resurrection, not his crucifixion. Accordingly, Pentecost was a Sunday, the day of the Lord, like the Resurrection whose meaning and liturgical celebration it completes. Adomnán gives no date for either of these related feasts in the year of Columba's death, but in his use of scriptural and liturgical language he places Columba's death on the feast of Pentecost. Although, citing Christ's promise, Columba had 'desired with desire' to enter his promised heavenly rest at Easter, he acknowledges at the opening of the final chapter that his death then would have turned the feast of the Resurrection into a time of sorrow for his community who wished to hold on to his physical presence. He deliberately postponed his death in order to explain it and thereby deepen their understanding of Christ's death and physical departure as the necessary means of the disciples sharing in his risen life and receiving the Holy Spirit. The narrative of Columba's remaining days, unfolded within the symbolic octave of Easter, therefore expounds the true meaning of the feast of the Resurrection and culminates in the death and entry into life at Pentecost of one whose very name, 'dove', showed him to be a dwelling-place of the Holy Spirit.

The time of Columba's death proposed here solely on the basis of Adomnán's use of the language of sacred time receives support from modern commentators' entirely separate interpretation of the hints in *VC* iii. 22 that Columba's pilgrimage on Iona began on the same date on which he died, thirty-four years later. Sharpe notes that the later tradition of the 12th-century Irish life of Columba specifically gives the date of his landing in Iona as the eve of Whitsunday:

> in 563 this day fell on 12 May according to the orthodox Easter calculation, but using the Irish table the date comes out as 9 June, the date of Columba's death [in the Ulster Chronicle]. Could this be coincidence? Or may we accept that later tradition was correct, preserving the date in relation to the Church's calendar, whether or not anyone remembered that the movable feasts would have all changed along with Easter? (Sharpe 1995, 371-2).

It is worth adding that the Irish life also states that Columba remained with his monks from Easter to Whitsun in his final year, to console them, and that 'when the bell for nocturns was rung on Whit Sunday night, he went to the church before everyone else' and sent forth his spirit (*ILCC* §§61, 64).

Adomnán, though personally persuaded of the 'Roman' calculation of Easter, was writing probably shortly before 700, some while before the rest of the Iona community conformed in 715 (*HE* v. 21, 22). Herbert has noted that 'the compilation of the *Vita* was designed, therefore, to be a unifying force within the Iona community' (1988, 144). The mention of either the Columban or Roman date of Easter and Pentecost would have frustrated this design. At no point does Adomnán refer to any method of calculating the date of Easter, even when recalling the evangelization of Northumbria (*VC* i. 1); the only explicit reference to the controversy, and then without mention of Northumbria and Whitby, is the saint's prophecy, inspired by revelation of the Holy Spirit, 'concerning the great dispute that after many days arose among the churches of Ireland over the diversity in time of the Easter festival' (*VC* i. 3). This prophecy, among other manifestations of his sanctity, occurred while he was a revered guest at the monastery of Clonmacnoise; it concludes the early chapter describing his rapturous reception there in a ceremonial *adventus* recalling Christ's entry into Jerusalem. The monastery was not a Columban foundation. The point would not have been lost on Adomnán's audience, particularly if Clonmacnoise had been among those Irish churches which had accepted the 'Roman' dating of Easter a generation before the Whitby debate. It has been seen that the last chapter opens with Columba blessing Iona to safeguard it from ever being harmed by the poison of serpents, an image of spiritual evil which could particularly refer to schism or heresy. His hilltop blessing of the monastery foresaw it would one day be honoured by 'not only the kings of the Irish with their peoples, but also the rulers of barbarous and foreign nations, with their subjects ... also especial reverence will be bestowed by saints even of other churches.' His final command to his spiritual sons was that they should have among themselves 'mutual and unfeigned charity, with peace', after the example of the holy fathers; his own intercession for them, and God's continued provision for their needs, required them to follow the divine commandments. Adomnán demonstrates that Columba's sanctity did not depend on his method of dating Easter but on the fact that he lived it and continued, after his death, to mediate its fruits.

The fear of the Lord

Adomnán's claim that the spirit of Columba continued to guide Iona's line of abbots is vividly expressed in his account of Columba's last action *before* vespers, namely his transcription of part of Ps 33. In the *Epistle* of Clement of Rome at the end of the 1st century, Ps 33. 12 was already interpreted as an invitation to eternal life issued by Christ: 'Come my children; listen to me, and I will teach you the fear of the Lord' (Staniforth 1968, 35). The verse opens Ambrose's *De Officiis Ministrorum*; it was used in baptismal catechesis (Whitaker 1960, 136), and formed part of a chain of texts on the spiritual life used by monastic writers. Cassian's *Institutes* and *Conferences* provide examples of monastic fathers whose words and deeds offered a sure guide to those seeking the way of perfection in the cenobitic life. One such holy abbot in the *Institutes* iv. 32-43 counsels a new monk that 'the fear of the Lord' (Prov 9.

10) is the beginning of salvation and inner conversion because it leads to compunction and the renunciation of worldly desires and preoccupations; in ascending this way of perfection the monk, no longer driven by dread but drawn by love of God, comes to fix his whole longing on the heavenly life. The quest for such purity of heart to understand the full meaning of 'the fear of the Lord' is described unambiguously in scriptural terms as being 'nailed with Christ to the Cross', being 'crucified to this world' (Gal 6. 14): 'You no longer live but he lives in you who was crucified for you' (Gal 2. 19-20). Cassian's holy abbot says, 'The fear of the Lord is our Cross', and shows that the way of the cross is reached through a monk's humble daily submission to the monastic rule, to his superior and the example of his elders (Gibson 1894, 230).

This spiritual process is famously described in the *Rule of St Benedict* (ch 7: Fry 1981, 193) through the image of ascending the ladder of humility whose first rung requires that a man always keep 'the fear of God before his eyes' (cf. Ps 35. 2). The rule affirms that 'all who fear God have everlasting life awaiting them'. In the description of the way of renunciation and mortification, Benedict identified the ladder of humility with Jacob's Ladder (Gen 28. 11-17; John 1. 51), an image used in exegesis of the cross which links heaven and earth and provides the means of God's descent and man's heavenward journey. The rungs of the monk's spiritual progress are marked by his daily obedience to the monastic rule and to his superior and bring him to the perfect love of God (John 4.18). It is the task of the abbot, with and through Christ, to teach his monks the way, hence the exhortation, both in the *Rule of the Master* and in the Prologue of the *Rule of St Benedict*: 'Come and listen to me, sons; I will teach you the fear of the Lord' (Ps 33. 12). In both rules this text follows the call to rise from sleep (Rom 13. 11) and is immediately followed by the command: 'Run while you have the light of life, that the darkness of death may not overtake you' (John 12. 35). Cassian had used another verse of Ps 33 in his *Conference* i. 13 to expound the text, 'The fear of the Lord is the beginning of wisdom' (Ps 110. 10), as an invitation to those seeking spiritual riches: 'O fear the Lord, all ye his saints; for they that fear him lack nothing' (Ps 33. 10). This divine promise is echoed in Ps 33. 11, the last words Columba wrote on the last day of his life before handing over to his successor the task of transcribing a psalter: 'Here, at the end of the page, I must stop. Let Baithéne write what follows.' Adomnán cites the psalm number, quotes the verse: 'But they that seek the Lord shall not want for anything that is good' (Ps 33. 11), and applies it to Columba:

> The last verse that he wrote aptly befits the holy predecessor, who will never lack eternal good things. And the verse that follows, 'Come, my sons, hear me; I will teach you the fear of the Lord' [Ps 33. 12], is

fittingly adapted to the successor [Baíthíne], the father of spiritual sons, a teacher, who, as his predecessor enjoined, succeeded him not in teaching only, but in writing also. After he had written the former verse, at the end of the page, the saint entered the church for the vesper office of the Lord's-night.

After vespers he returned to his lodging and recalled for the benefit of his monks the promised reward of 'eternal good things' awaiting those who follow the divine commandments.

Columba is presented as an exemplary abbot in providing his monks with a spiritual guide in the form of his own life and in forming and appointing a successor who, on Adomnán's testimony here, continued to teach Columba's spiritual sons 'the fear of the Lord'. For the next stage in the narrative the reader needs to turn back to the beginning of the book and the story of the young St Fintan (*VC* i. 2). He had just resolved to leave Ireland and seek out the holy Columba 'in order to live in pilgrimage' when two visiting monks arrived with the news of their founder's death. Fintan asked: 'Whom has he left as his successor?' They replied, 'Baithéne, his foster-son' and all present exclaimed, 'A worthy and fitting successor.' Fintan declared, 'If the Lord permits, I shall sail out to Baithéne, who is a wise and holy man; and if he receive me, I shall have him as my abbot.' The account of how Columba had designated Baíthíne (Baithéne) as his successor on his last day, reserved for *VC* iii. 23, thus forms a highly allusive closure to the story; in between several scenes reveal Baíthíne's spiritual formation under Columba, as the example in *VC* i. 37 has already illustrated.

Columba had praised Baíthíne for ensuring that the community of a church under his care was defended from the assaults of demons by the spiritual combat of fasts and prayers (*VC* iii. 8). Baíthíne, who was to take over from Columba the task of writing out Ps 33. 12, is early associated with Columba in the copying of Scripture and specifically of the psalms (*VC* i. 23). On the island of *Hinba*, the grace of the Holy Spirit was poured out on Columba for the space of three days and nights during which 'everything that in the sacred scriptures is dark and most difficult became plain, and was shown more clearly than the day to the eyes of his purest heart.' The saint 'lamented that his foster-son Baithéne was not there, who, if he had chanced to be present during those three days, would have written down from the mouth of the blessed man very many mysteries, both of past ages and of ages still to come, mysteries unknown to other men; and also a number of inter-pretations of the sacred books' (*VC* iii. 18). The account suggests that on other occasions Baíthíne may have had a privileged share in the fruits of Columba's contemplative experience and exposition of Scripture which was such a vital part of his charism as abbot.

Adomnán, like Báithíne, had succeeded to Columba's role as teacher. The traditional interpretation of Ps 33.12, which regarded those in spiritual authority as sharing in Christ's work of teaching 'the fear of the Lord', saw the task as the revelation of the continuing meaning of God's word for the believer. Modern study of the *DLS* and the *VC* is gradually documenting the degree of learning Adomnán was able to bring both to the explication of the literal text of Scripture and to its interpretation. Many books were ascribed to Columba; in the early commemorative poem, *Amra Coluim Cille,* he is praised as a pillar of learning, a formidable exegete, a reader of Basil and Cassian. In the monastic tradition shared with Cassian, however, Adomnán's portrait of Columba exalts his closeness to Christ, rather than his human learning. He depicts Columba as literally copying Scripture and receiving the direct inspiration of the Holy Spirit in its interpretation. Instead of quoting Columba's exegesis on particular scriptural passages, he shows how the saint exemplified their precepts. Adomnán's own considerable learning serves this larger purpose in some of the narrative episodes in the *VC*, and especially in the final chapter, where he too teaches the 'fear of the Lord', the beginning of wisdom, by showing how the spiritual interpretation of the Scriptures may be read in the life of Columba.

Columban Virgins:
Iconic Images of the Virgin and Child
in Insular Sculpture

Jane Hawkes

Images of the Virgin and Child surviving in insular art of the pre-Norman period have proved a constant source of interest, particularly since Kitzinger's study (1956) on the decoration of the late 7th-century wooden coffin of St Cuthbert. As a result of his work the Virgin and Child incised on one end of the casket (Fig 1) has been inextricably linked in the minds of most art historians, even of those not working ostensibly on insular art (e.g. Bergman 1990, 51-2), with the image of the Virgin and Child in the Book of Kells (Fig 2), dated most recently to c 800 (Meehan 1994, 91). Yet, in spite of the attention excited by these two images, other closely related Virgin and Child groups surviving in insular art, primarily in a sculptural medium, have been largely ignored.

A perceived rarity of insular Virgin and Child images, probably resulting from the tendency to treat the pre-Norman sculptural remains of Britain and Ireland as discrete entities (e.g. Allen & Anderson 1903; Cramp 1984; Bailey & Cramp 1988; Lang 1991; Harbison 1992; Tweddle 1996; cf. Clayton 1990, 142-78), has contributed to this general neglect of the subject. As Kelly points out in her survey of depictions of the Virgin and Child on Irish high crosses (1995, 197), the overwhelming number of portrayals carved on these monuments form part of narrative images of the Adoration of the Magi. They thus differ significantly from the strictly iconic images found on the coffin and in the Kells manuscript. The only iconic images of the Virgin and Child to have survived in Irish sculptural contexts appear on the cross at Drumcliff, Co. Sligo (Harbison 1992, fig 810), and possibly, as Kelly has argued, on a pillar at Carndonagh, Co. Donegal (Kelly 1995, fig 5), both variously dated to between the 9th and 11th centuries (Henry 1970, 123; Harbison 1992, 374-5; Kelly 1995, 202). In Scotland, the scheme is almost as rare. Apart from the Iona Group crosses of St Martin, St Oran and Kildalton on Islay (Figs 3-5), recently dated to the second half of the 8th century

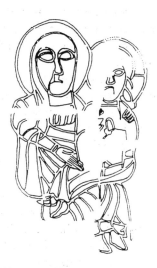

Figure 1 St. Cuthbert's coffin, Lindisfarne: Virgin and Child.

(RCAHMS 1982, 18, 197, 208; 1984, 29, 209), the only other carved monument in Scotland to preserve a Virgin and Child scheme is the 9th-century cross slab fragment at Brechin, Angus (Fig 6) (Allen & Anderson 1903 III, 249-50) (Map 2).

In Anglo-Saxon England, however, iconic images of the Virgin and Child are comparatively numerous. Among the pre-Scandinavian material from Northumbria the image is featured on a 9th-century fragment from Dewsbury, Yorkshire (Fig 7), and in Mercia it occurs on the roughly contemporary cross-shaft at Eyam, Derbyshire (Cramp 1977, 218-19, pl xxx; but cf. Routh 1937, 28; Radford 1961, 209), and at Sandbach, Cheshire. Here, two examples are extant: one on the east face of the north cross (Figs 8, 9), which can be dated to the early decades of the 9th century; the other on the west face of the south cross (Fig 10), dateable to the middle of that century (Hawkes 1989, 430-31). Two further images survive from late 10th- or 11th-century contexts at Derby (from the church of St Alkmund) and at Deerhurst, Gloucestershire (Radford 1976, 52-3, pl 9a; Cramp 1974, 145-6, Taf 68.3).[1] Four

1 The fragment recovered from the church of St Alkmund in Derby is extremely damaged and worn but appears to depict a seated woman and child which has been identified as the Virgin and Child and dated by Radford to the 9th century (1976, 52-3). However, a foliate motif above the Child's head, and similar motifs carved in the arch above the pair, resemble the thick acanthus-leaf ornament characteristic of later Anglo-Saxon art (e.g. Backhouse 1984, nos 23, 24, 131). This, together with the general appearance of the Virgin, which is comparable with that of the Inglesham panel in the way the shoulder is hunched and the head thrust forward, suggest that like the Inglesham carving it, too, reflects southern English art of the 10th and 11th centuries.

others survive from the 11th century: at Nunburnholme and Sutton-upon-Derwent, Yorkshire (Lang 1991, 189-93, 230-31, pls 711, 868), at Shelford, Nottinghamshire (Pattison 1973, 219, pl XLIVa), and at Inglesham, Wiltshire (Raw 1966, 43, pl II) (Map 2).

The number of carvings which have survived in Anglo-Saxon contexts, considered with those from elsewhere in Britain and Ireland, indicates that the scheme enjoyed some considerable popularity in the insular world in the pre-Norman period; this in itself is not without interest. More importantly, the arrangements and iconographic details used for many of these images, which range so widely in time and space, show some remarkable similarities (see Appendix). These suggest that awareness of a limited number of models lay behind their production. Furthermore, some of the earliest carved versions survive in 'Columban' contexts (at centres known to have been within, or at one time closely associated with, the Columban community). This raises a question about the possible role of these 'Columban' images in the production of Virgin and Child schemes elsewhere in the insular world.

THE QUESTION OF ICONOGRAPHIC TYPES

Iconic portrayals of the Virgin and Child surviving on insular monuments use a limited number of compositional types, which, with one or two exceptions, illustrate the Child held in such a way that his body crosses that of the Virgin. This 'complementary' pose was first discussed by Kitzinger (1956, 248-64) as a diagnostic iconographic feature, and has been subsequently invoked in most studies that attempt to ascertain the specific icon-type lying behind depictions of the Virgin and Child in insular art (for references see Alexander 1990, 280-81). This distinctive pose of the Virgin and Child, however, is not necessarily as significant as has been claimed. In iconic images portraying the Virgin actually holding the Child which survive in the early Christian art of both western Europe and the eastern Mediterranean, the Child is held in one of two ways: either across his mother's body, or fully frontally before her (see surveys in e.g. Schiller 1980; Belting 1994). So widespread are these attitudes that the 'complementary' pose is only of limited use in determining the specific nature of the iconographic model lying behind the insular images.

Furthermore, attempts to link the images of the Virgin and Child on the Cuthbert coffin and in the Book of Kells with specific types of icon, such as the seated *Hodegetria*, *Nikopoia* and *Maria Angelorum*, or the *Eleousa* and *Galaktotrophousa* (or *Maria Lactans*), may also be of limited use. The *Hodegetria* (The One Who Shows the Way), depicts the Child sitting on one of the frontally-set knees of the Virgin, while she indicates his presence by pointing

Figure 2 Book of Kells, folio 7v: Virgin and Child.

to him. The *Nikopoia* (Bringer of Victory), a more formal version of the *Hodegetria*, depicts the Christ Child seated centrally in front of the Virgin who faces rigidly forwards. The *Maria Angelorum* shows the pair flanked by two angels. Other icon-types show the Virgin and Child in more 'affectionate' terms. The *Eleousa* (Virgin of Mercy or Tenderness), for instance, depicts them cheek-to-cheek, while the *Lactans* (or *Galaktotrophousa*) shows the Virgin breast-feeding the Infant.[2] All were intended to express, to varying degrees, the mystery of the Incarnation by which the Divine was made human and to celebrate the Virgin's place in that process. The more 'affectionate' icon-types refer also to qualities specifically associated with the Virgin, highlighting her part in the Incarnation and her subsequent focal role as Intercessor (for discussions see Lazareff 1938; Shepherd 1969; Cutler 1987, 337-8; Sieger 1987; Deshman 1989; Bergman 1990; Belting 1994).

In the insular context attention to the iconographic details of these schemes, such as the positions of the Child's head and hands and the Virgin's arms, has led to speculation concerning their possible influence on the Cuthbert coffin and Kells images (e.g. Kitzinger 1956; Werner 1972; G Henderson 1987, 155). Belting's survey, however, has demonstrated that many of the details of these schemes were not iconographically inflexible in earlier medieval art, particularly in the West. The strictly formulaic nature associated with such icon-types came to be established only as the images were depicted more frequently in Byzantine and later medieval art (Belting 1994, 47-77; cf. Shepherd 1969; Bergman 1990). In Christian art of the 6th to 9th centuries produced in both the eastern Mediterranean and western Europe the *Hodegetria* and *Maria Lactans* could depict the Child seated frontally or half-turned (e.g. Schiller 1980, figs 411, 421; Bergman 1990, fig 16; Schiller 1980, fig 420; Rice 1963, pl 17), while the *Lactans* Child could be further varied by being seated upright or half-reclining in his mother's arms (e.g. Schiller 1980, fig 419; Bergman 1990, fig 16). In the *Maria Angelorum* the Virgin and Child could be shown in either the arrangement of the *Hodegetria*, or that of the *Nikopoia*, and sometimes as a *Lactans* (e.g. Schiller 1980, figs 413-14; Bergman 1990, fig 16). All these icon-types include portrayals of the Child empty-handed, holding a scroll and/or raising his hand in blessing; gestures towards his mother are also by no means limited to one type or another. Most of these iconic schemes illustrate the Virgin seated *en face*, but a few do portray her seated in profile. One such is an *Eleousa* preserved in MS

2 Most of these icon-types were present in the art of the eastern Mediterranean by the 6th century where literary expression of devotion to the Virgin first seems to have gained popularity. By the end of the 6th, or early in the 7th century, most of them were circulating in the West. The only exception seems to have been the *Maria Regina*, the crowned Virgin who does not always hold the Christ Child, which was developed in Rome during the 7th century.

Figure 3 Iona, St Martin's cross: Virgin and Child.

Figure 4 Iona, St Oran's cross: Virgin and Child.

Ashburnham 17 in the Laurentian Library in Florence, which, although itself of 11th-century date, is thought to preserve earlier iconographic features of 6th- and 7th-century work (Rosenthal 1969, 65-9, fig 14).[3]

Thus, attempts to distinguish the nature of the various models lying behind the insular schemes should probably consider, only in the most general terms, those details which distinguish one compositional type from another: the pose adopted by the Virgin (whether she is seated facing forwards or in profile) and that of the Child (whether his face is turned towards the spectator or his mother). From such a survey it may be possible to establish the various compositional types which were circulating in the insular world, as opposed to establishing the existence and identity of specific icon-types. In addition to being so varied, the iconographic details commonly associated with the iconic images of the Virgin and Child (such as the positions of their hands) are not always diagnostically relevant in an insular sculptural medium. The Virgin's arms, which have been highlighted in discussion of the Cuthbert coffin and Kells images in attempts to determine the nature of the iconographic type(s) lying behind them, are often unclear in the carved images. The positions of the Child's arms are sometimes clearer than in the case of the Virgin, but it is not always possible to determine whether they reveal the intended significance of the individual insular carving or the nature of the model from which it was ultimately derived.

INSULAR VIRGIN AND CHILD SCHEMES

Despite the overwhelming use of the 'complementary' arrangement for the Virgin and Child in insular sculpture, there were clearly some exceptions. The carving which differs most significantly from the 'norm' is on a panel, probably *in situ*, above the doorway of the church of St Mary at Deerhurst (Cramp 1974, 146, Taf 68.3). It depicts a woman standing within an architectural framework holding an elliptical medallion. This attribute serves to identify the image as a very distinctive icon-type which, originating in the art of the eastern Mediterranean, was circulating in western Europe from at least the 7th century. It is preserved, for instance, among the frescos of S Maria Antiqua in Rome.[4] In its general appearance the carving at Deerhurst clearly conforms to this tradition and can, therefore, probably be identified as the Virgin and Child, the Child originally having been painted onto the medallion (Lang 1990; Bailey 1996, 109). Although unique among the surviving

3 I am grateful to Jennifer O'Reilly for this reference. 4 This fresco has not been published, but is situated on the outer north-west wall of the Atrium area among frescos dated by Nordhagen (1962) to the 7th century.

insular schemes the panel does have a parallel in the narrative scene of the Adoration of the Magi carved on the Northumbrian Franks Casket, dated to the first half of the 8th century (Webster & Backhouse 1991, no 70). Here the Virgin is set under an architectural surround with a circular medallion before her containing the face of the Christ Child. The adaptation of the scheme into this narrative scene indicates the very early introduction of the type into the Anglo-Saxon world. It is unlikely, however, given the differences between the insular images (such as the shape of the medallion), that the Deerhurst panel looks back to the earlier version. This stone carving more probably indicates the continued use of the general type in the Christian art of western Europe and its re-introduction to Anglo-Saxon England in the 10th century.

Apart from the Deerhurst panel the only other exception to the 'complementary' pose adopted for the insular Virgin and Child schemes is the group carved at what is now the top of the west face of the cross-shaft at Eyam. Here the Virgin is seated fully *en face*; her feet, visible below the hem of her gown, point forwards. She holds the Child on her lap before her, her right arm supporting his body which is half-lost in the folds of her robe; her left arm is not indicated. The upper part of her veiled head is lost in the break at the top of the shaft, but immediately below her chin the short-haired, oval head of the Child faces strictly forwards. To his right he grasps a short

Figure 5 Kildalton, Islay: Virgin and Child.

Figure 6 Brechin, Angus: Virgin and Child.

floriated sceptre in both hands which crosses his and his mother's body at an angle. Presented in this manner the group clearly derives from a *Nikopoia*-type image depicting the Christ Child seated rigidly facing forwards in front of the Virgin's chest.[5]

The other extant insular portrayals of the Virgin and Child utilize the 'complementary' arrangement, but although they have this one feature in common their compositional details vary sufficiently to suggest the presence of a number of distinctive model-types circulating in the insular world between the 7th and 11th centuries. The most unusual is that depicted on the 9th-century cross slab at Brechin (Fig 6). Here the Virgin is portrayed seated, facing forwards, supporting the Child lying across her lap with her right arm, and holding him against her with her left, which passes over his body. The Child himself, uniquely in an insular context (and apparently in Christian art generally in iconic depictions of the Virgin and Child), is portrayed as a baby swathed tightly in swaddling clothes from which one hand emerges clasping a book (see further below). In all the other surviving iconic images Christ is represented as a child seated on his mother's lap.

5 The hieratic references implicit in the Eyam image are expanded in the figural scenes that have survived above in the cross-head (which is filled with angels), and below on the shaft where a figure displays an open scroll across his chest. This figure can most reasonably be identified as a prophet, such as Isaiah, foretelling the birth of the Messiah. Together, the images present a complex iconographic programme focusing on the mystery of the Divine made human at the Incarnation.

Another unusual version of the 'complementary type' of Virgin and Child scheme is that featured in the late Anglo-Saxon carvings from St Alkmund's, Derby, and Inglesham. Both show the Virgin seated in strict profile, with only her head turned to face the spectator. At Inglesham the Child also turns to gaze out at the spectator; his right hand is raised in blessing, and his left supports a book on his knee. Above his head the hand of God extends down from the broken edge of the stone. At St Alkmund's the carving is both damaged and worn, but it would seem that the head and torso of the Child faced strictly forwards; the lower portion of his body, if originally present, is now indecipherable. He holds what might be described as a long sceptre that crosses his mother's body at a slight angle. In their general arrangement (of the Virgin seated in strict profile) these two carvings have no real parallels in other surviving iconic depictions of the Virgin and Child in the insular world, or in Christian art generally (Raw 1966).

The remainder of the 'complementary pose' type of insular Virgin and Child images conform to one of two distinct compositional groups. One features the Virgin seated facing forwards. The other depicts her seated in the half-turned position she adopts on the Cuthbert coffin: her head faces forwards, her body is turned to accommodate the Child and her legs are seen in profile. Both these compositional schemes were varied in one of two ways: the Child seated across her lap turns his face either towards the spectator, or towards his mother.

Examples of the forward-facing Virgin with the Child turned towards her are comparatively rare in insular sculpture. They survive only on the Iona cross of St Martin and the fragment from Sutton-upon-Derwent. In the latter case the head of the Virgin has been lost. Her left arm supports the back of the Child, and her right, hanging down over his legs, holds him on her lap. He raises his head towards her and stretches both arms up towards her face. On St Martin's cross (Fig 3) the Child turns towards the Virgin (his long hair is visible hanging down the back of his head), but his face is not tipped up towards hers, and the position of his hand(s) is unclear. The Virgin's right arm can be seen bent across the body of the seated Child and her left hand may have supported his back, but this is far from certain.

The forward-facing Virgin holding the Child who turns his head towards the spectator occurs more frequently. The scheme is preserved on the St Oran's and Kildalton crosses, on the south cross at Sandbach, the cross at Drumcliff, and the fragment from Shelford.

At Shelford the scheme has survived in remarkably good condition. The Virgin supports the Child under his body with her right hand, her left hangs down behind his legs, while the Child, seated with his head against her right shoulder, holds a book firmly out before him. Unfortunately, the other versions of this compositional group are more worn and weathered, making it difficult to decipher their iconographic details with any certainty. Those carved on St Oran's cross and the Kildalton cross depict the Child with his head angled as though gazing up at his mother. On the cross of St Oran, however, the head is oval and crowned by a 'wig' of short hair (Fig 4). This, together with the difference it presents when compared to the Child's head on St Martin's cross, suggest the Child faces the observer. The cast of the Kildalton cross, held at the Royal Museum of Scotland in Edinburgh, shows the Child (with the same 'wig' of hair) clearly staring out at the spectator (cf. Fig 5). On both crosses the Virgin's left hand can be discerned supporting the Child's back, and her right arm seems to be stretched out towards the Child's body which half-reclines across her lap. The position of the Child's arms on the Kildalton cross is not clear, but on St Oran's cross his right arm can be seen flung out towards the Virgin's right shoulder.

At Drumcliff (Harbison 1992, fig 810), although the Virgin's feet turn to the right, the lower part of her body is set squarely forwards with the Child across her left knee. Her left hand is not visible, but just as on St Oran's cross, her right arm is stretched out towards the Child's body, and his left arm extends towards her.

The pair contained in the arched panel on the south cross at Sandbach are extremely weathered (Fig 10), and the Virgin is, moreover, not full-length. Nevertheless, in outline the overall relationship between the Virgin

Figure 7 Dewsbury, Yorkshire: Virgin and Child.

and Child compares (as a mirror image) with that featured on the Iona Group crosses, while the prominent round shape discernible by the Virgin's right shoulder indicates that the Child's head was nimbed and turned to face the spectator. Heads shown facing forwards and surrounded by a nimbus which are featured elsewhere on both the Sandbach crosses are clearly distinguishable from those shown in profile. The faces are regular oval shapes, with the circular halo set coherently round their heads; the type is still discernible in the head of the Virgin. The profile faces, on the other hand, are characterized by a prominent forehead that is continuous with a long nose, a sharply pointed chin, and a distinctive curve at the back of the head which is described with a double outline around the skull (Fig 8). In the context of the standard figural style used at Sandbach, therefore, the Child on the south cross can be identified as having faced the spectator. This depiction of the Virgin and Child derives from a model which, like that lying behind St Oran's and the Kildalton cross, showed both Virgin and Child facing forwards. The lower part of the Virgin's body was cut off by the arch of the panel below containing a similarly half-length image of Christ (Hawkes 1995a, fig 2).

The second distinctive compositional group of Virgin and Child images, depicting the Virgin seated in the half-turned pose, is not commonly featured in the carved stone monuments of the insular world, despite its use on the Cuthbert coffin and in the Book of Kells. The fragment at Dewsbury preserves one example of the type which illustrates the Child gazing out at the observer, while the Nunburnholme cross preserves another.

The Virgin at Dewsbury (Fig 7) appears to be seated *en face*, but her knees are set to one side of her body, suggesting an awkward attempt to illustrate her seated in a half-turned position. There is no sign of her left hand, but her right hand extends towards the Child. He is nimbed, holds a scroll with his left hand and, although the carving of his right side is very worn, can be seen, in suitable lighting, to raise his right hand in blessing. At Nunburnholme the Virgin's feet are lost, but the remains of her knee surviving to the right of the Child suggest she was originally (if awkwardly) shown with the lower part of her body seated sideways. She grasps the Child firmly behind the back with her left hand and round his knees with her right. He holds a book out before him with his left hand.

Carved versions of the Child turned to face his mother when she is seated in the half-turned position are even rarer. This is, of course, the pose preserved most famously in the Book of Kells, but the only other example to be found in insular art is that preserved on the north cross at Sandbach (Figs 8, 9). Here, in a rather curious image, the Virgin bends her right arm over the body of the Child. He raises his left hand up to, and bows his head down

Figure 8 Sandbach, Cheshire, north cross: Adoration of the Magi.

towards, her breast, which is visible above his hand; the lower part of his body is lost in a fold of her robe crossing over her knees (Fig 9).

The most noticeable feature of this carving is that, unlike the other depictions, it forms part of a narrative scene. To the right of the elaborate canopied throne surrounding the Virgin and Child are three niches formed by arches proceeding from the right-hand side of the 'column' supporting the canopy over the throne (Fig 8). Each of these niches contains a profile bust-length figure grasping a cylindrical object which is held out towards the couple seated on the throne; most of the lowermost figure is lost, but the upper portion of the object he held before him still remains.

Considered in isolation, many details in this scheme are unusual, but within the context of the monument as a whole, most conform to the style and layout of scenes adopted across the north and south crosses at Sandbach. The bosses on either side of the head of the middle figure, for instance, are two of the small circular pellets which fill most of the panels on this cross-shaft (one survives to the right of the Virgin and Child), and are probably skeuomorphs of rivets (Hawkes 1989, 427-9; 1995, 218, figs 2, 4; cf. Bailey 1996, 122-3). Likewise the round-headed niches in which the busts are placed are symptomatic of the general layout of both of the Sandbach crosses. In addition, the three figured busts themselves display the characteristics (described above) of the standard profile haloed figure used throughout the

Figure 9 Sandbach, Cheshire, north cross: Virgin and Child.

monuments. The short cylindrical objects held out before them are the standard motif used on the Sandbach crosses to illustrate scrolls.

The use of so many of these standardized motifs suggests that the scene, like others on this cross-shaft, was composed from a number of elements available to the sculptor (Hawkes 1995a, 215-17). In this case, the three standard profile figures were amalgamated with an image of the Virgin and Child in order to illustrate a 'processional' version of the narrative scene of the Adoration of the Magi. In such images, found in the Christian art of western Europe from the 4th century, the Virgin is shown seated to one side of the scene with the Child on her knee, while the Magi, half-bowed, approach from the other side (Schiller 1971, 100; Kelly 1995, 197-9). During the 7th century this iconographic type was modified to impose majesty on the non-centralized Child with the addition of architectural details and the elaboration of Mary's seat to give her more importance as the Throne of the Son of God. The scene at Sandbach, despite its many idiosyncrasies, carries the hallmarks of this modified iconographic type indicating some knowledge of its distinctive details among those responsible for its production. The differences, however, are significant: the Child, for instance, neither faces the Magi nor the spectator, as would be expected in such images; the 'Magi' do not approach in file, but are reduced to half-length figures set one above the other; and the cylindrical objects 'presented' by the Magi do not resemble the gifts most often presented by them. Together these features indicate that although the scene was, in all likelihood, being adapted to fit the limited field available within the confines of the top of the cross-shaft, a model illustrating the narrative scene was probably not available to those responsible for its production. Instead, three half-length versions of the profile, scroll-bearing figures widely used on the monument were amalgamated with an image portraying only the Virgin and Child in an attempt (albeit with limited success) to illustrate the narrative scene of the Adoration of the Magi.[6]

Thus, although the Sandbach carving incorporates the Virgin and Child into a scene illustrating a narrative event, the details of this scene indicate that a model depicting only the Virgin and Child was available to the sculptor. Furthermore, they suggest that that image illustrated the Virgin seated in the half-turned position with the Child turned to face her. If it had depicted the Child looking out at the spectator, as, for instance, on the Cuthbert coffin (Fig 1), there would have been no need to change the position of the Child's head so radically that he turns to face and bow towards his mother; a Child facing the onlooker would be much more appropriate to the Magi scene into which the Virgin and Child have been incorporated.

Interpretation

This extensive survey of sculptural insular Virgin and Child schemes has revealed the existence of a number of different compositional types circulating in Britain and Ireland during the pre-Norman period. Some of these were apparently unique productions, such as those carved on the panel at Deerhurst, the cross-shaft at Eyam, and the cross slab at Brechin. The vast majority, however, conform very generally to two main compositional types which depict the Child set across his mother's lap. In these the seated Virgin is depicted either facing forwards or in a half-turned pose, and the Child's face is turned to gaze either at his mother or at the spectator.

Most of the carved images (seven in all) feature the Virgin facing forwards. Four are in clearly Columban contexts on the crosses of Iona, Islay and Drumcliff; the other three survive at Sandbach in Anglo-Saxon Mercia, and in 11th-century contexts at Sutton-upon-Derwent and Shelford. The few images which depict the Virgin seated in the more unusual half-turned pose survive in two pre-Scandinavian Anglo-Saxon contexts: at Dewsbury in Northumbria, and Sandbach in Mercia. The other is preserved on the 11th-century cross-shaft at Nunburnholme.

The recurrent use of these compositional types may, of course, be a

---

6 The uppermost of the 'Magi' at Sandbach has been carved upside-down. A possible explanation for this is that it represents an attempt to correct the fact that if the figure had been carved upright he would have presented his gift over the top of the canopied throne containing the Virgin and Child.

Figure 10 Sandbach, Cheshire, south cross: Virgin and Child.

coincidence, and there is always the possibility that the images were produced using similar, but unrelated, models. This would imply the presence
of an impressive number of images of the Virgin and Child circulating in the
insular world. When, however, the varying iconographic details of the general compositional types carved between the 7th and 9th centuries are considered, along with the other two insular images (on the Cuthbert coffin and
in the Book of Kells), a very different pattern emerges. The four compositional
types outlined above resolve themselves into three very distinct groups.

One group includes the image at Dewsbury (Fig 7) which is most closely
paralleled by that incised on the Cuthbert coffin (Fig 1) in both its arrangement and iconographic details. The two schemes show the Virgin half-turned,
with the Child seated across her lap gazing out at the spectator. In one hand
he holds a scroll. On the coffin the other hand is lost, but incisions to the left
of the scroll suggest his right hand may have been raised in blessing, while at
Dewsbury the Child's right hand was raised in the standard gesture of the
Latin benediction. On the coffin the Virgin supports the Child's back with
one hand and places the other across his body in a gesture which cannot be
clearly interpreted as supporting him. If this 'supportive' attitude was depicted in the model from which the image on the coffin was derived, it has
been rendered ambiguous in the Northumbrian wood-carving and could be
interpreted either as an 'incompetent' portrayal of the Virgin holding the

Child, or as a depiction of the Virgin 'pointing out' the Child to the onlooker, in a manner which was standard in the *Hodegetria*-type icons. At Dewsbury, the Virgin was not shown supporting the Child with her left hand, but is depicted pointing towards him with her right.

Whatever the exact nature of the gestures made by the Virgin on the coffin and at Dewsbury, the overall iconography of the two images clearly presents the Child in a hieratic manner, despite the expression of his humanity conveyed by the fact that he is seated on his mother's knee (and that, on the coffin, she supports him with at least one hand). The way the Child's head is surrounded by the nimbus (cruciform on the coffin), the manner in which it is turned fully to confront the onlooker, and the presence of his scroll, representative of the New Law of Christ's salvation, all serve to communicate the Child's status as the Son of God incarnate, the Divine made human. The gesture of benediction (clear at Dewsbury), serves only to accentuate this aspect of the scheme, as would the Virgin's right hand, if it was positioned in order to indicate (or present) the 'real' nature and identity of the Child seated on her lap.

A second distinct iconographic group of carved Virgin and Child images centres on those featured on the Iona Group crosses of St Martin, St Oran and Kildalton on Islay (Figs 3-5). Here, the compositional type favoured was that characterized by the *en face* Virgin, and, while St Martin's cross depicts the Child turned to face his mother, the schemes preserved on St Oran's and the Kildalton cross depict him gazing out at the spectator. Despite the variation in the attitude of the Child's head it has been generally assumed in the extensive literature surrounding the Iona monuments and their relationship with the Book of Kells and Pictish sculpture, that these three images depend ultimately on a common model-type (for summaries see RCAHMS 1982, 192-213; RCAHMS 1984, 206-12; cf. Henderson 1982; 1983; Mac Lean 1986; 1991; 1993). It is not certain if this illustrated the Child facing his mother or the spectator. On constructional grounds St Oran's and the Kildalton cross (featuring the forward-facing Child) are thought to have been produced before St Martin's cross, which features the Child facing his mother (RCAHMS 1982, 192-208; RCAHMS 1984, 208-10; Kelly 1993). It could, therefore, be argued that the model on which the images were based featured the Child facing forwards. Whichever was depicted on the model, it was clearly altered for one of the variations produced on the Iona crosses.[7]

7 Trying to ascertain the nature of the icon-type lying behind the Iona Group images involves as much speculation as is involved in discussions surrounding the Cuthbert coffin and Kells images. It too depends very much on ascertaining which version most closely resembles the model on which the images were based. The 'tipped-back' attitude of the Child, present on St Oran's and the Kildalton cross might suggest a *Lactans* type image, but against this possibility is the position of the Virgin's arms which, consistently in all three images, seems to portray her either indicating his presence or holding the

One implication of this local adaptation of a model-type is that the potential significances of the iconography of the Virgin and Child were being deliberately exploited by those responsible for the production of the monuments. In this respect the contrast with the type of image found on the Cuthbert coffin and at Dewsbury is instructive. On all three crosses the Virgin and Child are flanked by angels whose wings provide a canopy for them, and at least one of whom carries a book. These accompanying figures are clearly absent from the Cuthbert coffin type of image. Although archangels feature elsewhere on the coffin, and the Dewsbury carving is too fragmentary to tell whether angels were placed outside the architectural surround containing the Virgin and Child, the close relationship between the angels and Virgin and Child featured on the Iona crosses is distinctly absent from those images. Furthermore the Child on the crosses lacks a nimbus, does not carry a scroll, and does not have his hand raised in benediction.

Set against the coffin and the Dewsbury fragment the iconography of the Iona Group images is clearly more complex. On the one hand the humanity of Christ is given more emphasis, but this is not achieved at the expense of his divinity. On St Oran's and the Kildalton cross (Figs 4, 5) the way the Child turns to confront the onlooker recalls the authoritative pose of the Child featured on the Northumbrian carvings. But the hieratic connotations conveyed by the position of the Child's face are balanced by the details expressive of his humanity: the fact that he does not raise his hand in blessing; that he lacks attributes, such as the halo, book or scroll; the way the Virgin bends her head to his; and the way he almost reclines across his mother's lap. In the Iona scheme the overt expression of Christ's divine nature is instead conveyed and emphasised by the angels, the figures whose function in Christian art is (as the servants of God) to articulate his divine authority.

On the cross of St Martin (Fig 3) the nature of the Christ Child is given a slightly different iconographic treatment. His humanity, as elsewhere, is expressed through the absence of halo and attributes, but it is further emphasised in the way his head is turned away from the spectator, towards his mother. Unlike his pose on St Oran's and the Kildalton cross, however, the St Martin's Child sits upright. His head is not tipped backwards and the Virgin does not incline her head towards him; the number of angels flanking the pair has been increased to four. These details accentuate the divinity of Christ. Despite such differences between the St Martin's scheme and that

Child on her lap, rather than holding her breast (a constant detail in *Lactans* images). The position of the Virgin's arms on the Iona Group crosses, along with the profile view of the head of the St Martin's Child, might alternatively suggest the influence of an *Eleousa*-type image.

depicted on the other Iona Group crosses the overall effect of the iconography is still a carefully balanced presentation of the mysteries inherent in the Incarnation. As in the other Iona images the scheme expresses the eternal nature of Christ's divinity and the human reality of his theophany.

The potential iconographic significance of the Virgin and Child is not limited to Christological concerns on these crosses. The comparatively hieratic presentation of Mary not only sets off the increased emphasis on her close relationship with Christ (suggested in the way he turns his head towards her), but also contains a potentially explicit reference to the Virgin as the Mother of God, the instrument of, and hence one of the most important elements in, the Incarnation. The elevation of the Virgin to the status of *Theotokos* (Mother of God) in AD 435, which is reflected in all the iconic images of the Virgin and Child, was a result of her self-confessed role as Handmaiden of the Lord in the process of the Incarnation (Luke 1.38). It was these notions (of Mary's identity as the Mother of God, and as the Servant of God) which formed the basis of subsequent interest in the Virgin as Intercessor. In the individual attainment of salvation, service to the Virgin, the Servant of God, was regarded as particularly apt (Shepherd 1969, 105; Sieger 1987, 84-6; Deshman 1990, 39-41; Leveto 1990, 410-12). The literature associated with the Columban community during the 8th and 9th centuries demonstrates that these ideas were current at the time the crosses were being constructed. The song, *Cantemus in Omni Die*, composed by Cú Chuimne of Iona (obit 747 *AU*), for instance, describes Mary in terms using language which, by the 8th century, was well established in Christian literature devoted to Marian concerns and to service to the Virgin as a means of personal salvation (Bernard & Atkinson 1898 I, 32-4; II, 124-5; Herbert 1988, 9-35, 43-5; Clancy & Márkus 1995, 177-92; cf. Carney 1964, 47).

The difference in iconographic detail in the St Martin's version of the Virgin and Child scheme suggests that these concerns may have been intentionally made more explicit on that monument than they are in the other Iona Group images. They are, of course, implicit in any depiction of the Virgin and Child, particularly when attendant figures are included – the angels function, not only as signifiers of Christ's divine nature, but also as references to the service owed (by the onlooker, the faithful Christian) to the Virgin and, by extension, to Christ. The iconographic difference is one of emphasis. It probably results from the fact that the schemes are set in different positions on the monuments and associated with different sets of images. At Kildalton and on St Oran's cross the Virgin and Child are placed below the cross-head at the point where the shaft and cross-head meet; they are one of three figural scenes set round the cross-head. On the cross of St Martin, however, they are set at the centre of the cross-head, where the image functions as the apogee of a complex programme of narrative images placed up the length of the shaft.[8]

Apart from the iconographic distinctions made in the Iona images of the Virgin and Child, however, they do present versions of the same compositional type, and closely similar types are also found elsewhere in insular sculpture: at Drumcliff and Sandbach. The general arrangement and iconographic details of the Drumcliff carving indicate that it too was based on an image which illustrated the Virgin seated, facing forwards, with the Child set across her knee facing the spectator. As on St Oran's cross the Child has his arm stretched out towards her. The carving is comparatively naïve and lacks the attendant angels, but in its general arrangement and iconographic details it bears all the hallmarks of the Iona scheme. Likewise, the group on the south cross at Sandbach (Fig 10) resembles those on St Oran's and the Kildalton cross. Here the Child is shown with his head in close contact with that of the Virgin, slightly tipped back, and turned to face the spectator. Kneeling figures, rather than angels, flank the Virgin and Child in separate niches, but as on the Iona Group crosses they too serve to attest the divine nature of Christ-made-Man and the appropriateness of 'servitude' in their attitude of veneration; a pair of angels is set in two arched panels further down the face of the shaft (Hawkes 1995a, fig 2).

The third distinctive group of Virgin and Child images is that character-

---

8 The overall significance of the iconographic programme presented by these figural scenes is not easy to ascertain as the identity of the figures in the lowermost panel cannot be identified with any certainty. One explanation, suggested by Henderson (1986, 95), is to identify them as David and Goliath (on the left), and David before Saul (on the right). If this is so, viewed in conjunction with the other images, of David as the Psalmist, the Sacrifice of Isaac and Daniel in the Lions' Den, they present a series of references, linked in a number of ways in biblical passages such as Paul's Letter to the Hebrews (11-12). Here, mention is made of a number of Old Testament figures (including those portrayed on St Martin's cross) who are deemed noteworthy both because they foretold the coming of the Messiah, and because, in adversity, they remained firm in their belief in God. The passage culminates with an articulation and celebration of the nature of Christ incarnate. Read in this way, together with the lions in the cross-arms and the snake-and-boss motifs which form saltire-cross and lozenge shapes elsewhere on the monument and which can be understood as symbols of the Resurrection and the universality of Christ's salvation (e.g. Lindsay 1911 II, iv; Kessler 1977, 51-8; Dynes 1981, 38-9; Nees 1983, 76-9; Mac Lean 1986, 185; but cf. Mac Lean 1993), the Virgin and Child image at the centre of the cross-head is both integral to, and a culmination of, an extended iconographic programme expressing the complexities of Christ's nature, his Church and its sacraments, and their relevance to the Christian community on earth (e.g. Shepherd 1969; Bailey 1978a, 10-12; I Henderson 1987, 64-5; Sieger 1987; Bergman 1990; Deshman 1990; Leveto 1990; O'Reilly 1993; 1995). Similar iconographic references were probably also being made through the images at Kildalton and on St Oran's cross, although here more use was made of the non-figural motifs and the scenes themselves were varied, both in their positions on the monuments, and in their selection (Hawkes, forthcoming).

ized by the half-turned Virgin holding the Child who turns to face her. This is the compositional type featured in the Book of Kells (Fig 2). The north cross at Sandbach preserves the only other example to survive from a 'pre-Scandinavian' context in Anglo-Saxon England (Figs 8, 9). Certainly the body of the Sandbach Child differs from that depicted in the manuscript in being 'seated' upright on the Virgin's knee, while the head, instead of being tipped back to look up at her, is bowed. In its other iconographic details, however, the Sandbach image bears a remarkable similarity to that in the Book of Kells: the Child's hand is raised towards the area of the Virgin's breast, which is distinguishable in the carving, and her right arm crosses his body. These features, together with the compositional type which is used for both schemes, invite comparison of the two images.

Viewed in this manner, therefore, the surviving carved Virgin and Child images suggest that there were three main compositional types of the 'complementary pose' scheme circulating in the insular world between the 7th and 9th centuries. Furthermore, the earliest extant versions of these three types survive at centres associated in some way with the Columban Church: Lindisfarne and Iona (and possibly Kells). This pattern of occurrence raises the question of the role(s) these 'Columban' images may have played in the production of the other carved insular Virgin and Child schemes.

'COLUMBAN VIRGINS'

The earliest of the extant insular images of the Virgin and Child is that incised on the Cuthbert coffin produced at Lindisfarne (Fig 1). This was, of course, the Northumbrian centre founded by monks sent from the Columban community on Iona. And although direct *familia* links between the two centres were probably no longer in existence by the late 7th century when the coffin was made, this was the time when ecclesiastical and royal links between Northumbria and Iona were being reaffirmed after the Synod of Whitby, under the aegis of Adomnán and Aldfrith, the king of Northumbria who had spent some years in exile on that island (Herbert 1988, 47-56). The potential relevance of this specific cultural milieu to the iconographic signifiers of the coffin has not been ignored. Forty years ago Kitzinger (1956, 273-7) noted that along with references to the Church of Rome (cf. Higgitt 1989), the iconographic programme of the coffin also makes allusions to the liturgy of the Irish Church in the unusual series of archangels set along one side. Although the coffin cannot be considered a 'Columban' artefact in the way the crosses on Iona might be, its iconography does seem to invoke the Irish Columban inheritance of the Lindisfarne community.

In an insular sculptural context, the closest parallel to the Virgin and

Child depicted on the coffin is that at Dewsbury (Fig 7). These two images are separated from each other by some one hundred years. Yet they are the only examples of this particular version of the Virgin and Child to have survived in insular art from the pre-Viking period. Furthermore, they both use the same iconographic details which are by no means universal to such images. These similarities could be viewed as significant. At the very least they can be interpreted as revealing knowledge of the same compositional type. It could be speculated, however, that in the light of the apparently close relationship between these two images and the status accorded Cuthbert's shrine throughout the Anglo-Saxon period, knowledge of the general iconographic features of the image incised on the saint's coffin may have influenced the image carved on the fragment at Dewsbury.

The influence of the Iona Group monuments (Figs 3-5) is not such a matter of speculation. Indeed, it would be surprising if they had not had an impact on artefacts produced elsewhere, given their impressive appearance and association with the Columban Church, one of the most influential ecclesiastical communities in the early insular world. The relationship of their non-figural motifs to sculpture elsewhere in Scotland and to the decoration of the Book of Kells, has long been the subject of academic enquiry (Macalister 1928; Curle 1940, 94-6; Radford 1942, 4-6; Stevenson 1955, 117-18; 1956; 1971, 71; Henry 1974, 178, 218; Robertson 1975, 117-21; Calvert 1978, 160-67, 246-55; Henderson 1982, 103-5; 1983, 236-7; I Henderson 1987; RCAHMS 1982, 18-19, 192-209; RCAHMS 1984, 209-10; Mac Lean 1986; 1993; Ritchie 1989, 34). Their figural carvings have also generated some interest, although these have been less extensively explored (Curle 1940, 96-7; Henderson 1982, 103; 1986, 94-5; Calvert 1978, 160-66; Mac Lean 1986, 177-9; Mac Lean 1991). In such studies, however, the Virgin and Child schemes have been comparatively neglected as they do not appear to be related to the carved figural schemes featured more commonly in both Irish and Scottish contexts. Nevertheless, the one indisputable depiction of the Virgin and Child surviving on an Irish cross (at the Columban centre of Drumcliff) displays the same general features.[9]

Here, the comparatively naïve rendition of the figures, and their position at the end of the cross-arm, indicate that the scheme plays a less prominent role in the overall iconographic programme of the cross than it does on the Iona Group crosses, and a directly dependent relationship between the Drumcliff cross and those on Iona and Islay is unlikely. The strong similarities in compositional type and general appearance do, however, suggest that some memory of the Iona scheme may have influenced the production of the

9 If, as argued by Kelly (1995), the Carndonagh pillar also illustrates the Virgin and Child, the proximity of that site to the main Columban foundation at Derry (Herbert 1988, 73-4, 109-23) may account for its presence.

image at Drumcliff. Indeed, the association of Virgin and Child iconography with the crosses of the Columban foundation on Iona may explain the presence of this scheme on the Drumcliff cross, while its other figural carvings indicate a very different set of cultural links. As Harbison has pointed out (1992, 373-6), the narrative scenes depicted on the cross constitute a specific selection which marks the monument as an outlier of the Ulster Group of Irish high crosses. In this context, setting the Virgin and Child, not on either of the main faces, but on the end of one of the cross-arms, could have served as a reminder of other cultural and ecclesiastical affinities of the community at Drumcliff.

This use of the scheme, as a deliberate (visual) invocation of the original foundation of the Columban community, may also provide an explanation for the production of the Virgin and Child group at Brechin (Fig 6). This ecclesiastical centre first enters the written records in the 10th century at the end of the reign of Cináed (971-95). Prior to that it seems to have been the seat of a *Céli Dé* ('Culdee') community established during the 9th century, possibly at the site of a pre-existing church located on an ancient pilgrimage way linking Iona and Lindisfarne (Jervise 1860, 28-31; Jamieson 1890, 15-84; Simpson 1963, 279-80; Lines 1992, 19; Atkinson 1994, 14). Against this background the production of a cross slab featuring an iconic image of the Virgin and Child, at a time contemporary with the presumed establishment of the *Céli Dé* community at Brechin, could be viewed as the visual expression of an affinity with Iona and all that it represented. Here, the image does not present a copying of the Iona scheme – rather the reproduction of a scheme closely associated with Iona itself.[10]

More problematic is the speculation that the two Virgin and Child schemes

10 Stylistically the Brechin slab is related to other stones in Angus (Lines 1992, 19), although the beaded medallion containing the Virgin and Child is most closely paralleled on a lost cross-head from Hoddom (Radford 1953, pl III). It also differs from the Iona monuments iconographically. The Child, depicted as an infant, graphically and realistically expresses Christ's humanity, while the standard features of turning to face the onlooker and presenting the book of the New Law convey his divine authority. Angels standing in the horizontal cross-arms holding and presenting the medallion emphasise the divine nature of the Child. The bird set in the upper cross-arm could be interpreted either as an eagle (in which case it refers potentially to the resurrection of Christ, and by extension, the general resurrection available to all the faithful), or as a dove. In this case (apart from oblique references to Columba and his community), it would represent the Holy Spirit, again alluding to the hidden nature of Christ as the Divine made human. The two figures set in the lower cross-arm can probably be identified as Peter and Paul; the figure on the left holds keys, the standard symbols of Peter (Higgitt 1989; cf. Hoddom cross-head in Radford 1953, fig 2). Depictions of these two were usually intended to refer generally to Christ's Church on earth (Kinder-Carr 1978, 69-73; Hawkes 1989, 400-5). When associated with the Child held by the Virgin (e.g. the early 8th-century mosaics at St Peter's, Rome) they are understood to connect service to the Mother of Christ with the sacraments of the Church (Deshman 1989, 42). As in the mosaics an inscription at Brechin relates the

featured on the Sandbach crosses can be related in any way to the 'Columban' images featured on the Iona Group crosses and in the Book of Kells. That depicted on the south Sandbach cross (Fig 10) is, with two main differences, broadly comparable with the images found on the Iona Group. One difference lies in the absence of angels. This can best be explained as the result of the different principles of design and the different roles the images play within the overall iconographic programmes presented on the monuments. On the south cross at Sandbach the Virgin and Child is one of three figural groups centred on the adoration and veneration of Christ, and it is not the foremost. The focal point of the programme is the theophany of the Transfiguration placed above the Virgin and Child (Hawkes 1995a, 217-18).

The other difference between the schemes is the fact that the group on the south cross at Sandbach comprises a 'mirror image' of that depicted on the Iona crosses. This could imply dependence on a different model – although this is not necessarily the case as the use of patterns and templates easily explains the phenomenon (Bailey 1978b; 1996, 111-18; Lang 1986). Nevertheless, in attempting to assess the likelihood of dependence on a different model at Sandbach a number of matters need to be considered. Firstly, even if a different model was used, it was certainly of the same compositional type as that used for the Columban crosses. This means that, secondly, it was of a very different type from that used on the north cross, a phenomenon which is all the more remarkable given that other scenes carved on the south cross were copied from the north cross (Hawkes 1995a, 216-17). Thirdly, these two Sandbach schemes are, in themselves, different from all the others which have survived in pre-Scandinavian Anglo-Saxon contexts, even that found elsewhere in Mercia on the roughly contemporary cross-shaft at Eyam. Their closest parallels are with images which have survived in Columban contexts. The use of one such scheme at Sandbach could be viewed as no more than coincidence. Two such images are at least a matter for speculation.

Other decorative features are also common to the Sandbach monuments and those found elsewhere in the Columban world. Foremost among these is the distinctive profile figural style used throughout the two crosses (see

image to the Virgin: .S. MARIA. MR. XPI (*Sancta Maria Mater Christi*) (Allen & Anderson 1903 III, 249-50). Such references to the Church and its sacraments are extended on the cross slab in the four full-length, book-bearing and winged evangelist symbols standing in the spandrels of the cross-arms. Set around a cross in this manner they indicate the universal nature of Christ's message of salvation preserved in the gospels, and available through the Church and its sacraments (Hawkes 1989, 386-91, 521-34; 1995b, 264-5). The iconography of the Brechin slab, therefore, focusing on the central image of Christ and his mother, which in itself conveys the complexity of the mysteries inherent in the Incarnation, re-inforces the significances of that scheme and extends it to refer to the Church of Christ and its sacraments, and their relevance to the Christian community on earth.

above). This cannot be easily paralleled in any other group of Anglo-Saxon monuments produced in the pre-Scandinavian period, even outside Mercia, although there are some comparisons to be made with figural carvings of the Viking age in the Peak District and Trent Valley (e.g. Hope and Norbury, Derbyshire: Routh 1937, pls XV, XVII.B). But the closest contemporary parallels to the Sandbach figural style are those featured most famously in the Book of Kells, as on folios 7v (Fig 2) and 124r (Henry 1974, pl 47), and on some of the Scottish monuments (for summary see Calvert 1978, 160-67; Henderson 1982, 94-5). Another distinctive feature of the Sandbach monuments is the thin panel of interlace used to border the west and east faces of the south cross. Again, this is not something which is easily paralleled in a sculptural medium among the stone monuments of Anglo-Saxon England; used in this way it is rare throughout the insular world. Interlace is, however, used in an exactly comparable position, as a border, on the cross of St Oran on Iona, where it frames the image of the Virgin and Child (RCAHMS 1982, 194, fig A).

Research into the decoration of manuscripts of the late 8th and 9th centuries has demonstrated numerous similarities between the Book of Kells and manuscripts produced at Canterbury when it was under Mercian control (Brown 1994). Such similarities imply a shared cultural heritage which is explained by the (documented) influence of the 'Irish' Church in Mercia and its continuing presence in the region during the late 8th and early decades of the 9th century (Brown 1994, 342; cf. Hughes 1971; Cubitt 1990, 340, 422). Such documentary and art-historical evidence does not, of course, constitute proof of direct contact between the ecclesiastical centre responsible for the Sandbach crosses and the Columban community (in either Iona or Ireland) in the early 9th century. Taken together with the iconographic and stylistic concerns of the carved monuments, however, it does add up to an impressive body of evidence (albeit circumstantial) suggesting, at the very least, that knowledge of figural schemes featured in the art of north-western Britain and Ireland was not an impossibility in Mercia in the first half of the 9th century (cf. Mac Lean 1985, 350; 1986, 183; Henderson 1986, 105-8). The similarities between the Sandbach and 'Columban type' schemes (similarities which are not easily found elsewhere in the extant art of the insular world) may indicate that knowledge of the images associated with prestigious Columban artefacts played a part in the production of the Virgin and Child images on the Sandbach crosses.

This hypothesis certainly provides an explanation for the similarities between the Virgin and Child on the north Sandbach cross (Figs 8, 9) and that in the Book of Kells (Fig 2). The carved image probably depends most immediately on a model which, like that lying behind the Ashburnham miniature of the *Eleousa* (see above), illustrated the Virgin seated, half-turned, with her right arm bent across the Child's body. As on the Sandbach cross, the lower half of the Child is not depicted in that manuscript, and he bows his head onto his mother's left shoulder (Rosenthal 1969, fig 14). These details imply the influence at Sandbach of a model displaying similar features. Such a derivation, however, does not explain the details the Sandbach scheme has in common with the Kells image: the highlighting of the Virgin's breast and the distinctive gesture of the Child's left arm reaching up towards it. These details may suggest the influence of a *Lactans*-type image, but this is unlikely. Surviving examples of this iconographic scheme do not show the Child bowing his head onto the Virgin's breast; he is usually depicted looking up towards her. Nor do they illustrate the Child reaching out towards the breast; usually the Virgin presents it, to the viewer as much as to the Child, as evidence of the Child's humanity (see surveys in Schiller 1980; Belting 1994). The emphasis on these details at Sandbach is thus more convincingly explained as the result of adapting another type of iconographic image, such as the Ashburnam *Eleousa*. Furthermore, the fact that the Virgin's breast and the position of the Child's left arm constitute details which are common to the Mercian cross-shaft and the Kells image but appear to be absent from other surviving portrayals of the Virgin and Child, strongly suggests that the Sandbach image, or the model on which it was directly based, was adapted with some knowledge of the iconography preserved in the manuscript.

Such speculation aside, iconic depictions of the Virgin and Child were clearly popular in the sculptural art of the insular world throughout the pre-Norman period. A number of iconographic and compositional types were available and the arrangements which were used most frequently have some iconographic details in common. This implies a shared knowledge of a very limited number of model-types, particularly in the pre-Scandinavian period in Anglo-Saxon England. These may have been associated, at an early date, with artefacts which emerged from a Columban context, the prestige of that community perhaps explaining the far-reaching influence of the images.

It is unlikely, however, that the similarities between the later, 11th-century, Anglo-Saxon carvings and the 'Columban-influenced' images can also be explained in this way. The Nunburnholme scheme has been interpreted as depending on a locally-available model (Pattison 1973, 227-32; Lang 1978b; 1991, 189-93), and the similarities that scheme bears to the Dewsbury (and Cuthbert coffin) images, in its arrangement and detail, suggest that it was these schemes which continued to exert an influence on the iconography of the Virgin and Child in the region (cf. Raw 1966, 46; Kitzinger 1956, 264). The Shelford image may also have been produced under these conditions. Although the general arrangement of the group conforms (as a mirror image) to the Iona scheme featuring the Virgin facing forwards and the Child, seated across her lap, turned to face the spectator, the Shelford Child holds a book out before him, as he does at Nunburnholme. Moreover, these two carvings are very closely related stylistically. It is more likely, therefore, that, together with the carving at Nunburnholme, the Shelford image reflects an interest in the Virgin and Child current in the area at the time. They probably derived some of their inspiration from earlier portrayals of the group, like those surviving at Dewsbury and on the Cuthbert coffin. While Columban associations may have played a part in the production of these earlier carvings, such considerations are unlikely to have influenced the later versions.

At this period the re-introduction of iconic images also played a part in the development of the iconography of the Virgin and Child. The carving at Sutton-upon-Derwent, although of the same compositional type as on St Martin's cross, with the *en face* Virgin and the Child turned towards her, is probably not related to that Columban image. This was, in all likelihood, adapted from a type which featured the Child looking out at the spectator. Furthermore, the very distinctive gestures of the Child at Sutton-upon-Derwent, not preserved in other insular depictions of the group, closely resemble those made by the Child in some of the later medieval *Eleousa*-type icons, dating from the late 10th and 11th centuries, where the Child raises his face and arms towards his mother (e.g. Belting 1994, 261-96, fig 173). This carving, therefore, like that at Deerhurst, probably represents the introduction of a specific icon-type into the late Anglo-Saxon world (cf. Raw 1966, 45).

In an insular context, therefore, carved images of the Virgin and Child in Northumbria were more probably influenced by the association of the scheme with the cult of St Cuthbert than with the Columban Church, although the image on the Cuthbert coffin was itself produced at a time when contacts between the Columban and Northumbrian Churches were strong. Elsewhere, however, it is arguable that an association of images of the Virgin and Child with carved monuments set up in the original foundation of the Columban community on Iona had a mnemonic effect on other insular versions of the scheme. The association may have affected the decision to produce such an image at Drumcliff and Brechin. Furthermore, at Drumcliff, memory of the Iona scheme may have inspired the general arrangement and iconographic details of the image figured on the end of the cross-arm. If such considerations also played a part in the production of the carvings at Sandbach, the prestige of the Columban Church must have extended beyond the regions normally deemed to have been within its sphere of influence in the first half of the 9th century.

ACKNOWLEDGEMENTS

I would like to thank John Higgitt, Doug Mac Lean, Jennifer O'Reilly, Ross Trench-Jellicoe and Niamh Whitfield for their critical comments and advice made during the preparation of this chapter.

Appendix

Iconic Images of the Virgin and Child in Insular Sculpture

Carved iconic images of the Virgin & Child: 'complementary' pose	Virgin's body			Child's face		Child's hands			
	facing forwards	half-turned	strict profile	facing forwards	turned to mother	holding attribute	raised blessing	raised to mother	empty handed
Cuthbert coffin, Lindisfne, late C7th		•		•		scroll	•		
St Oran's cross, Iona, mid-late C8th	•			•					•
St Martin's cross, Iona, mid-late C8th	•				•				•
Kildalton, Islay, mid-late C8th		•		•					•
Dewsbury, Yks, early C9th	•					scroll	•		
Sandbach, north cross, Cheshire, early C9th	•				•			•	
Sandbach, south cross, Cheshire, mid C9th			•	•		[not available]			
Drumcliff, Co. Sligo, C9th	•			•					•
St Alkmund's, Derby, C9th–C11th	•			•		sceptre?			
Nunburnholme, Yks, C11th		•		•		book			
Sutton-upon-Derwent, Yks, C11th	•				•			•	

	Virgin's body			Child's face		Child's hands			
Carved iconic images of the Virgin & Child: 'complementary' pose	facing forwards	half-turned	strict profile	facing forwards	turned to mother	holding attribute	raised blessing	raised to mother	empty handed
Shelford, Notts., C11th	•			•		book			
Inglesham, Wilts, C11th			•	•		book	•		
Associated Images									
Franks Casket, Nthba, late C7th	•			•		[not available]			
Book of Kells, late C8th	•			•				•	
Eyam, Derbyshire, C9th		•			•	sceptre			
Brechin, Angus, C9th	•			•		book			
Deerhurst, Gloucs, C10th	•			[not available]		[not available]			
Carndonagh, Co. Donegal, C11th	•			[not available]		[not available]			

Insignia Columbae I

Raghnall Ó Floinn

*This and the following chapter treat of the relics and reliquaries linked with
Columba's name. Insignia I considers the corporeal relics of the saint and an array
of cult accessories. Bells and croziers are considered separately in Insignia II.*

Of the trinity of Irish 'national' saints – Patrick, Brigid and Columba (Fig 1)
– the latter stands out as the most historical figure. Patrick is unrepresented
in any contemporary source other than the two texts attributed to him, and
little is known about his origins or the period in which he lived. Brigid is an
even less visible figure and there is some doubt as to whether indeed she ever
existed. By contrast, we know who exactly Columba was and when he died
(597 *AI*; 595 *AU*). Moreover, his life – the *Vita Columbae* (*VC*) – was written
by Adomnán within a century of his death. Through the various lives of the
saint, other historical sources and the surviving sites and artefacts associated
with him, the origins and development of his cult can be traced, albeit
sketchily. The standard reference in this regard to date has been Reeves
(1857, 318-34). In recent years some of the relics and reliquaries associated
with Columba have been re-examined, firstly in a major paper on the role of
relics in the Columban community (Bannerman 1993), secondly in my own
paper on metalwork associated with Donegal, much of it with Columban
connections (Ó Floinn 1995a).

Surprisingly, no corporeal relics of the saint are known to exist today. In
contrast there are a number of reliquaries which purport to contain portions
of the mortal remains of both St Patrick and St Brigid (although it is unlikely
that any of these are earlier than the later medieval period). Adomnán (*VC*
iii. 23) records that Columba's grave at Iona was, in his time, marked by a
simple pillow stone. When his remains were first enshrined is uncertain but
it is likely that a portable shrine containing them was in existence by the
mid-8th century, when the *Law* of Columba was promulgated on a number
of occasions by Irish kings and the abbots of Iona (753, 757, 778 *AU*). By the
early 9th century there seems to have already existed a rival tradition that his

Figure 1 The *Fiacail Pádraig*: Patrick and Columba (the figure of Brigid, originally to Patrick's right, is now missing).

bones were kept at Saul, Co. Down. This piece of Armagh propaganda is contained in the supplementary notes to Tírechán's life of Patrick contained in the Book of Armagh. Here it is claimed that Columba, in addition to showing that Patrick's grave was at Saul, also 'confirms ... there is the coming together of the martyrs, that is, of the bones of Columb Cille from Britain and of all the saints of Ireland on the day of Judgement' (Bieler 1979, 164-5). This may well be linked to an interpolated entry at 553 *AU*, citing the Book of Cuanu, in which Columba uncovers Patrick's grave and places his remains in a shrine, *scrín*, while an angel gives one of Patrick's relics, *minna*, to Columba and divides the others between Down and Armagh.

The earliest reference to a shrine of Columba is in 818 *CS*, when the abbot of Iona brings *scrín Coluim Cille* from Ireland to Scotland. This is the first of a series of accounts which distinguish the shrine of the saint's corporeal remains, *scrín*, from his other insignia, *minda*. A shrine containing his corporeal remains was certainly in existence by 825 *AU* when, during a Viking raid on Iona, Blathmac, a member of the monastic community, was martyred for refusing to divulge where Columba's shrine, *arca*, had been buried. From an account of Blathmac's death by Walafrid Strabo written soon after the event, we learn that this shrine was composed of 'precious metals wherein lie the holy bones of St Columba', *pretiosa metalla ... queis sancti sancta Columbae ossa jacent* (Reeves 1857, 315; Anderson 1922 I, 263-5), and we might well imagine that it consisted of a full-size wooden sarcophagus ornamented with metal mounts and finials not unlike those preserved today at St Germain-en-Laye (Youngs 1989, no 138) (and similar fragments from a Viking grave at Gausel, Norway). These are ornamented with snake-and-boss ornament which has artistic links with both the Book of Kells and the Pictish cross slab at Nigg, Easter Ross, and may, as Fisher has pointed out (1994, 45), have an Iona provenance. Bannerman has suggested (1993, 20) that Walafrid Strabo's account would indicate that the shrine was placed on pediments, *sedes* (Reeves 1857, 315), implying both size and weight. The small oratory-like structure located to the north-west of the medieval abbey church at Iona and known as 'St Columba's Shrine' was described in the 17th century as enclosing the final resting place of the saint. While this is evidently a misnomer, it may mark the *site* of the saint's grave before his bones were translated (Sharpe 1995, 374-5; *RCAHMS* 1982, 42, 137-8).

The fate of Columba's shrine and of his mortal remains after the raid of 825 remains uncertain. Reliquaries of the saint travelled between Ireland and Scotland on a number of occasions in the mid-9th century. Their nature is unspecified but they were brought by Diarmait, abbot of Iona, from Ireland to Scotland in 829 *AU* and returned with him in 831 *AU*. Indrechtach, abbot of Iona, brought them out of Scotland to Ireland again in 849 *AU*. The term used in all these accounts is *mindaibh/minnaibh*, a word which can be translated as 'badge', 'emblem', 'insignia', 'halidom' or 'venerated object' (*DIL* sv 1 *mind*). It is not a word particularly used in association with the corporeal remains of a saint or with reliquaries containing such remains: in the 11th century, the *minnaibh* of Columba brought from Tír Conaill are specifically glossed (1090 *ATig*) as *Clog na Rígh, ocus an Chuillebaigh, ocus in da soiscelo*: the 'bell of the kings', the *Cuilebad* (flabellum) and two gospel books. The *minnaibh* which travelled back and forth between Ireland and Scotland in the 9th century may not therefore have included the shrine containing the remains of Columba. But the importance of these references is in showing that a group of reliquaries collectively associated with the saint was already in existence by the early 9th century which accompanied the abbots of Iona on their travels. We may presume that they included some of the saint's insignia – his bell, staff and gospel book – and perhaps, in addition, his tunic.

Indrechtach's journey to Ireland with the relics of Columba in 849 may have had another significance, namely the division of the relics between Ireland and Scotland. In 849 Cináed mac Alpín, having united the kingdoms of the Scots and Picts, 'transported the relics of Columba to a church that he had built', which was probably at Dunkeld (Smyth 1984, 187-8).

The travels of the saint's relics did not, however, end there, for in 878 *AU* the shrine of Columba and his other reliquaries, *scrín Coluim Cille 7 a minna olchena*, arrived in Ireland, 'having been taken in flight to escape the foreigners'. It has been suggested that these represent the Columban relics brought to Dunkeld in 849 and sent to Ireland to avoid capture by Vikings raiding eastern Scotland (Bannerman 1993, 43; RCAHMS 1982, 48, 271, n 123) The annalist is clearly making a distinction here between the shrine of the saint and the other relics associated with him. The same distinction is made in the report of disturbances at Tailtiu in 831 *AU* in the presence of the shrine, *scrín*, of Mac Cuilinn and the relics, *minda*, of Patrick. Elsewhere in *AU*, where the context is sufficiently clear, the term *scrín* appears to indicate a reliquary housing the corporeal remains of a saint. We are told, for example, how in 824 the Vikings raided Bangor, destroyed its oratory, *a derthagi*, 'and shook the relics of Comgall from their shrine', *reilgi Comghaill do crothadh asa scrin*. A Latin gloss on the word *scrín* is implied by two entries in succeeding years in the same compilation:

> 800 *AU* *Positio reliquiarum Conlaid hi scrin oir 7 airgait*
> The placing of the relics of Conláed in a shrine/casket of gold and silver.
> 801 *AU* *Positio reliquiarum Ronaen filii Berich in arca auri 7 argenti*
> The placing of the relics of Rónán son of Berach in a shrine/casket of gold and silver.

It is clear that in both cases it is the corporeal remains that are being translated and that the Irish word *scrín* was considered equivalent to the Latin *arca*, a reliquary normally reserved for corporeal remains; *arca* is the very term used by Walafrid Strabo for the shrine that held Columba's bones.

If the 'shrine' of Columba brought to Ireland in 878 is equated with the reliquary which held the saint's bones then Ireland is its last *recorded* resting place. Attempts to trace its later history are hampered by the fact that the phrase *scrín Coluim Cille* can refer either to a reliquary or to a place: Skreen, Co. Meath, Skreen, Co. Sligo, Ballynascreen, Co. Derry, and Scrín in Arda (Ardmagilligan or Tamlaghtard), Co. Derry (Map 3). Skreen, Co. Meath, first appears in written sources in 976 (Bhreathnach 1996, 41). Gwynn and Hadcock (1970, 44), following Reeves (1857, 315), accept that Columba's shrine was placed there after its arrival in Ireland in 878, but there seems to be no evidence to support this other than the place-name itself, and it would seem most likely that the shrine was brought to Kells. In the Irish life of Adomnán, reference is made to the opening of the *erdamh* of Columba – *Oslaiccidh in [n]-erdamh do Cholum Chilli* – apparently to exorcize a devil by the power of his relics (*BAd* §16 (12)). It has been shown that this life is a Kells composition of the 10th century (Herbert 1988, 151-79), and its editors conclude that the term *erdamh* (*DIL* sv *airdam*) 'manifestly refers to the building containing the corporeal and other relics of Colum Cille (his *cella memoriae?*)' (*BAd* 84, n 224). They point out that the word *erdamh/airdam* denotes a building or part of a building, and that the same word is used in *AU* to describe the building at Kells from which the Book of Kells was stolen in 1007 and which is mentioned again in 1156 *AFM* II. The precise meaning of the term is uncertain, but it does appear to describe an architectural feature in which relics were sometimes housed, perhaps a treasury (Ó Floinn 1995b, 255) or a *Westwerk* (O'Keeffe 1995, 267-8). Thus, while the episode is one of a number supposedly set in Iona in the 7th century, it is likely that it actually reflects the existence of such a structure at Kells in the 10th. The stone-roofed oratory at Kells, called 'St Columb's House', could well have been known as *erdamh Coluim Cille* in the early middle ages. There is, besides, a reference at 1127 *AFM* II to the theft of the shrine of Columba by the Vikings of Dublin 'which was buried again in a month in its house'. Taken at face value this suggests that a portable reliquary called the shrine of Columba was stolen, and the location might have been Skreen, Co. Meath, but the account is found in no other source and cannot be taken as proof that Skreen possessed a shrine containing the bones of Columba (although it probably held some other relics of the saint). One wonders whether the *tech*, 'house', in which the shrine was kept in 1127 might be identical with the *erdamh* at Kells.

Ardmagilligan or Tamlaghtard, Co. Derry, is probably the place in which a reliquary of the saint called *scrín Coluim Cille* was preserved, according to a passage in Ó Domhnaill's 16th-century life (*BCC*). This contained a copy of the gospels and many relics of saints, including portion of the hair of the Virgin, 'And this shrine is the chief relic of Columcille in the place from that time to this, doing wonders and miracles' (*BCC* §146). The contents of the shrine bears a striking resemblance to those mentioned in a poem ascribed to Adomnán (see below).

The corporeal remains of Columba reappear in dramatic circumstances at the close of the 12th century. Their rediscovery is linked directly to the Anglo-Norman conquest of Ulster and to John de Courcy in particular. In 1177 de Courcy captured and fortified Downpatrick. The king of the Ulaid attacked de Courcy's position but was repulsed, and in his flight many relics, including the croziers of Finnian (of Clonard?) and of Rónán Find (of Lann Rónáin Fhind, now Magheralin, Co. Down) were left behind (sa 1178 *MIA*). Later the same year (1177) the Ulaid returned with a larger force of the kings of Ulster but were defeated at Downpatrick without striking a blow. De Courcy seized the abbot of Armagh and his clergy along with a host of relics including the Book of Armagh, two bells associated with Armagh and Patrick, the crozier of Comgall (of Bangor, Co. Down), the bell of Tigernach (of Clones, Co. Monaghan?), and the croziers of Da Chiaróg (of Errigal, Co. Tyrone), Éimíne (of Monasterevin, Co. Kildare) and Muru (of Fahan, Co.

Donegal). Only the Book of Armagh and Tigernach's bell were returned (sa
1178 *MIA*). De Courcy retained the others, either to ransom or to enhance
the prestige of Downpatrick, where he established his *caput*. The papal legate, Cardinal Vivian, had witnessed the battle (Scott & Martin 1978, 174-5).

As well as being a brilliant strategist, John de Courcy was to the forefront
of the reform movement in the Irish Church. In 1183 he granted land to
Chester Abbey in order to found a Benedictine priory at Downpatrick in
place of the older monastic church (Gwynn & Hadcock 1970, 105-6). In
1185 he staged one of the most famous of all translations of Irish saints at
Downpatrick. In the presence of Cardinal Vivian and other distinguished
ecclesiastics, the bones of Patrick, Brigid and Columba were placed in a new
shrine, their location in the cathedral church having been miraculously revealed to the bishop of Downpatrick, Malachias III (Reeves 1847, 227;
O'Laverty 1878, 285-9). The translation is not found in any native Irish
source. It is mentioned by Giraldus Cambrensis and by Jocelin of Furness,
commissioned by de Courcy to write a life of Patrick in 1185/6. The most
detailed account of the *inventio* or discovery of these relics by Malachias is
found in the *Office of Translation of the Relics of SS Patrick, Columba and
Brigid*, printed in Paris in 1620 and synopsised by O'Donovan (*AFM* III, p
457-8, n f). Malachias prayed that God would reveal to him where the

Figure 2 The shrine of St Thomas Becket as depicted in a 13th-century
stained-glass window at Canterbury (after Kendall 1970).

remains were buried. On a certain night a light appeared in the church and fixed on the spot; Malachias had the place excavated and the remains uncovered, which he then ordered to be placed in three distinct boxes or coffins. He communicated the discovery to John de Courcy, who sought permission from Pope Urban III for their translation and had them enshrined with great ceremony in the presence of the papal legate on, significantly, the feast-day of St Columba.

It would appear from the accounts available that a quantity of bones was unearthed, and any reliquary designed to accommodate such remains would have been of substantial proportions. One can only speculate on the form that the reliquary designed to house the Downpatrick relics might have taken. Given that de Courcy's foundation at Downpatrick was an attempt to counter the influence of the pre-Norman Church represented by Armagh, it is unlikely that the reliquary took the gabled form of St Manchán's shrine, and it most likely resembled the large gabled *châsses* so commonly found in German cathedral treasuries – of which the most famous is probably the shrine of the Three Kings preserved in Cologne Cathedral (Lasko 1972, pl 293) – or the reliquary preserved at Troyes (Aube) which houses the remains of St Bernard and St Malachy (Ó Fiaich 1986, pl 6). The Downpatrick shrine might equally have resembled the shrine of St Thomas at Canterbury (Fig 2).

Maghnas Ó Domhnaill, quoting 'the holy Berchan' as his source, relates how the body of Columba came to be at Down. After burial in Iona the grave was plundered by Vikings, under Mandar son of the king of Lochlann, who made off with the wooden coffin, thinking it contained gold; on opening it and finding that it held only bones they cast the coffin into the sea and it came ashore at Down, where its contents were placed by the abbot in a tomb alongside the remains of Patrick and Brigid (*BCC* §371). This story is clearly an attempt to link Walafrid Strabo's account of the plundering of Iona in 825 with the known presence of the relics of the three saints at Downpatrick. It must therefore post-date the 1185 translation but credits the enshrinement to an unnamed abbot of Downpatrick and ignores John de Courcy's role.

It is a remarkable fact that all references to the remains of Columba subsequent to the 1185 translation are linked directly or indirectly to the remains of Patrick and Brigid. This suggests strongly that they derive from the division of the relics contained in the Downpatrick shrine and that the mortal remains of the saint transferred to Ireland (probably to Kells) in 878 had disappeared long since. In fact, the latter must have been lost by 1185, as it is difficult to believe that the discovery of Columba's remains could have been staged if his shrine was still venerated at Kells.

A second translation of the relics of Patrick, Columba and Brigid is recorded in 1293 *AFM* III; *AU*[1]. In this case they were placed in a shrine by

Figure 3 The shrine of St Patrick's hand.

the abbot of Armagh, Nicholas Mac Máelíosa, after it was revealed to him that they were buried at Saul. This second translation is somewhat puzzling: it is not clear whether the location of the discovery refers to the Augustinian house at Saul, Co. Down (Gwynn & Hadcock 1970, 194) or, as O'Laverty has suggested (1878, 289), to a church called Saul (*Saball*) at Armagh. O'Donovan suggested (*AFM* III, p 458, n f) that this event was a counter-scheme of the anti-English party in the Irish Church. Whatever the reason, the relics of Patrick, Brigid and Columba were preserved at Downpatrick until the Reformation. In 1538 *AU*[1] the English justiciar, Lord Leonard Gray, burnt the monastery of Down and took with him the relics, *taissi*, of the three saints and an image of St Catherine. The latter was taken to the green of Dundrum Castle but the annals do not record the fate of the former.

There are a number of later medieval inventories of church treasuries which mention the presence of small fragments of Columba's remains. A 15th-century inventory of the relics in Christ Church Cathedral, Dublin, lists *os de ossibus sancti Columbe abbatis* (Crosthwaite 1844, 3). That relics of St Patrick and St Brigid are listed immediately before and after this single bone of Columba in the inventory suggests that the relics of all three may have been acquired from Downpatrick at some stage after their translation by John de Courcy in 1185.

Relics of Columba are, in the later middle ages, found in a number of

English church treasuries. The church at Leominster, Herefordshire, contained the relics of a number of Irish saints including some of the earth in which lay the bones of Patrick, Finnian, Ciarán, Féichíne, Columba, Brigid, Conláed, Colmán and Ultán (Lehmann-Brockhaus 1956, §2301). Durham Cathedral treasury contained, according to a 14th-century inventory, ... *ossibus et reliquiis s. Columkelli abbatis* (idem 1955, §1491). In both cases the churches contained relics of other Irish saints, including Patrick and Brigid, so that they do not seem to indicate a particular Columban devotion and, as at Christ Church, the relics may well have been acquired as part of the division of the contents of the Downpatrick shrine and may thus have arrived subsequent to de Courcy's translation.

An episode contained in Ó Domhnaill's life, in which the saint gives Cormac ua Liatháin, of the community of Durrow, the tip of his finger as a relic, may indicate that a reliquary containing a finger-bone of the saint was actually preserved at Durrow by the later middle ages (*BCC* §276). Sharpe has observed (1995, 342, n 323) that this episode is found in a Middle Irish poem and in the notes to the *Félire Óengusso*, which suggests that the relic may have been already in existence by the 12th century. Reliquaries containing finger-bones are known from Ireland – the silver shrine of St Patrick's thumb, still containing its relic and preserved at Drogheda, is of 18th-century date (Bourke 1993, 55), while a copper-alloy casing in the shape of a finger might have been detached from an arm-reliquary (Crawford 1923, 93, fig 6).

Iona appears to have been in possession of an arm-reliquary of St Columba in the 15th century. According to the Book of Clanranald, Donald, Lord of the Isles, made 'a covering of gold and silver for the relic of the hand (or arm) of Columba' (Steer & Bannerman 1977, 145). According to the same source he was a benefactor of Iona and was buried there in St Oran's Church on his death in 1421 (ibid., 209; RCAHMS 1982, 249-50). This reliquary no doubt resembled the contemporary shrine of St Patrick's hand (Bourke 1993, 51) (Fig 3).

In Scotland, two principal relics of Columba were preserved in the middle ages; his crozier, called *Cathbhuaidh* on account of its use, like the *Cathach*, as a battle talisman and another object termed the *Breccbennach*. The latter is known from a number of documents relating to the monastery of Arbroath, which was granted the lands of Forglen (where a church was dedicated to Adomnán) in north-east Banffshire 'given to God and to St Columba and to the *Breccbennach*', the keepers of the said *Breccbennach* being required to render military service in the king's army. The abbot of the monastery conferred the lands of Forglen 'which pertain to the *Breccbennach*' on Malcolm

Figure 4 Tomb-shaped shrine, Monymusk, Aberdeenshire.

Figure 5 Seal of Scone Abbey, Perthshire.

Figure 6 Cross-shaft, Hoddom, Dumfriesshire.

of Monymusk in 1315 (Reeves 1857, 330-2; Anderson 1881, 196, n 1, 241-250).

Several writers in the past have attempted to identify the *Breccbennach* on the basis of its name. Reeves (1857, 331-2) considered the object to have been a banner. But a small tomb-shaped shrine, in the possession of the Monymusk family and acquired by the National Museum of Scotland in 1933, may with confidence be regarded as the *Breccbennach* of the medieval sources (Fig 4). Joseph Anderson (1881, 245), in his masterly description of the Monymusk shrine, stopped short of identifying the *Breccbennach* with the reliquary, but in view of its association with Monymusk House and the fact that it is the only surviving reliquary of its kind from Scotland there is little room for doubt. That there were other reliquaries of this type in Scotland in the middle ages can hardly be questioned. Bannerman notes (1993, 21) the existence of a reliquary known as the *Mórbrecc* at St Andrews at the beginning of the 13th century. He has also argued (1989, 127-31) that the *Breccbennach* might be depicted on a 13th-century seal of Scone Abbey portraying the inauguration of Alexander III (Fig 5). It is worth noting that what appears to be the roof of a tomb-shaped shrine is shown on the base of a cross-shaft from Hoddom, Dumfriesshire (Allen & Anderson 1903 III, 439-40) (Fig 6),[1] a site which has also produced two crozier fragments of Irish type (Radford 1954, 115-19; Michelli 1986, 392, illus 7-11). It should come as no surprise that Hoddom is dedicated to St Kentigern, missionary to the Britons of Strathclyde (Lowe et al 1991, 11-12), and the presence of two crozier fragments and the representation of a tomb-shaped shrine is evidence of a flourishing cult of relics at that site.

In the absence of any contemporary description it is only by considering its name – *Breccbennach Coluim Cille* – that we can suggest what this Columban heirloom contained. Anderson argued (1881, 245) that the name signified 'blessed breac' and that the word *brecc* signified a special class of reliquary in the form of an oratory on the basis that the only other reliquary with the name *brecc* is the *Brecc Máedóic*, a tomb-shaped shrine associated with Drumlane, Co. Cavan. He rejected the suggestion that the name might signify a banner. In further defence of Anderson's arguments, it is likely that the second word in the name – *bennach* – derives not from the word *bennaithe* 'blessed' but rather from the word *benn*, 'peak', 'gable', 'ridge', as suggested by Watson (1926, 281) and Bannerman (1993, 21).

The Monymusk reliquary is now empty and none of the medieval sources describe its former contents. I have argued elsewhere that these small shrines, usually called 'house-shaped' shrines but more properly described as tomb-shaped, had a particular function as containers for relics of the saints and martyrs of the early Church, and that they are to be regarded as being distinct from reliquaries containing the bones of a saint (Ó Floinn 1990, 53-5). Bannerman makes a similar distinction (1993, 21), but considers the portable 'house-shaped' shrines to be single-relic shrines, presumably on the basis of their size. But the practice of sub-dividing relics, which was common throughout the medieval period, allows for a multiplicity to be placed in very small shrines. A reliquary-pendant of c 1200 with a Scottish (Whithorn?) provenance, measuring only 5 cm across, contained, according to its inscription, the relics of some nine different saints (Radford 1954, 119-23; Zarnecki

---

1 I am grateful to the Editor for this reference, brought to his attention by Katherine Forsyth.

et al 1984, 289). Bannerman also suggests (1993, 21) that the component *brecc*, 'speckled', 'clearly describes the effect of the decorative metalwork'. But the evidence points to the conclusion that these portable shrines functioned as containers for relics of the saints and martyrs of the early Church (Ó Floinn 1990, 53-4). This is supported by an early medieval explanation of the word *brecc* in a context specifically relating to a relic. The epithet *brecc* ('speckled, spotted; variegated; patterned, ornamented': *DIL* sv 1 *brecc*) is, in the case of the *Brecc Máedóic*, explained in the life of Máedóc:

> and this is why the name Brec (variegated) was given to it, because of the variegated arrangement together of the relics of the saints and virgins which had been united and made fast in it, after being collected and gathered together from the bosom of marvellous Molaise on the corner of Maedoc's mantle, as the Life of Molaise relates (Plummer 1922 I, 266; II, 258, §232).

Earlier in the same paragraph these relics are listed as those of 'the saints and patriarchs, namely relics of the martyr Stephen, and Lawrence, and Clement, the ankle of Martin, and some of the hair of the Virgin Mary, and many other relics of saints and holy virgins besides' (ibid.).

A poem, sometimes known as *The Shrine of Adomnán*, purports, according to one version, to list the relics collected by Adomnán and placed by him in a single shrine. A 12th-century note equates this shrine with the shrine of Adomnán which was brought to Ireland in 727 *AU* (Carney 1983, 26-7). Carney considered this to be too literal an interpretation of the poem, preferring to see the 'relics' of Christ, the Virgin and the early Church fathers along with those of Irish and Scottish saints as metaphors for the gospels, the teachings of the early fathers and the accounts of the lives of the saints. He believed that the 'shrine of Adomnán' referred to in 727 and again in 730 *AU* most likely contained the human remains of Adomnán rather than relics collected by him. Given what has been said above about *scrín Coluim Cille*, it is indeed more likely that Adomnán's shrine contained his corporeal remains. *Scrín Adomnáin* was taken by the Vikings from Donaghmoyne, Co. Monaghan, in 832 *AU*.

Notwithstanding Carney's caveats, the collection of 'relics' referred to in the poem does read like the contents of a shrine containing multiple relics of the type represented by the *Brecc Máedóic*. Of the twenty-six articles referred to, eight consist of fragments of garments – of the Virgin, Christ and St Martin of Tours, the hair shirts of Brigid and Columba, the curly-haired tunic of Senach or Senán (of Scattery Island, Co. Clare), the chasubles of Énna (Enda) (of Aran, Co. Galway) and Cainnech (of Aghaboe, Co. Laois). These could equally be regarded as *brandea*, fragments of cloth which touched the relics of the holy men and women concerned and which thus became relics in themselves. Another eight relate to corporeal relics – relics of the teeth of Patrick and Déclán (of Ardmore, Co. Waterford), a rib of Fínán Cam (of Kinnitty, Co. Offaly), the knee-cap of Donnán (of Eigg), the shoulder of Columb mac Crimthainn (of Terryglass, Co. Tipperary) and portions of the skulls of Mochuta (of Lismore, Co. Waterford) and Mochóe or Mochóemóc (of Liathmore, Co. Tipperary?). Portion of the True Cross and the belt of St Paul are also included. These are exactly the kind of relics which one would expect to have been housed in a tomb-shaped shrine of the type represented by *Breccbennach Coluim Cille*.

Columba's clothing was considered to be a prized relic, perhaps next in importance to the physical remains of the saint. Apart from his books, the only other object explicitly kept and revered as a miracle-working relic described by Adomnán is Columba's tunic. In order to induce rain after a prolonged drought, it was decided, after some debate, to walk in procession through the fields holding aloft the white tunic, *candida ... tunica*, which Columba wore at his death, to shake it three times and to read aloud from his books (*VC* ii. 44). On another occasion, the saint's vestments and books, ... *vestimenta et libros*, were laid on the altar to ensure favourable winds (*VC* ii. 45). It is significant that Adomnán mentions the tunic's colour, for among the textiles retrieved from St Cuthbert's tomb were portions of a weft-patterned tunic of white silk with decorated braided edges (Granger-Taylor 1989). Dating to c 800, this object may have been added to the tomb in Durham as late as the early 12th century (ibid., 327). Closer in date to Columba's time is the late 7th-century tunic of St Bathilde preserved at Chelles (Seine et Marne) (Roth 1979, Abb 239).

The saint's cowl or cloak was also endowed with magical powers. Adomnán recounts (*VC* ii. 24) how one of Columba's companions, intercepting an assassin's spear, was protected from injury because he wore the saint's cowl, *cucula*. Unlike the tunic, however, Adomnán makes no reference to the cowl being preserved after Columba's death.

Garments associated with Columba are mentioned in the later lives. In the 12th-century Irish life written about 1150 in Derry (Herbert 1988, 192; but cf. Bannerman 1993, 41, who argues in favour of Armagh), reference is made to his tunic, *léne*, which Cainnech (of Aghaboe, Co. Laois) had acquired as part of the division of his garments (*ILCC* §57). Elsewhere in the same text (§47), a youth removes portion of the saint's garment, *étach*, as a keepsake. The latter recalls the relic known as *Étach Pátraic*, Patrick's 'garment' or 'cloth', seized by the Vikings of Lough Neagh in 895 *AFM* I. In the poem attributed to Adomnán cited above, reference is made to the hair shirt, *féslène*, of Columba (Carney 1983, 35, line 14).

Another garment, the saint's cloak or cowl, *cochall*, is mentioned in the mid-11th/early 12th-century *Bórama* saga where the northern Uí Néill king, Áed mac Ainmuirech, wears it to protect himself from the Leinstermen (*LL* V, 1298). In the 12th-century life (*ILCC* §40) and in Ó Domhnaill's life (*BCC* §98), the *cochall* is blessed by Columba and given to Áed Sláine, king of Tara. It was believed to have magical powers, protecting the wearer from injury. According to Ó Domhnaill it was preserved at Kilmacrenan 'in a right worshipful shrine covered with gold and silver. And so it is a high relic of Columcille, working wonders and miracles in Cill mic Nenain to this day' (*BCC* §355h). It may well have been preserved in *Teach Coluim Cille* at Kilmacrenan which was plundered in 1129 *AU*.

Curiously, John O'Donovan, writing in 1838 from Ballycroy, Co. Mayo (*OSLM* I, 333-5), refers to a tradition of a relic in the locality some seventy years earlier, which was called *Cochall Coluim Cille* and on which people had the habit of swearing. It was in the possession of two old men named Clery and Freel and was described as consisting of a box with some gems inserted in the cover. This would, however, appear to relate to the shrine of the *Cathach*, which in *BCC* §275 is glossed his 'cowl of purity', and this may explain the confusion.

The shrine of the *Cathach*, interestingly enough, did contain small fragments of cloth (unspecified), supposed to have been a relic of Columba's garment, behind one of its crystal mounts when opened by Sir William Betham in 1814. The crystal and the cloth behind it were, however, lost by 1874 (Armstrong 1916, 394).

From the beginning books and book production seem to have played a key role in the Columban legend. Three of the ten surviving Irish manuscripts of pre-1000 date, and two of the eight surviving book-shrines, are associated with the Columban tradition. It has been noted above how books believed to have been written by the saint were placed on the altar at Iona. Although he does not say that these books were enshrined, Adomnán was familiar with the concept of a book-shrine or cover: he recounts two instances of how books recovered from rivers in Ireland were ruined, save only those parts written in Columba's own hand which were miraculously protected as if kept in a cover or case, *in scriniolo* (*VC* ii. 8); *in scrinio* (*VC* ii. 9). Almost a thousand years later, Conell Mageoghegan was to write, in his translation of the *Annals of Clonmacnoise*, how a manuscript written by the saint:

w[ch] I have seen partly myselfe of that book of them which is at Dorow in the K^s County, for I saw the Ignorant man that had the same in his Custody, when sickness came upon cattle, for their Remedy putt water on the booke & suffered it to rest there a while & saw alsoe cattle returne thereby to their former or pristin state & the book to receave no loss (Murphy 1896, 96).

This was undoubtedly the 7th-century Book of Durrow which contains a later colophon attributing its writing to Columba. The earliest modern description of this manuscript is of the early 17th century when it was known as the 'Book of Columcille, i.e. the Book of Durmhaigh ... with a binding of silver and gems' (Luce 1960, 66). Other accounts speak of this covering as being composed of silver plates and adorned with a silver cross bearing an inscription (ibid., 32-3). Part of this read as follows:

+*Oroit acus bendacht choluimb chille do Flaund macc Mailsechnaill do righerenn la sa ndernad a cumddach so*

A prayer and the blessing of Columba on Flann mac Máelsechnaill on the king of Ireland who caused this cover to be made.

The description of the cover is in keeping with other early book-shrines which have survived, most obviously the shrine of the Stowe Missal of the early 11th century, which is covered with silver plates and a cross bearing an inscription. The inscription on the Book of Durrow has always been taken to refer to Flann Sinna and therefore to imply a date between 879 and 916. Recently, however, it has been suggested that the inscription may refer to a Flann mac Máelsechlainn who died in 1013 or to another who died in 1041 (Michelli 1996, 28-30). But it is clear from the formula that the Flann mentioned in the inscription actually claimed the title of high king rather than being either an aspirant to the title or the son of a high king. The formula *or do x do y* is frequently used in early Irish inscriptions where *y* gives the title of the person named *x*. Thus, on the shrine of the Stowe Missal the inscription – *Or do Dondchad macc Briain do rig hErend ocus do Maccraith hU Dondchada do rig Cassil. Or do Dunchad hU Taccain do Muintir Cluana dorigni* – asks for prayers for Donnchadh mac Briain, king of Ireland, Maccraith Ua Dúnchada, king of Cashel and Donnchadh Ua Taccain of the community of Clonmacnoise. There was only one Flann mac Máelsechnaill who was king of Ireland and that was Flann Sinna. Michelli further argues (1996, 30) that the inscription may be even later, on the basis of the rendering of Máelsechnaill's name as *Mailsechnaill*, which is 'impossible for the pre-Norman period'. This does not take into account either an error by the craftsman (see the two versions of the name *Donnchadh* on the shrine of the

Figure 7 Shrine of the *Cathach*.

Figure 8 The *Misach*.

Stowe Missal above) or by the transcriber. Moreover, although not common, the forms *Mail-* and *Mel-* are found in pre-Norman sources, in inscriptions (Macalister 1949, nos 588, 700), annalistic references (867.8, 912.4, 970.4, 1013.1.2.13 *AU*) and genealogies (O'Brien 1962, 58, 64, 67).

It can hardly be doubted that the Book of Kells is to be equated with the 'great gospel book' of Columba, *Soiscelae mor Coluim Cille*, which was stolen, as we have seen, from the western *erdamh* (treasury?) of Kells in 1007 *AU*. Described as 'the chief relic of the western world' it was stolen on account of its cover, *comhdaigh doendi*. Ryan has recently reviewed the possible meanings of the latter term (1994, 273-4), which has been interpreted as indicating that the book-cover, *cumdach*, had human ornamentation, and has concluded that this cannot be demonstrated and that the term *doendi* probably has some sense such as 'wrought'. The annalist informs us that the manuscript was recovered, 'its gold having been taken from it', some months later.

The manuscript known as the *Cathach* or 'battler' of Columba bears the unique distinction of being the only extant relic which is contemporary with the saint and was therefore possibly even penned by him. It consists of a psalter of late 6th- or early 7th-century date to which a cover was added at Kells sometime between 1062 and 1098 (Fig 7). By tradition, this battle talisman of the O'Donnells is said to be the very manuscript copied by Columba which led to the battle of Cúil Dreimne. I have argued elsewhere (Ó Floinn 1995a, 117-25) that there is no reference to the *Cathach* of Columba before the 13th century and that none of these traditions appear to be earlier than this, although the manuscript was certainly part of the relic cult of Columba by the late 11th century when it was enshrined at Kells. I have suggested the possibility that it may be identified with the Gospels of Martin of Tours, the *Soscéla Martain*, one of the chief relics of Derry in the 12th century (last heard of in 1182 *AFM* III, when carried off by the Anglo-Normans after the battle of Drumbo, Co. Antrim, where it was used as a battle talisman or *cathach*), and that the relic reappears in the 13th century as the *Cathach* of Columba. In the early 19th century Sir William Betham reported a tradition that the shrine of the *Cathach* had been sealed by Col Daniel O'Donnell 'under an idea that it contained the bones of St. Columkill himself' (1826, 110).

Another gospel book, the Gospels of the Angel, was one of the three relics of Patrick recovered by Columba from Patrick's grave. In the division of these relics, Columba retained the gospel book. The account is given at 553 *AU* in a passage interpolated from the Book of Cuanu. If the latter may be ascribed to Cuanu, abbot of Louth, exiled to Munster in 818 *AU*, then we may suppose that a book called the Gospels of the Angel was preserved at Iona by the early 9th century. Reeves has suggested (1857, 326) that the book was identical with the Gospels of Martin of Tours, but this is by no means certain.

The book-shrine known as the *Misach* (Fig 7) was a late addition to the Columban cult. Its history has recently been dealt with elsewhere (Ó Floinn 1995a, 126-31). It was known as *Misach Cairnigh* in the 12th century, by which stage it appears to have been transferred to a northern church, most probably Derry. Cairnech – a Briton from Cornwall – had his principal church at Dulane, Co. Meath, some 3 km from Kells. It is likely that when the Uí Uchtáin, one of the ecclesiastical families associated with Dulane, assumed high office at Kells in the early 11th century this Dulane relic was transferred, eventually being brought north with other relics when Kells was replaced by Derry as the head of the Columban monastic federation. By the early 17th century all knowledge of the object's association with Cairnech was lost, for an inquisition of 1609 found that Donogh O'Morreeson, erenagh of Clonmany was 'keeper of the missagh or ornaments left by Columkill'.

Derry appears, therefore, to have been in possession of at least two important books – the *Misach* of Cairnech and the Gospels of Martin. We may add to these the belt of St Mobí of Glasnevin, Co. Dublin, mentioned in both the 12th-century life of Columba (*ILCC* §32) and that of Ó Domhnaill (*BCC* §77) in relation to the foundation of Derry. It was apparently used for the swearing of oaths, for, according to Ó Domhnaill, 'never was it opened for gluttony and never was it closed upon a lie'.

The 'great cross' of Columba is first mentioned in the preface, dated to the 10th or 11th century, to the *Altus Prosator*, a Latin hymn describing the Creation, Fall and Last Judgement, which is ascribed to Columba. Here it is described as *in mor-Gemm Coluim cille, ocus cross esside indiu*, 'the great gem of Columba (which is a cross at the present day)', which had been sent to him by Pope Gregory the Great along with a book of hymns and other gifts (Reeves 1857, 318-19; Kenney 1929, 263-5). The episode is expanded in Ó Domhnaill's life, to the effect that the cross was made of wood which Gregory had received from angels of God, and that 'to this day it is called the Great Cross of Columcille. And it is the chief treasure of Columcille in Tory, working wonders and marvels from that day to this in the north of Erin, whither Columcille sent it westward from Iona' (*BCC* §215). It appears to have been of some size, as it is reported, in 1542 *AFM* V, that it was 'broken' by Brian Mac Conmhidhe, who died as a result 'through the miracles of God, and the curse of Ó Robhartaigh'. The latter was presumably its hereditary keeper.

It would appear, therefore, that a large, jewelled wooden cross which tradition held was a gift from Gregory the Great to Columba was in existence by the 10th/11th centuries, that it was originally at Iona but was transferred at some unknown date to Tory Island. Gregory was a contemporary of Columba's and had, through his initiation of the Augustinian mission to England in 597, a direct link with the insular Church. In addition it has been pointed out that Gregory's writings, particularly his *Dialogues*, were known at Iona in Adomnán's time – the episode in which Columba's tunic and books are brought into the fields to induce rain relies heavily on a similar account in Gregory's life of Benedict of Nursia (Sharpe 1995, 59; O'Reilly this vol). It is therefore possible that there was some historical foundation to the legend. If this is the case, then it is likely that the cross reputedly received from Gregory contained a portion of the True Cross. Relics of the True Cross were known to have been in Ireland since at least the 9th century (868 *FAI*). Gregory was in possession of such relics; a cross containing pieces of the True Cross was given by him, along with a precious gospel book and other objects, to the Lombardic queen Theodolinde and was preserved in the cathedral treasury at Monza (*NCE* 335). The cross does not survive but the golden covers of the gospel book of Queen Theodolinde, dated to c 600 and bearing on each face a *crux gemmata* in the form of a Latin cross with expanded terminals – inlaid with antique cameos, precious stones, pearls and cloisonné enamel – perhaps give an idea of what the 'great gem' of Columba might have looked like (Backes & Dölling 1969, 18-19; Hubert et al 1969, 231, fig 241).

A second cross is described in a letter from Sir John Perrott to Lord Burleigh as 'holy Collamkille's cross, a god of great veneration with Sorleyboy and all Ulster' which Perrott acquired following the seizure in 1584 of Somhairle Buidhe Mac Domhnaill's stronghold at Dunluce Castle, Co. Antrim (McNeill 1943, 12). Perrott sent the relic to Burleigh in the hope that 'you may, if you please, bestow him upon my good Lady Wallsingham or my Lady Sydney to wear as a jewel of weight and bigness, and not of price and goodness, upon some solemn feast or triumph day at the court' (ibid.). From this it appears that the relic was enclosed in a jewelled cross capable of being worn around the neck. It is uncertain whether this is to be equated with the 'great gem' preserved at Tory Island. It is more likely, if there is any connection between the two, that the Dunluce relic contained a fragment of the Tory cross.

Columba's flabellum or liturgical fan, *Cuilebad Coluim Cille*, is first mentioned in 1034 *AU* when it was reputedly lost at sea, along with three relics of Patrick, *tri minna do minnaib Patraicc*, while in the custody of Maicnia Ua Uchtáin, lector of Kells, who was returning from Scotland. It appears to have been recovered (or replaced), for in 1090 *ATig* it is reckoned as one of the relics of the saint which came south from Tír Conaill together with 140

Figure 9 The flabellum in use, as depicted in a Rouen
manuscript of the 13th century (after Way 1848).

ounces of silver. Bannerman suggests (1993, 44) that these relics were on
circuit in the north and that the silver was paid in tribute by the Cenél
Conaill. The fact that they were in the possession of a Kells official, Óengus
Ua Domnalláin, would tend to support this and to indicate that they were
normally kept at Kells. Further evidence for the presence of this object at
Kells is found in the voyage tale *Immram Snédgusa ocus Maic Ríagla*, of
which two versions survive, a poetical version of 9th- or 10th-century date
and a prose account dating to the 11th century (Kenney 1929, 447-8). Both
recount how the two clerics, Snédgus and Mac Ríagla, are carried to an
island while returning from Ireland to Iona. On the island is an immense tree
with a flock of white birds. A great bird with a golden head and silver wings
gives them a leaf as large as the hide of an ox, bidding them to place it on
Columba's altar. However, only in the later prose account does the following
gloss appear: *Conid hi cuilefaid Coluim Chille andiu, i Ceannandus atásaide*
(Van Hamel 1941, 84), 'and it is Colum Cille's *Cuilefaidh* at this day in
Cennanas.' The identification of the leaf brought back from an island off the
coast of Scotland with the *Cuilebad Coluim Cille* at Kells in the 11th-century
prose version may have been necessary to explain the recovery of a relic
which had been reported lost in 1034.

Some writers, such as McRoberts (1961) and Richardson (1993), have
attempted to suggest that flabella were in use in the Celtic Church from an

early date, although Wilson has convincingly dismissed most of McRoberts arguments (1973, 118-20). The earliest occurrence of the word in an Irish context is contained in glosses dated to the mid-9th century in the Karlsruhe *Soliloquia* of St Augustine (Stokes & Strachan 1903, x-xi) where the word *flabellum* is glossed *culebath* (ibid., 8). Richardson states (1993, 30) that the flabellum 'was in use in Ireland in the 7th and 8th centuries and very probably earlier', and that an 'indication of the early date when the fan flourished in Ireland is the connection with ecclesiastics mainly of the 6th century'. She offers no proof in support of these statements other than the mistaken belief that historical characters associated with flabella may be used to date their currency in Ireland, and the supposition that flabella were used in the western Church from an early date. The flabellum preserved in Canossa, northern Italy, dates to the 12th century but is traditionally associated with the 6th-century St Sabinus (Braun 1932, 654). Although flabella are known in the eastern Church from the 5th century, the earliest recorded occurrences in the West date from 831 (ibid., 651-2) (Fig 9). Flabella are said to be represented on a number of Irish cross slabs (Higgins 1987, 109-13), most notably the carved pillar at Carndonagh, Co. Donegal (Henry 1965, pl 59), and in the Book of Kells (McRoberts 1961, pl xxix-xxx; Richardson 1993, fig 3.7). However, although these *may* be representations of flabella, the identification is by no means certain (see Braun 1932, 652). Many of the crosses said by

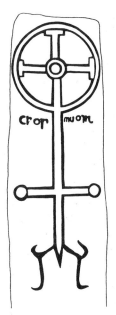

Figure 10 Slab with disc-headed cross, Temple Brecan, Aran, Co Galway
(after Higgins 1987).

Higgins (1987, figs 38-9) to be derived from the flabellum may simply be disc-headed crosses which bear only superficial resemblance to the liturgical fan.

Braun (1932, 653-6) divides medieval flabella into two types, the first being made of light materials such as vellum and ivory which were used as fans to keep flies off the altar. The earliest surviving fan-type flabellum from the West is that from the monastery of St Philibert, Tournus (Sâone-et-Loire) (in the Bargello Museum, Florence), dated to the 9th century (Gaborit-Chopin 1978, 188, fig 49; Lasko 1972, 46-7). It is circular, composed of folded sheets of illuminated vellum with a bone and ivory handle. Three others are known from the West, all from Italy and dating to the 12th century (Swarzenski 1969, 487-8, fig 6; Braun 1932, 654). Braun's second type is composed of metal discs in the shape of flabella which developed later and which served as processional or altar crosses, often in pairs (ibid., 655-6). The disc-shaped heads were provided with pointed tangs to enable them to be set on a long staff for processional use and into a stand to be used on the altar. These are more numerous in the West and date mostly to the 12th century. They usually consist of discs of gilt copper, either solid or open-work, and are sometimes covered with precious stones and filigree. Many have as their central motif an equal-armed cross (Legner 1982, 82-3, pls 348-51). A disc cross of this very type is represented on a carved slab at Temple Brecan, Inismore, Co. Galway: a disc-headed cross pattée on a long shaft with a pointed tang in its base is set into a stand with splayed feet (Fig 10). It is directly comparable with the late 12th-century disc cross made in England or Saxony and kept in the treasury at Kremsmünster, Austria (Legner 1982, pl 350). The Temple Brecan slab bears an inscription which has been variously read as *cronmael* / *cronmaol* / *cronmaoin* (Higgins 1987, 363). It could, however, be read as *cros maoir* or *cros maeir*, 'cross of the hereditary keeper' or 'steward', indicating that it indeed depicts a processional cross. A similar disc cross on a stand is carved on a slab at Cill na Seacht nIníon, Inisheer (Higgins 1987, fig 78), suggesting that both represent a metal cross (perhaps a continental import?) preserved somewhere on Aran around the 12th century. In the context of Columba, none of the texts which mention *Cuilebad Coluim Cille* are earlier than the 11th century. It is possible that the latter may have been a disc cross of this type, fixed in a stand and placed on, or beside, an altar at Kells.

Adomnán relates (*VC* ii 39) how Columba gave a monk, Librán, a sword 'decorated with ivory', *macheram beluinis ornatam dolatis ... dentibus*, in order that the latter might buy his freedom. The sword was, in the event, returned to Columba. The description is clearly that of a sword with a carved element such as a hilt or sheath of walrus ivory. Surviving walrus ivory carving of such an early date is rare, but – if the sword indeed ever existed – the raw material of its decorated elements suggests they were most probably of north European workmanship, resembling perhaps the early 8th-century ivory sheath of the so-called 'dagger' of St Peter preserved in the cathedral treasury at Bamberg, northern Germany (Gaborit-Chopin 1978, pl 31).

It is not possible to say whether the sword of Adomnán's story bears any relationship to the sword with special powers which was preserved at Durrow, according to the 12th-century life (*ILCC* §37). In Ó Domhnaill's account of the same object the sword is attributed to Colmán Mór mac Diarmada, eponymous ancestor of the Clann Cholmáin kings of Midhe (*BCC* §96). The special power which this sword possessed was that whoever had it could not die. Although not specifically associated with the saint, the sword acquired its magical powers through his intercession and should therefore be reckoned as a relic.

Swords associated with important secular patrons are not unknown in church treasuries elsewhere in medieval Europe – the treasury of St-Denis contained the legendary sword of Charlemagne (Gaborit-Chopin 1991, 204-9), while Essen Cathedral housed the sword of the abbesses of Essen (Swarzenski 1967, fig 100). While not strictly speaking a relic of Columba, a sword which received its power through his blessing would have possessed the same magical properties as his cloak.

Such is the nature of the diverse sources used in this survey – saint's lives, annalistic entries, charters, inventories of church property, inscriptions, prose texts and texts in verse, and folk traditions, some far removed in time from the events they purport to describe – that it is impossible to compare the weight of one piece of evidence against the next.

With the possible exception of Patrick, the relic cult of Columba was one of the most prolific in medieval Ireland. His cult was widespread in Scotland also but does not appear to have extended in any notable way to the rest of Britain. Unlike the cults of Patrick and Brigid, devotion to Columban relics does not appear to have spread to the continent. Another peculiarity is that relics of other saints were subsumed into Columba's cult. These included the *Misach*, which, as we have seen, was originally associated with Cairnech of Dulane.

Scholars are divided as to when the remains of the saint were enshrined and venerated after his death. Adomnán refers (*VC* ii. 45) to his tunic and books being placed on the altar in Iona but is equivocal on his actual remains. Bannerman (1993, 22-3) is doubtful whether Columba's remains could have remained undisturbed until after Adomnán's time, in view of the rapid trans-

lation of those of other saints, and indeed Adomnán's own relics were placed
in a shrine within a generation of his death (727, 730 *AU*) (cf. MacDonald
this vol). Doubts over the location of Columba's remains arise as early as the
9th century with the claim that he was buried at Saul. These rival claims
recall those associated with the burial place of Patrick and reflect a widespread medieval phenomenon, which includes the competing claims over the
remains of St Martin of Tours, whose life, written by Sulpicius Severus, had
so much influence on early Irish hagiography.

Because Iona, as the principal foundation of the Columban federation,
was located across the sea from the Irish foundations, many of the early
references to the saint's insignia relate to their movements back and forth
across the North Channel before most appear to have rested at Kells from
the later 9th century. Kells seems to have been in possession of the principal
relics after their division in the mid-9th century, the saint's shrine, along
with his flabellum and a number of manuscripts, including the *Cathach* and
the Book of Kells, being recorded there between then and the late 11th
century. Later, in the 12th century, some at least were transferred to Derry.
The insignia, *miondaibh*, of Columba were present, along with the *Bachall
Ísu*, the principal relic of Armagh, as witnesses to a treaty in 1152 *AFM* II,
but we are not told in whose possession they were. Other named relics were
kept at Dunkeld, Monymusk, Durrow, Downpatrick, Dublin, Tory Island,
Gartan, Kilmacrenan and Tamlaghtard (Maps 3, 4). No doubt others of his
foundations, such as Swords, Co. Dublin, burnt in 1130 *AU*, *cona thempaill
7 co minnaibh imdaibh*, 'with its church and many halidoms', contained some
Columban insignia.

It is a remarkable fact that enshrined corporeal remains figure little in the
Irish cult of relics. The shrine of St Manchán is the only pre-Norman reliquary containing the bones of an Irish saint. The practice of placing corporeal remains in portable reliquaries of precious metal which were liable to be
plundered rather than in more durable stone tombs may, in part, account for
this. In fact, references to stone shrines in contemporary sources are rare.
One such relates to the translation in 1207 *AFM* III, nine years after his
death, of the remains of Ruaidhrí Ua Conchobair, king of Connacht, and
their deposition in a stone shrine: *taissi ... do thabhairt a talmain, 7 a ccur hi
sccrín chloiche*. While tomb-shrines of stone of undoubtedly early form are
known from Ireland, it has yet to be convincingly demonstrated that these
belong to 'founder saints' rather than being those of prominent ecclesiastics
or secular patrons (*pace* Herity 1993). Columba's *scrín* is last heard of in 878
AU and the shrines containing the remains of Brigid, Patrick (last mentioned
in 1066 *AU*), Adomnán (last mentioned in 832 *AU*) and others, disappear
from native written sources by the 12th century. Their actual disappearance
no doubt allowed de Courcy to stage the invention and translation of the

Triadis Thaumaturgae in 1185. With the possible exception of a relic containing his tooth, all surviving corporeal relics of Patrick need be no earlier than the 15th century (Bourke 1993, 48-55). The same is true of Columba – his arm or hand enshrined at Iona in the 15th century, and a possible thumb-shrine preserved at Durrow at an unknown date prior to the compilation of Ó Domhnaill's life in 1532. The latter is the richest quarry for information on Columba's relics. It is also the latest, being a compilation of other texts of different periods, but without a modern critical edition it is impossible to date many of the events it records. In particular, it would be useful to know when the various eyewitness accounts were written – those of Columba's *scrín*, containing a gospel book and a lock of the Virgin's hair, and of the shrine of his cowl, kept at Kilmacrenan, the latter encased in gold and silver.

ACKNOWLEDGEMENTS

I am grateful to Edel Bhreathnach and Cormac Bourke for their many useful comments and observations.

Insignia Columbae II

Cormac Bourke

Nowhere in Scotland is the survival of three ancient hand-bells attested in such close proximity as in Glen Lyon, Perthshire (Map 4). In this captivating valley, dominated by Ben Lawers to the south and Carn Gorm to the north, where Perthshire Gaelic survived within living memory, Joseph Anderson saw three bronze-coated iron bells towards the end of the 19th century (1881, 178-82). One of them, since lost, had been found in 1870 at Balnahanaid (Baile na hAnnaide), which is to be identified as a church site by its name (Watson 1926, 251-4; MacDonald 1973). The second remains where Anderson saw it in the parish church at Fortingall. The third was preserved in his day in Cladh Bhranno graveyard, at first in the open, latterly in a locked niche which can still be seen in the graveyard wall. It is exhibited today in Glen Lyon or Innerwick church and there identified as St Adomnán's bell.

Anderson records (1881, 179, n 2):

> The fair at Dull [near Fortingall] was called Feil Eonan, and held on 6th October, which is St. Adamnan's day, old style. There is also a well called Tobar Eonan, and on the top of Craig Euny a natural fissure, traditionally styled the foot-mark of St. Eonan or Adamnan. The mill-town of Balvoulin Eonan [Baile Mhuilinn Eódhnain] in Glenlyon also preserves the saint's name, and ... up to a very recent period the mill always stopped work on the saint's day.

To this concentration of nomenclature Watson adds Magh Eódhnain, 'Adomnán's plain', in Glen Lyon, and Ard-Eódhnaig (Ardewnan), 'Adomnán's height', south of Loch Tay. He reports that the story of how Adomnán stayed a great plague 'is still told in Glen Lyon, and the spot where he planted his crozier, thus setting a limit to the plague, is pointed out at Craigianie' (1926, 270-71).

The existence of Columban monasteries among the Picts is confirmed by Adomnán (*VC* ii. 46), supported by Bede (*HE* iii. 3), although none is named and even their location is uncertain. But it is tempting to speculate that monks from Iona were active in Glen Lyon and that dependent monasteries were founded here, among the southern Picts, in the lifetime of Adomnán if not of Columba himself. Oblique references in the *Amra Coluim Cille* say of Columba that he taught 'the tribes of the Tay', *túatha Toí*, and that 'his blessing turned them ... the fierce ones who lived on the Tay' (Clancy & Márkus 1995, 104-5, i.15, 112-13, viii. 5-6). Glen Lyon is immediately north of Loch Tay, and these words, if not 'poetic circumlocution' (Herbert 1988, 11), may reflect the contact which the dedications to Adomnán and the three Glen Lyon bells seem to attest.[1]

Adomnán, writing in the 690s, is among our earliest witnesses to the ringing of bells in the early insular Church. He refers to the use of a bell to signal the beginning of the midnight office and to call the community to assembly. A note attributed to his contemporary Tírechán says of Patrick that he took with him across the Shannon 'fifty bells, fifty patens, fifty chalices, altar stones, books of the law, books of the Gospels and left them in the new places' (Bieler 1979, 122-3).

This exaggerated picture of Patrick as quartermaster extraordinaire at least reveals Tírechán's own familiarity with the listed accoutrements. There can be no doubt that by the late 7th century they were part of a complement in regular use, including also the wine-strainer, the pastoral staff, the tomb-shaped reliquary and clerical vestments. Probably all were employed in the Churches of Gaul and Britain when Irish Christianity was established, seemingly by impulses from both places, in the course of the 5th century. Tírechán provides our first intimation that any or all of them could be hallowed by association, referring to patens (or covers for patens) made by Patrick's metalworker, which he saw with his own eyes, as well as to a chasuble of Bishop Brón preserved in the church which bears his name, Killaspugbrone, Co. Sligo (Bieler 1979, 140-41, 158-9). Adamnán, similarly, mentions that the garment of Columba was taken on a circuit on Iona to induce favourable weather (*VC* ii. 44). His account of the Holy Places, *De Locis Sanctis* (*DLS*), shows an appreciation of the developing cults of the relics of Christ and of the saints, and there is ample evidence that such cults were imitated in the West.

It is a truism of the cults of the saints that allusion to the material things of their lives is retrospective. Saints' *lives*, in the sense of their written 'biographies', were almost invariably written *post mortem*, and every attribution is open to question: the greater the distance in time between hagiogra-

---

1 Aidan MacDonald points out (pers comm) that dedications to Adomnán in central Perthshire might be due to the later influence of Dunkeld. But there are signs that the Scottish bells fall into two successive series, and that those of bronze (including a bell from Little Dunkeld) are later than those of iron. The latter are more widely distributed and have some claim to greater antiquity. If the expulsion of the community of Iona beyond the 'Spine of Britain' by the king of the Picts in 717 *AU* was effective (but cf. Smyth 1984, 139), one might hazard a guess that the three Glen Lyon bells predate it (see note 2).

pher and subject the greater the element of doubt. A similar doubt attends the annalistic record: a reference at 1123 *AU* to the destruction of the bell of Ailbe of Emly, Co. Tipperary (obit 527 *AU*), is evidence only that a bell existed which was attributed to that saint, but not that he himself necessarily used it. On occasion, however, we approach a seeming reality, even if the articles referred to have not survived. Besides the vestments of Brón and Columba, one might cite the staff of Columbanus (obit 615), said in the 830s to have been bequeathed on his deathbed in Bobbio to his follower Gallus (Krusch 1902, 304-5, §26; Joynt 1926, 101) and the bell of Fer Dá Chrích, said in a note added to the *Félire Óengusso* to have been brought to Tallaght, Co. Dublin, by Máel Ruain (obit 792 *AU*) (Stokes 1905, 186-7). In the case of Moninne of Killeevy, Co. Armagh, her relics – badger-skin garment, comb and hoe (Heist 1965, 89, §19; de Paor 1993, 288) – have such an aura of the personal as to appear plausibly authentic in our eyes. The transmission of non-corporeal relics might have been guaranteed on occasion by their committal to the grave with the body of the sainted person, to be recovered in the event of the translation of the bones to a sarcophagus or shrine above ground. That the tomb of Patrick was said to have been located and opened by Columba, revealing, besides his mortal remains, a chalice, book and bell, may be a reminiscence of such discoveries (553 *AU*; Smyth 1972, 47). The actuality is attested in Anglo-Saxon England in the case of St Cuthbert, who was buried at Lindisfarne in 687 accompanied by his pectoral cross, and to whose tomb further relics were added on the translation of his remains in 698 (Battiscombe 1956a, 25). Thus, while there is no difficulty in accepting that material things might indeed have been transmitted from the age of the great monastic founders, we yet lack any item confidently attributable to a 6th-century figure – unless the *Cathach* of Columba is one such – much less to any 5th-century figure such as Patrick. Our inheritance is discontinuous, and the plagues of the 7th century, which Tírechán and Adomnán mention (Bieler 1979, 42, 142-3; *VC* ii. 46) and which intervened before the cults of the 6th-century saints were yet fully established, might be among the causes.

The relative chronology of iron and bronze bells is somewhat uncertain, although the likelihood is that the earliest insular bells were made of iron. Iron bells alone were eventually enshrined (with the ambiguous exception of the bronze bell of St Muru, which is contemporary with its 11th-century mounts), and several bronze bells from Ireland are certainly of 9th- or 10th-century date (Bourke 1980).[2] Thus it is that *iron* bells are probably referred to in our 7th-century sources. Small bells of both metals – those of iron four-

---

2 The bronze bells of Scotland are more uniform than their Irish counterparts and less comparable in their morphology with those of iron. They may form a 10th-century cluster (Bourke 1983).

Figure 1 Killadeas, Co Fermanagh: figure with staff and bell.

sided, those of bronze four-sided or round – are a commonplace in the material culture of the Roman world in contexts sepulchral, domestic and equestrian. The earliest available reference to the bell in a specifically Christian milieu is in a letter from Ferrandus, a deacon in Carthage, to Eugippius, abbot of Luccolano near Naples. Writing about 535 Ferrandus recommends the use of a bell, *campana*, and describes bell-ringing as a 'holy custom' among monks (Wölfflin 1900; Williams 1985, 20, 195). Such a custom must have arisen from the need to regulate the monastic day, and bells are likely to have been adopted in Ireland either in the earliest years of the Church or in the context of the 6th-century flowering of monasticism. The *Apgitir Chrábaid*, *Alphabet of Devotion*, an Irish text of c 600, cites attention to the bell, *cloc*, as a requirement of monastic discipline (Hull 1968, 63, §10; Ó Corráin 1994, 13-14; Clancy & Márkus 1995, 201).[3] In daylight no doubt, weather permitting, bells were used in conjunction with sundials.

The balance of probability must be that Columba took with him to Iona equipment essential to the monastic life, or else saw to its manufacture or acquisition on his arrival. Adamnán paints a realistic picture of a bell being rung routinely on Iona to mark the hours (*VC* iii. 23) or to call the monks

---

3 On the basis of the date now accepted for the *Apgitir Chrábaid*, this is the earliest reference to a bell in the Irish documentary sources.

together on Columba's specific instruction (*VC* i. 8; ii. 42; iii. 13). He refers twice to the bell, *cloca*, and twice to the bell or to its sound, *signum*. It is worth observing that early insular quadrangular bells, whether of bronze-coated sheet iron or of cast bronze, were not rung by striking, despite assertions to that effect, and were universally provided with clappers. They have suspension loops internally – in iron bells a continuous bar penetrates the crown to form both loop and handle, and bronze bells typically show internal wear caused by the clapper's action. Indeed the end of a clapper is visible below the lip in the case of bells depicted in carvings at Killadeas, Co. Fermanagh (Fig 1), Kinnitty, Co. Offaly, and Carndonagh, Co. Donegal. That clappers rarely survive need not surprise, given the ease with which they might have been detached and lost. Further evidence, were it needed, could be gleaned from the lives of the saints, in which pre-ordained locations are pointed out by a bell ringing of its own accord. Exceptionally, it is true, a *tongueless* bell is specified, but only to underscore the miraculous nature of the sound (Plummer 1910 I, clxxvii, n 5).

The point is of both general relevance and of specific importance in understanding one usage of Adomnán, for the belief that early bells were rung by striking has misled his translators. Thus Columba is said to have issued to his assistant Diarmait the instruction 'strike the bell', and to have hastened to the church minutes before his death 'when the beaten bell re-sounded at midnight' (Anderson & Anderson 1961, 227, 529; Sharpe 1995, 119). The verb Adomnán uses, *pulso*, has the primary meaning in Classical Latin 'to push, strike, beat', but is also used of musical instruments in the sense 'to play upon' (*LDO* sv). In medieval Latin it is used commonly with reference to bells (*GMIL, MLLM* sv *pulsare*), as is its equivalent, *benaid*, 'beats, strikes', in Old Irish sources (*DIL* sv). Thus, in a typical instance, the phrase *Ro triallsat a cclucca 7 a cceolana do bein*, is translated by Plummer 'They proceeded to *ring* their bells, both large and small ...' (1922 I, 323; II, 314, §36). In Modern Irish the phrase *bain an clog* translates 'ring the bell', and given that the archaeology of the bells is unambiguous, this is precisely the command, *clocam pulsa*, attributed to Columba by Adomnán.

Whatever the reasons underlying the specialized use of Latin *pulso* and Old Irish *benaid* to mean 'ring', this is certainly their sense. It may be significant that both usages are appropriate to the *semantron*, a wooden board or beam sounded by striking and used in early monasteries in the eastern Mediterranean (Williams 1985, 10-17) Two 'ringing rocks', which were similarly sounded, are said to exist on Iona (MacArthur 1995, 13; cf. Purser 1992, 38).

The bell and staff are represented in insular sources as the twin insignia of early ecclesiastics of rank. Associated pairs survive from Inishmurray, Co. Sligo (Bourke 1985), Fahan, Co. Donegal (Ó Floinn 1995a, 113-16) and Glen Dochart, Perthshire (Watson 1926, 265), attributed respectively to Molaisse,

Muru and Fillan. In the case of Columba no 'pair' can be recognised and these cult accessories were separately preserved.[4]

For our purposes the background of the staff, like that of the bell, lies in the Mediterranean world, where Osiris, god of the Egyptians, holds symbolic crook and flail in his role as guarantor of the fertility of flocks and crops in the Nile valley, and where Christ, Moses and Peter can appear in mural and relief staff in hand. The staff, whether straight, crook-headed or otherwise distinguished, is essentially timeless, an extension of the person which is at once both simple and potent.

As we have seen, the bell is represented by Adomnán as communal property, being rung routinely and in emergencies, perhaps on occasion by Columba himself (*VC* ii. 42; iii. 13). The staff, *baculus*, by contrast, which Adomnán attributes to Columba only once (*VC* i. 33), is represented by the context as something personal to him, used spontaneously to strike the ground near the seashore on Skye. Cainnech's staff, accidentally left behind after a visit to Iona, is represented in similar terms (*VC* ii. 14). The staff was something habitually carried, probably as much for support as for any connotation or symbolism, and need not have been adorned with metal mounts. Although it was far from Adomnán's intention to describe the material context of Columba's life, he might have envisaged nothing more elaborate than the straight, finely finished walking stick recovered from a 7th-century context in the ditch of the monastic *vallum* on Iona, of which Barber observed that 'the section which shows that the circuit of the staff is eccentric to the growth rings indicates the deliberate and careful nature of its preparation' (1981a, 343, fig 34. 447/06). Jocelin of Furness said of Kentigern in the 12th century that 'he bore a pastoral staff (*virga*) not rounded and gilded and gemmed, as may be seen now-a-days, but of simple wood, and merely bent' (Forbes 1874, 57, 184).

The distinction between the bell as 'communal' and the staff as 'personal' is a real one which can be read between the lines of Adomnán, although blurred later by iconography, which shows them together, and by hagiography and vernacular tradition, which treat them as twin insignia (Fig 1). Such they certainly became, and the difference of nuance in their primary roles has been eclipsed by a process of assimilation. It could hardly have been otherwise, given that bells are vocal, not quite inanimate, and that churches typically possessed no more than one.

At the extreme of its symbolic range the pastoral staff is a manifestation of the True Cross, whereby the bearer is identified with the eternal priesthood of Christ.[5] Evidence for this is multifarious, and it will suffice to

---

4 But see below pp 176-7. 5 Despite this sacerdotal reference Irish tradition ascribes the crozier to women on occasion: the crozier of St Brónach, *baculus Bromanae*, of Kilbroney,

mention the tradition of the miraculous flowering of the True Cross at the
moment of Christ's death (O'Reilly 1987, 154), as anticipated in the budding
of the rod of the first priest Aaron (Num 17. 8) and recapitulated in the
flowering staffs of numerous medieval saints (Plummer 1910 I, cliv, n 4).
The priesthood of Columba is referred to by Adomnán (*VC* i. 44; iii. 12, 17)
(if only, in the first case cited, to illustrate his humility towards a bishop); the
12th-century Irish life refers to Columba as *uasalshacart innse Goedel*, 'the
noble priest of the island of Ireland' (*ILCC* §10), and in Maghnas Ó Domhnaill's
account of the taking of Glencolumbkille, Co. Donegal, in a life of Columba
compiled in 1532, a holly javelin thrown by a devil is thrown back by the
saint and takes root where it strikes the ground (*BCC* §132). The land was
'yielded to him' to the length of the cast, as Tory was claimed by the cast of
his staff, *trostán*, metamorphosed in the throwing into a spear or dart: *dorindedh
ga no fogha ar siubal anairde do ...* (*BCC* §111). It is noted, in passing, that a
7th-century praise poem refers to Columba metaphorically as a cast or throw:
ba hé roüt ... (Clancy & Márkus 1995, 138-9).

No bell attributed to Columba has survived outside Ireland, and of those
extant none has a claim which is other than traditional, however favourably
such claims are viewed. The traditions embrace bells attributed to the saint
and those he was believed to have bestowed on others. All are associated with
sites otherwise linked with his name: Glencolumbkille, Termonmaguirk, Gartan,
Drumcolumb and Tory (Map 3).

The *Dub Duaibsech*, 'black gloomy [bell]', is mentioned by Ó Domhnaill
in the context of the saint's expulsion of devils from Glencolumbkille, the
same devils, we are told, which Patrick had earlier expelled from Cruachán
Aigle (Croagh Patrick) (*BCC* §132). As Patrick threw the *Bernán Brigte* (the
Bernán Padruic in *BCC* §120), so Columba flings the *Dub Duaibsech* to compass the devils' undoing. The name is typical of the battery of pet names
attached to the insignia of the saints; the adjective *dub*, 'black', might suggest
a bell of iron from which much of the bronze had been lost. It appears that
the *Dub Duaibsech* was extant in Glencolumbkille when Ó Domhnaill wrote
and used for cursing in the manner of both the *clocha breacha* on Inishmurray
and of seemingly analogous stones which once existed on Iona (RCAHMS
1982, 250, 280). The bell no longer survives; in the 1830s John O'Donovan

Co. Down, was extant in the 15th century (Reeves 1847, 115-16, n q, 309) (a bronze bell
with the same attribution survives); the crozier of St Scíre, *bachall Scíre*, of Kilskeer, Co.
Meath, was one of the sureties in a property transaction recorded in an 11th-century
charter in the Book of Kells (O'Donovan 1846, 134-5; Mac Niocaill 1961, 18). It is
possible, however, that such pieces came into being as the regalia of these patrons' *male*
successors (but cf. note 16 below).

Figure 2   Iron bell, Termonmaguirk, Co Tyrone (after Wilson 1863).

was told the unlikely story that its clapper had been converted into nails (*OSLD* 216).

Another bell, termed the *Dub Díglach*, 'black vengeful [bell]', is mentioned in the 13th-century Book of Fenagh as the gift of Caillín of Fenagh to Adomnán and is linked with north Connacht where Skreen (Scrín Adomnáin, 'Adomnán's shrine'), Co. Sligo, preserves his name (Hennessy & Kelly 1875, 412-13). A late medieval poem ascribed to Columba's authorship has the saint refer to his 'dear, gloomy, vengeful black [bell]', *mo Dub-díglach duaibsech dil* (Bodleian Laud MS 615, 28-9; Reeves 1857, 330), but perhaps referring with poetic licence to a bell of composite identity rather than to any specific example. In the Book of Fenagh the bell is called alternatively *Clogán Adomnáin*, 'Adomnán's little bell', so it appears that *this* bell, if indeed it ever existed, was attributed by tradition to the ninth abbot of Iona and not the first.

The *Dub Duaibsech* is apparently unconnected with an iron bell (Fig 2)[6] called variously in 19th-century accounts the 'Dia Dheultagh' (McCloskey 1821, 117), 'Dia Deeltagh' (*OSLL* 178), 'Diadeltah' (Bell n.d., 64v) and 'Dia Dioghaltus' (Wilson 1863, 463), a name which has been interpreted as *Dé Diongbhálta*, 'steadfast God' (Ó Ceallaigh 1951, 57), and *Dia Díoltais*, 'God of vengeance' (Ó Floinn 1995a, 112), although a form such as *Dia Díoltach*, 'vengeful god', perhaps agrees better with the 19th-century witnesses.[7] The bell was associated by tradition with Columba and was acquired by John Bell at Termonmaguirk, Co. Tyrone, in the 19th century from its hereditary keepers the McGuirks, erenaghs (*airchennaigh*) of that parish.[8] Oral tradition

6 Royal Museum of Scotland KB 2, now on loan to the Ulster Museum, Belfast. 7 cf. *DIL* sv 2 *día*, 'god, goddess, supernatural being, object of worship'; *dígaltach*, 'vengeful, vindictive'. 8 In 1837 the bell was kept at Sluggan, near Carrickmore in the parish of Termonmaguirk (Lewis 1837 II, 620), but had been acquired by John Bell by 1852, in

collected by the Ordnance Survey in the 1830s suggests that the bell was
alternately or successively held by the McGillians of Ballynascreen and the
McGuirks of Termon (*OSLL* 178; *OSM* 9, 27), and John Bell (n.d., 76v)
cites evidence of intermarriage between the two families. Ballynascreen opinion maintained as early as 1821 that the bell of that place had been 'removed
to Tyrone' (McCloskey 1821, 117); in the 1830s it was said to be 'yet at
Termon McGuirk' (*OSLL* 179).[9] By tradition both churches belonged to a
group of nine established by Columba in the Sperrins, and Ballynascreen
(Baile na Scríne, formerly Scrín Coluim Cille), as its name attests, was the
repository of Columban relics, whether in a fixed or a portable shrine. The
common affiliation of Termon and Ballynascreen would support the view
that but one bell is in question.[10] The Termonmaguirk bell, like so many
made of iron, is poorly preserved, lacking its handle, suspension loop (and
clapper) and part of one face and one side.

Another extant bell (Fig 3)[11] is that obtained by a collector from its
(unnamed) hereditary keeper at Gartan, Co. Donegal, in 1847, with an attribution to Columba but without supporting data. Gartan is significant as the
traditional birthplace of the saint; as the 12th-century Irish life has it: *Gortán
didiu ainm in luicc in ro genir* (*ILCC* §20). Maghnas Ó Domhnaill describes
the traditions of Columba's youth in that area, including his baptism by
Cruithnechán at Templedouglas (Tulach Dubhghlaise) (*BCC* §54). He says
nothing of the Gartan bell, unless the term *cloch ruad*, 'red stone', masks an
original *clog ruad*, 'red bell', in his sources; the former, we are told, was
preserved at Gartan, having been brought forth by Columba's mother at his
birth (*BCC* §52). A poem (Bodleian Laud MS 615, p 95), meanwhile, identifies as the 'red stone' the stone with which the saint exorcized
Glencolumbkille, although that function is performed by his bell and a 'round
green stone', *cloch cruind glass*, in *BCC* §132 (Reeves 1857, 330). Ó Náan
(Nawn), the coarb and erenagh of Gartan, was said in 1609 to have
'Collumkillie's read stone' (Ó Floinn 1995a, 109), which would suggest (un-

which year it was exhibited in Belfast (BAAS 1852 [Appendix], 11). John Bell died in
1861. 9 This information is in conflict with a further statement in the OS memoir that the
Ballynascreen bell 'is now [1836] in the possession of a man in the parish of Lisdress,
county Tyrone' (*OSM* 9). No parish or townland of that name is recorded in Co. Tyrone
(or in any other county) (*TI*), although there is a townland of Listress near Claudy, Co.
Derry. The picture is further complicated by John Bell's statement that the bell of
Ballynascreen 'was brought to ... Donomony [Dunamony] wood near Dungannon by a
woman of the name of Gillion [.] [S]he married a man of the name of Mallen' (Bell n.d.,
87v). Since the same collector also acquired a bell from the O'*Mellans* at Donaghmore,
near Dungannon, it appears that the records of various bells and keepers have been con-
founded. 10 'There was confusion of later origin between the bell of Tearmonn and that
of Baile na Scríne, two parishes away. Both bells had the same name. Or perhaps they were
one and the same ...' (Ó Ceallaigh 1951, 57, n 14). 11 National Museum of Ireland
1883:122 (Wk 202).

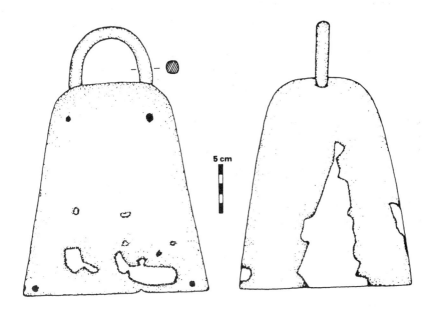

Figure 3　Bronze bell, Gartan, Co Donegal.

less one invokes further misunderstanding) that the stone did indeed have independent existence. Be that as it may, one cannot doubt the relevance of the Gartan bell to the cult of Columba, at least in recent centuries. By the same token, the place-name Tullanascreen (Tulach na Scríne), between Templedouglas and Gartan, seems not to figure in our sources, although an association with some Columban shrine is surely plausible.[12]

The Gartan bell is an imperfect bronze casting and therefore of some technical interest. Parts of its surfaces are discrete round-edged pieces riveted individually to plates of sheet iron which line the bell internally. It is clear that some mishap befell the manufacturing process: that insufficient bronze was poured into the mould, that the mould began to disintegrate or that the cavity within was partially blocked. It says much for the value of the bell that it was reinforced internally rather than broken up, melted down and reconstituted. Perhaps a taboo attended its making so that the casting process was in the nature of a rite which it was inappropriate to perform more than once.

Ó Domhnaill records that Columba appointed Finbar to head his foundation at Druim Coluimcille (Drumcolumb), Co. Sligo, leaving there the *Glassán*, described as *a chloc fen*, 'his own bell', and erecting a cross, prophesying that

12 The place-name is interpreted as Talamh na Scríne, 'land of the shrine', in the *OSNB* (sn *Tullanascreen*).

'so long as that cross and the *Glassán* were there, there should be happiness in that church' (*BCC* §154). This is perhaps evidence enough that the *Glassán*, the 'little green [bell]' was extant at Druim in Ó Domhnaill's day. There is no record of its subsequent fate.

Tradition asserts, too, the former existence of a bell ascribed to Columba on Tory Island, an important Columban monastery and repository of the 'great cross', *Cross Mór Coluim Cille*, in the later middle ages. According to O'Donovan (although he did not visit the island) the bell was no more than a memory in the 1830s (*OSLD* 90); a more recent author asserts that it was kept on St John's altar near the round tower until somehow lost, but he refutes the rumour that the bell was ultimately sold to a tinker (Ó Colm 1971, 82)

Connected to Columba, but at one remove, are three bells referred to by Ó Domhnaill (*BCC* §321). The three are said to have been made by Senach of Lower Lough Erne from a mass of iron with which he had earlier choked a sea monster threatening the saint. The bells are styled the *Glunán Senaigh*, 'Senach's little knee', the *Gerr an Curuigh*, 'the little short [bell] of the currach', and the bell of Náile. The first was presumably associated with the smith's own church at Derrybrusk, Co. Fermanagh, and the third can be identified with that of which the handle survived in the care of its hereditary keeper near Kinawley (Cill Náile) in the same county until the early 19th century (*OSLF* 83). According to Ó Domhnaill, when the three bells were manufactured 'God's name and Columcille's and the name of Senach the old smith were magnified thereby'.

There are no grounds for identifying any of the bells we have just passed under review with *Clog na Rígh*, the 'bell of the kings', which is mentioned in 1090 *ATig*: 'Colomb cille's reliquaries (*minda*), to wit, the Bell of the Kings, and the Flabellum, and the two Gospels, were brought out of Tyrconnell, together with seven score ounces of silver. And Óengus Húa Domnalláin was he that brought them from the North.' It is probable that their destination was Kells (where Óengus Ua Domnalláin was an official), that one of the 'gospels' was the *Cathach* and that the dispatch of that manuscript to Kells was the occasion of its enshrinement, for the shrine of the *Cathach* bears the name of Domnall Ua Robartaigh, abbot of Kells from 1062 to 1094/98 (Henry 1970, 89; Ó Floinn 1995a, 120, 144, n 177).[13] While the subsequent

---

13 It should, however, be stressed in this context that the entry at 1090 *ATig* does not mention the *Cathach* by name, does not disclose the function of the accompanying silver, does not say that the *minda* were dispatched for the purposes of enshrinement and does not say that their dispatch was temporary. Henry (1970, 89, n 6) cites an entry at 1089 (*recte* 1090) *AU* naming Kells as the destination of the material, but those annals contain no such entry. She and others, following Reeves, mention '120' ounces of silver, but the entry in *ATig* (as published) refers to *vii. fichit uinge*, 'seven score ounces' (= 140) (cf. Ó Floinn this vol).

Figure 4   Seal of Dunkeld Cathedral, Perthshire.

history of the 'bell of the kings' has not been established, there is no reason to follow Henry (1970, 90-91, 93-4) in identifying it with the bell of St Muru of Fahan, although the latter certainly belongs to this period and its mounts and the shrine of the *Cathach* are made in the same style. The only other 'bell of the kings' known to Irish tradition is that formerly preserved at Foxfield, Co. Leitrim, and associated with St Caillín of Fenagh (Hynes 1931, 51-3).[14] But this bell, as I hope to show elsewhere, is adapted from the bowl of a 12th-century chalice or drinking cup and cannot be the 'bell of the kings' which is linked with Columba's name.[15]

No staff attributed to Columba has survived outside Ireland, but a crozier termed the *Cathbhuaidh*, 'battle victory', which appears to have been kept at Dunkeld, Perthshire, was so attributed (Reeves 1857, 332-4).[16] It was taken

14 The bell is now in the Ardagh and Clonmacnoise Diocesan Museum in Longford. A second bell from Fenagh is the four-sided iron bell know as *Clog na Fola*, the 'bell of the blood', in the Primate Robinson Library in Armagh. 15 Bannerman notes (1993, 45) that the *Clog na Rígh* mentioned in 1090 'ought to have accompanied the transfer of *comarbus Coluim Chille* from Kells to Derry in 1150' but 'was presumably lost in the interval'. Some transference of its associations to the bell of Caillín may have been facilitated by its loss. 16 As Ó Floinn points out (1995a, 124), the term *cathbuadach* is used of a musical pipe associated with St Brigid and described as her 'episcopal staff', *a bachall epscoip* (Thurneysen

into battle by the army of Fortriu in a contest with Vikings in 918 *FAI*, the same talismanic use accorded to such Columban insignia as the *Breccbennach* in Scotland and the *Cathach* in Ireland. As Henderson has argued (1987, 190), the *Cathbhuaidh* must be the crozier shown on a 13th-century seal of the chapter of Dunkeld Cathedral, atop, or standing behind, an elaborate architectural shrine (Fig 4). Only the crook and upper shaft are represented, their surfaces covered in a pattern of lozenges. The image is schematic to the extent that the roof of the shrine is similarly treated, but fields of lozenges are in fact characteristic of the crooks of insular croziers, including that of St Fillan from Glen Dochart, Perthshire. Assuming its detail to be reliable, the seal shows a crook with an even curvature and a continuous decorative scheme; by contrast the crozier of St Fillan (both primary crook and secondary casing), as is the universal norm, has an extremity differentiated by both its angle and its ornament. I have argued elsewhere (Bourke 1993, 18) that the extremity or 'drop', thus differentiated, was developed in 8th-century Armagh to enshrine a fragment of a staff attributed to Christ, that the crozier thus modified, the *Bachall Ísu*, was absorbed by the cult of Patrick, and that all extant insular croziers are based on this prototype. The *Cathbhuaidh*, if it was in reality as it appears on the seal, might predate these developments, might have existed before the removal of the relics of Columba, apparently to Dunkeld, in 849 (Anderson 1973, 250; 1982, 117) and might therefore have been made on Iona.[17] On the other hand, there is evidence (see below) that the *Cathbhuaidh* is represented on the seal in 12th-century guise.

Whether the crozier was more than a prestige emblem of office for the coarbs of Columba and was in fact a reliquary of the founder's staff is a moot point. Archaeology can not yet show that any extant crozier is the enshrined staff of an early saint; in some cases it can demonstrate a contrary likelihood: a crozier from Lemanaghan, Co. Offaly, has a finely finished wooden core with a worked dowel at one end which is tailored to receive its metal furniture, and the core of a crozier from Prosperous, Co. Kildare, tapers to a fine point which never saw service independently of the ferrule enclosing it.

According to Henderson (1987, 190), a chain attached to the end of the

1933, 120). The term *cathbuaid* is used in its literal sense in an interpolation in the 12th-century life of Columba (*ILCC* §5). 17 The *Cathbhuaidh* is thus plausibly to be identified as one of the Columban *reliquiae* housed by Cináed mac Alpín in a church which he built (?for that purpose) in 849. But there is no evidence to associate any of the extant Irish bells or the sole surviving Irish Columban crozier (see below) with a visit to Ireland by the abbot of Iona 'with the halidoms (*mindaibh*) of Colum Cille' in the same year (*AU*) or with similar journeys to and from Scotland undertaken by his predecessor in 829 and 831 *AU* respectively. Neither is there any demonstrable connection with the removal to Ireland of the shrine, *scrín*, of Columba and 'his other halidoms', *a minna olchena*, to escape the attentions of the Vikings in 878 *AU*. The material in Ireland is presumably of Irish origin.

Figure 5 Crozier drop, Loch Shiel, Inverness-shire.

crook on the Dunkeld seal 'secures the head of the crozier to a small cross on the roof-ridge of the reliquary'. It might be, however, that the cross *hangs* by the chain, and that this unusual conjunction of cross and crook was a reality in 13th-century Dunkeld. Ó Floinn has recently reviewed the evidence for the attribution of a crozier and chain to both Muru of Fahan, Co. Donegal, and to Lommán of Portloman (Port Lommáin), Co. Westmeath (1995a, 113-16). Only the former are extant; the crook displays no obvious point of attachment and the 'chain' has been shown to be a piece of late medieval mail. While one acknowledges Ó Floinn's proviso that the attribution of the two objects might have been transferred from one saint to the other, these records and the Dunkeld seal could attest a detail of some early croziers which has hitherto not been recognised. A 12th-century crozier drop found in 1993 near the shore of Loch Shiel, Inverness-shire, has a small loop on the base or distal surface which corresponds to that from which the chain on the seal is shown to hang (Fig 5).[18] It must have served some purpose. Conceivably it anticipates the occasional late medieval practice of hanging a napkin

18 The drop, brought to my attention by David Caldwell, is closed to the front by a sliding plate and was clearly designed to hold relics. On Eilean Fhionain in Loch Shiel, adjacent to the find-spot, is preserved a 10th-century bronze bell attributed to St Finan (Fínán Lobur) which is among the finest in Scotland. The drop probably relates to the same site.

Figure 6 Bell-shrine, Kilmichael-Glassary, Argyll (after Wilson 1863).

from the crook (apparently to save the crozier from direct contact with the
hand) (de Fleury 1889, 107), but it is more likely that, as on the seal, a light
chain and cross were appended. Granted that this is plausible, the *origin* of
the usage is uncertain: the *Cathbhuaidh* of Columba might have set an early
precedent or itself been subject to 12th-century modification.

The accuracy of the image on the Dunkeld seal is further borne out by
the evidence of the bell-shrine found at (or near) Kilmichael Glassary, Argyll,
c 1814 (Anderson 1881, 206) (Fig 6).[19] The shrine is provided with suspension points at the sides and with a pierced *dextra Dei* on the front, and an
associated chain is attached to the terminal loop on one arm of an equal-
armed cross. The cross has similar loops on two other arms. The three loops
together may correspond to the points of attachment on the shrine, and three
lengths of chain may have linked them. The shrine (which contains a diminutive iron bell) is, like the Loch Shiel drop, of 12th-century date and the
Cathbhuaidh was probably contemporary, at least in its final form. So distinctive is the conjunction of chain(s) and equal-armed cross that the bell-shrine

19 The relevance of the bell-shrine to this discussion was brought to my attention by
David Caldwell. There are conflicting accounts of its discovery at Torbhlaran ('Torrebhlaurn')
and at Kilmichael Glassary itself (Campbell & Sandeman 1962, 82). The latter seems to
have the stronger claim.

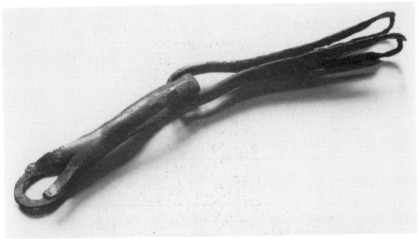

Figure 7 Bronze chain links, Drumcliff, Co Sligo.

and the *Cathbhuaidh* might well have been specifically connected. Is it beyond the bounds of possibility that they were made *en suite* for 12th-century
Dunkeld, that the shrine was rescued from destruction there in 1560 (see
below) and taken for safe-keeping to the west, and that the bell housed inside
it was revered as a relic of Columba?

A further crozier associated with Columba is mentioned in the 12th-
century life of St Kentigern by Jocelin of Furness. According to Jocelin a
staff, *baculus* (seemingly distinct from that 'of simple wood' he has earlier
described), was preserved at Ripon, Yorkshire, which Kentigern received
from Columba in exchange for his own (Forbes 1874, 109, 232). In the nature
of things the transaction cannot be historical, but it may be, as Henderson
suggests (1987, 190, 194), that the staff (or a relic thereof) was presented to
the church of St Wilfrid by Abbot Sléibíne of Iona when he visited Ripon in
the middle of the 8th century. In the 1440s the crozier, *cambo*, was said by
Walter Bower to be extant in Ripon, encrusted with gold and pearls (Watt
1989, 80-81).[20] Another relic of Kentigern is attested after the manner of the
Cathbhuaidh, for his bell (now lost) appears on the 14th-century corporation
and chapter seals of Glasgow (Renwick & Lindsay 1921, 25, pls opp pp 116,
148, 384). The fate of neither the *Cathbhuaidh* nor the crozier of Kentigern
has been recorded; the former was probably destroyed in the sacking of
Dunkeld Cathedral during the Reformation in 1560, the latter in the sacking
of Ripon Cathedral during the Civil War in 1643.

The 12th-century Irish life of Columba claims that the saint gave to Mo
Thoria, whom he installed in Drumcliff, a staff made by his own hand:

20 This reference has sometimes been attributed to John of Fordun (1320-85) but is
original to Bower's *Scotichronicon* (Watt 1989, 227).

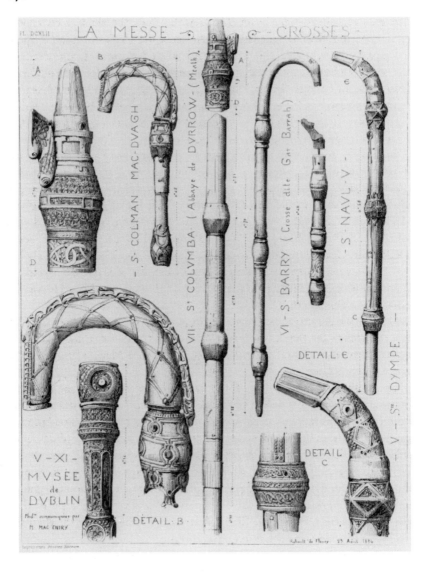

Figure 8 Irish croziers: that from Durrow, Co Offaly,
at centre and top left (after de Fleury 1889).

fácbais occa bachaill do-rígne fessin (*ILCC* §48). While the claim is retrospective, and the foundation of Drumcliff must post-date Columba's time, there is no reason to doubt that the staff existed when the life was composed. A round tower and free-standing cross at Drumcliff attest its former command of resources; no trace of the staff has survived, but part of a bronze loop-in-loop chain 'found at Druncliffe (sic), Co. Sligo', is presumably from within the confines of the site (Bruce 1880, no 494) (Fig 7). Such chains are distinctive and are known in association with shrines.

One crozier alone with an ascription to Columba has come down to us, that associated with Durrow, Co. Offaly, founded by the saint in the 580s and his principal Irish church (Figs 8-10).[21] The *Mór-bachall*, 'great staff', is mentioned in some texts of the 12th-century Irish life as having been given by Columba to Scandlán of Ossory on his release from captivity at the convention of Druim Cet (*ILCC* §9). Ó Domhnaill records, more circumstantially, that Scandlán was instructed to 'show', *taisben*, the staff to Laisrén, abbot of Durrow, when he returned to his own kingdom (*BCC* §§348-9). Colgan repeated this information in the 17th century, from which Reeves justifiably concluded 'that this reliquary was preserved in Durrow' (1857, 324). It is beyond reasonable doubt that this is the same crozier acquired in the 19th century by the Royal Irish Academy after it had passed to a Mr Nugent from Sir Richard Nagle, a descendant of the MacGeoghegans who had been its hereditary keepers.

Though the crook is lost (but for a fragment) together with the foot, the Durrow crozier is of very heavy proportions and could aptly be described by the epithet *Mór-bachall*. Its construction is otherwise typical: a wooden core is cased in rolled tubes of sheet bronze (or brass) and subdivided by three cast knops, perhaps originally by four. The longitudinal seams in the tubing were closed originally by sealing strips, all of them now lost. That the core is broken raises the possibility that parts of *two* croziers are in question, but as the two sections are of equal and above average thickness (c 3.5-4 cm) they will be interpreted here as one. They were so interpreted in 1826 when the crozier was first described (Brewer 1826, 256).

The lowermost[22] knop (Fig 9a) is biconical and decorated with interlaced animals which process in opposite directions above and below. The interlace is badly abraded but retains locally a covering of silver, keyed in median grooves, and the background is hatched to receive an inlay, apparently of niello, of which minute traces survive. Thus an original scheme of zoomorphic silver ribbons set in a lustrous black surface can be reconstructed in the mind's eye. The central knop (Fig 9b) is likewise biconical but distinguished

---

21 National Museum of Ireland W 8. 22 The shaft is described in terms of its conventional orientation.

b   a

Figure 9   Durrow crozier: (a) lower knop; (b) central knop.

by the remains of a beading of silver in a circumferential groove. The surfaces of the knop bear apparent traces of incised decoration. The uppermost
knop (Fig 10), mounted on the detached extremity of the core, is formally
similar to the others but decorated with rows of interlaced knots, three above
and two below a recessed interlaced band. Its surfaces bear traces of gilding.

A cylindrical sleeve below the upper knop has four figure-of-eight animals in false openwork whose heads (of which two remain) project in low
relief from the lower margin. Above the knop the end of the crook, which is
all that survives, is composed of openwork frames. The sleeve compares both
in form and in the nature of its ornament with the central mount on the
shrine of St Lachtaín's arm, associated with Donaghmore, Co. Cork (Ryan
1983, no 80) (Fig 11), and the lowermost knop is allied in style. An animal
head from which the crest of the crook originally sprang compares equally
closely with that in the same position on an unprovenanced crook, probably
from the south of Ireland (Raftery 1941, pl 86). This crook and the crook of
the Lismore, Co. Waterford, crozier (which has a comparable animal head in
the same position) (Ryan 1983, no 81) are designed to receive ornamental
panels in recessed, though not openwork, right-angled frames. The crook of
the Durrow crozier, when complete, was probably similar. The shrine of St
Lachtaín's arm and the Lismore crozier are dated by their inscriptions to the
early 12th century and these four components of the Durrow crozier – the

Figure 10 Durrow crozier: upper knop.

Figure 11 The shrine of St Lachtaín's arm: central mount.

crook, the terminal of the crest, the sleeve and the lower knop – must be contemporary.

The upper knop is set apart from these four components by its gilding and non-zoomorphic interlace and might have been fitted before them. The central knop could pertain to either of these potential phases or independently to a third. However, this is not to preclude the possibility that the crozier is a confection of parts either reused or sourced separately in a *single* phase, and that all the cast components are in this sense contemporary. It is an economical proposal and our preferred hypothesis that the primary phase of the Durrow crozier is manifest in its 12th-century parts.

At least four substantial sections of rolled sheet tubing on the lower shaft appear to be primary and are likely to be contemporary with some or all of the castings. There are besides at least five secondary pieces of tubing of copper or copper alloy, to some of which fragments of sheet silver are secured, and the torn edge of a more substantial silver covering projects from under the upper edge of the central knop (Fig 9b). Clearly the crozier has been subjected over the centuries to several interventions, some of them destructive, others aimed at repair or embellishment and performed with varying levels of skill. The high degree of ware sustained by two of the knops can be attributed to the crozier's role as relic: as such, no doubt, it was rubbed and touched repeatedly by the faithful.

The shorter, upper section of the wooden core is largely enclosed by the fragment of the crook, by the upper knop and sleeve and by a piece of rolled tubing inside them (Fig 10). The projecting extremity of the core is smoothly tapered and seemingly complete, and of sufficient length only to have anchored the crook. Indeed that the crook was cast in one piece, rather than in two C-sectioned halves, urges the conclusion that a wooden crook never existed, for no wooden crook could have been manoeuvred into a crook of the same shape made of metal. The lower end of the core is truncated but was presumably enclosed originally by a tapered ferrule, perhaps integral with or adjoining an additional knop. The date of the core is unknown; on the interpretation favoured here it is a structural component of a piece of 12th-century Columban regalia and not a relic of the 6th-century saint, although some such relic (a small one) might once have been housed in the drop.

The loss of the sealing strips from the shaft of the Durrow crozier is to be regretted, because an inscription on one or more might have disclosed the identity of the craftsman and of the patron or patrons by whom he was employed. We lack this information, but the production of the crozier can plausibly be associated with the ecclesiastical reforms of the early 12th century, in which dioceses were drawn up and the claims of churches to episcopal status were bolstered and broadcast. Fine metalwork, like architecture, could further ambition. Durrow was not to become the centre of a diocese but its leadership might well have wished otherwise.

The messenger of the gods in classical Greece, Hermes, has as attribute a herald's staff, a sceptre, a whip for driving cattle or a golden wand with magical powers to put to sleep or to awaken the sleeping. He is a go-between, mediator or intermediary between heaven and earth and his role has been argued, on linguistic grounds (Watkins 1970, 348), to anticipate that of Columba as 'messenger of the Lord', *Fiadat foidiam*, in the *Amra Coluim Cille*, the earliest eulogy of the saint that we possess (Clancy & Márkus 1995, 104-5, i. 12). In medieval tradition Columba was larger than life (cf. *VC* i.1; Smyth 1984, 84) and his cult was a focus of investment. The Durrow crozier, though battered and incomplete, is both witness to and symbol of his role.

ACKNOWLEDGEMENTS

I am grateful to the many people who have facilitated my access to original material over the years even if I cannot acknowledge them individually here. But in specific relation to this chapter I must thank David Caldwell for his comments on the Kilmichael Glassary shrine, Máire Herbert for generously sending me her transcript of the poem mentioning the *Dub Díglach* in Bodleian MS Laud 615, Michael Kauffmann for supplying photographs of the relevant pages, Bill Foster for advice on the history of Ripon, Sally Foster for help with sources and Adam Bowie and Georgina McGregor for their guidance in Glen Lyon in 1982 and 1996 respectively.

A Note on the Delg Aidechta

Cormac Bourke

The *Delg Aidechta* is the subject of a single reference in the story of the death of Brandub mac Echach, king of Leinster (obit 605 *AU*; 608 *AI*), a text dated linguistically to the 11th or 12th century and preserved in the early 15th-century Book of Lecan (Mulchrone 1937, 193rb. 8ff). It is recorded there that Columba joined Máedóc[1] in a struggle with devils for Brandub's soul, rising from his writing-desk and sticking his stylus, *graib*, in his cloak. As the combatants passed over Rome the stylus fell to the ground and was picked up by Pope Gregory the Great. Thereafter Columba spent some time with Gregory 'and brought away Gregory's brooch with him, and it is the hereditary brooch [*Delg Aidechta*] of the coarb of Columkille to this day. And he left his style [stylus] with Gregory' (Reeves 1857, 205, n a, 323, n d).[2]

This is an example of a widespread formula of hagiography whereby objects of significance are obtained either in Rome, miraculously, by exchange between saints or by a combination of these mechanisms. A 10th- or 11th-century Irish preface to *Altus Prosator* records the belief that this Latin hymn was sent to Gregory by Columba in exchange for a book of hymns and the cross known as the *Mór-gemm*, 'great gem' (otherwise *Cross Mór Coluim Cille*), which was formerly kept in the Columban monastery on Tory Island (Reeves 1857, 318-19; Kenney 1929, 263-5; Bernard & Atkinson 1898 I, 62-3; II, 140-41).[3] The life of Kentigern by Jocelin of Furness, to cite one

---

1 Either Máedóc of Ferns, Co. Wexford (and Drumlane, Co. Cavan), or Máedóc of Clonmore, Co. Carlow, might be in question (Doherty 1987). 2 As Reeves pointed out (1857, 359, n k), parallel incidents occur in the lives of Cainnech of Aghaboe and of Ruadán of Lorrha. In the Latin life of Cainnech a *graffium*, 'stylus', which had fallen from Columba's cloak when he joined that saint in an aerial battle, is returned to him through the agency of Baíthíne (Plummer 1910 I, 160, §22; Heist 1965 188-9, §27). Latin and Irish texts of the life of Ruadán describe a writing-tablet or -tablets, *pugillaris/manuail* (cf. O'Neill this vol), in a similar context (Plummer 1910 II, 251-2, §29; 1922 I, 328, §§56-8; Heist 1965, 167, §§23-4). 3 The Lecan text mentions Columba's composition of *Altus Prosator* (Mulchrone 1937, 193va.1ff) as a sequel to his acquisition of the *Delg Aidechta*, but does not refer to the *Cross Mór* of Tory Island. The name of a small bay on the island, Port an Deilg, is explained by a story about Balor of the Evil Eye (Ó Colm 1971, 44) and has no apparent connection with the subject of this essay. The name Cell Deilge/Cill Dealga (Kildalkey), Co. Meath, not far from Kells, has been translated 'church of the thorn' (Flanagan & Flanagan 1994, 224).

further instance, has that saint and Columba exchanging staffs to seal their friendship (Forbes 1874, 109, 232). In the present case there is no reason to doubt the existence of the *Delg Aidechta* or that the story was devised to explain a reality. Its name, as Reeves pointed out, allows comparison with the *Clog ind Aidechta*, the 'bell of the testament', which, by implication, was believed to have been willed by Patrick to his successors (cf. Carney 1961, 121, n 1; Bannerman 1993, 14-15). Valuables owned by the Church are likely to have been subject to formal mechanisms of bequest, and there is evidence not only in the two names mentioned but in the death-bed bequest of his staff by Columbanus to Gallus in 615 (Krusch 1902, 304-5, §26; Joynt 1927, 101) and, implicitly, in the removal to Tallaght by Máel Ruain of the bell of his late uncle Fer Dá Chrích (Stokes 1905, 186-7). An Irish text on John the Baptist, perhaps of the 11th century (Kenney 1929, 739), refers to a bequest of the shrine of the saint's head to a *comarba udachta*, 'testamentary successor' (*DIL* sv *aidacht*; Müller-Lisowski 1923, 152; Herbert & McNamara 1989, 59). Early continental precedent is to be found in the will of St Rémi, who left a silver-mounted staff to his nephew in the middle of the 6th century (*DACL* 2235; Jones et al 1957). The *Delg Aidechta* was, therefore, a monastic heirloom when it was incorporated as a motif in the Brandub story, although not necessarily of great age: the Book of Armagh, written in 807, was enshrined in 937 *AFM* II in confirmation of its role as Patrician relic and *vexillum* of the Armagh abbacy. The nature of the *Delg Aidechta* is the subject of the following speculation.

It is, seemingly, essential to the story of its acquisition that the *Delg Aidechta* and the stylus were approximate equivalents and interchangeable in reciprocal gift-giving. Any stylus might serve *ad hoc* as a dress-fastener, and Anglo-Saxon styli of some refinement are known from Whitby, North Yorkshire, and Flixborough, South Humberside, one from the former site made of silver, one from the latter made of bronze but with die-stamped silver foil applied to the head (Webster & Backhouse 1991, nos 107 c, 69 v). The Irish material includes an accomplished bronze specimen (unprovenanced) (Erichsen & Brockhoff 1989, no 139) and a distinct series with loose rings below drawn-out, flattened heads (Wilde 1861, 561, fig 458; Armstrong 1922, 75, pl xi, fig 1. 3, 5, 7). These probably date to the 7th-10th centuries and are best regarded, as Read may have been the first explicitly to suggest (quoted in Armstrong 1922, 75, n 3), as dual-purpose stylus-pins.[4] Unique among them is one, apparently from Dublin, with the remains of a die-stamped, interlace-decorated silver panel on the head, and with a ring modelled on the hoop of a brooch (as in the so-called 'ring brooch' or 'brooch-pin' class)

---

4 That stylus-pins of this form are known from the crannógs of Lough Ravel, Co. Antrim (Fig 1a), and Lagore, Co. Meath (Armstrong 1922, pl xii, fig 1.7), might be evidence for literacy in secular sites of high status.

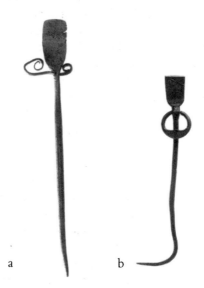

a   b

Figure 1   Stylus-pins: (a) Lough Ravel, Derryhollagh,
Co Antrim (length 14.7 cm); (b) Dublin (original length 16.5 cm).

(Armstrong 1909) (Fig 1b). The form of their heads rendered all such styli
and stylus-pins suitable equally for writing and for making erasures on wax,
and one of these instruments might be the *stilus* attributed to Columba by
Adomnán when he refers (loosely) to books ... *stilo ipsius descriptis* (*VC* ii. 44)
(Lambert 1991, 159, n 6). The use of wax tablets is also mentioned by
Adomnán (*VC* i. 35; *DLS* i. 2), and a set of six tablets of 7th-century date,
from Ballyhutherland, Co. Antrim, has survived (Webster & Backhouse 1991,
no 64).[5] That Columba was thought to have used a bronze stylus-pin might
be consistent with the terms of the story of the *Delg Aidechta*, but these
objects are relatively simple and hardly worthy to be exchanged, even in
literary *topos*, for an object of evident value with the bishop of Rome.

Columba's stylus, although not described in the text, is more likely to be
conjured up by a further allusion in the story of the birth of Brandub mac
Echach and Áedán mac Gabráin (Meyer 1899). This story, probably of the
10th or 11th century and therefore somewhat earlier than the first, is preserved in the 12th-century manuscript Rawlinson B.502.[6] In this case we
read of Áedán's maternity being proven by a grain of gold, *gráinne óir*, taken

5 Inscribed slates have been found at Nendrum, Co. Down, together with iron styli
appropriate to the medium. Several bear decorative motifs; one has outline sketches of
brooches; another (now lost) had lettering (Lawlor 1925; O'Meadhra 1979). 6 This manuscript also has a version of the same story in verse (Best 1927, 381-2).

from the head of his mother's 'writing-style', *delg graiph*, and placed under his skin in his infancy.[7] This grain of gold suggests the presence of granulation on the head of the instrument, a form of applied decoration used typically in association with gold and silver filigree and widely attested (though in a limited range of contexts) in late 7th- to 10th-century insular metalwork. No Irish stylus (or stylus-pin) with such a decorated head is known to exist, although the example from Dublin approaches this level of sophistication. The details call to mind the Alfred Jewel and a related series of elaborate terminals of indeterminate function from Anglo-Saxon England. These have been identified as, *inter alia*, the heads of *aestel*s, interpreted as manuscript pointers or bookmarks, which were circulated with copies of the *Pastoral Care* of Gregory the Great to the bishoprics of England in the 890s. The terminals are distinguished by elaborate gold granulation and in their potential functions they pertain, like the stylus, to writing and the written word.[8]

The story of the *birth* of Brandub is sufficient to attest the existence in Ireland at the time of its composition of elaborate styli with heads bearing gold (or silver) granulation. The story of the *death* of Brandub attributes to Columba a stylus or stylus-pin plausibly of similar refinement. In the *Tripartite Life* Patrick's *graif* falls from his cloak as he destroys the idols of Mag Slecht: *Dorochair dano agraif abrut Patraic ...* (Stokes 1887, 92-3). This instrument, *graif* (*graib*), from Latin *graphium* (McGrath 1979, 88-9; Lambert 1991, 162), must be a stylus or stylus-pin, even if translated 'pin' by *DIL* (sv 2 *graif*) ; it is attributed to both Columba and Patrick and each carries the instrument, in the manner of a dress-fastener, in his cloak.[9]

Speculation as to the form of the *Delg Aidechta* must be entirely inferential. It can have been made no later than the 11th or 12th century, on the basis of the apparent *termini ante quos* of the date of the text in which it figures and the date suggested for the stylus for which it was allegedly exchanged. The story of the death of Brandub refers only to the *delg* of Gregory and not specifically to a writing instrument, and, as we have seen,

---

7 The Yellow Book of Lecan has a version of the story from which this episode is omitted (Best 1927, 385). The motif recurs in the 11th- or 12th-century text *Fled Dúin na nGéd* (in the same manuscript) (Lehmann 1964, 26; Dillon 1946, 41, 63), but without reference to the source of the grain of gold. 8 Besides the Alfred Jewel, from North Petherton, Somerset, the group includes terminals from Minster Lovell, Oxfordshire, and Bowleaze Cove, Dorset (Webster & Backhouse 1991, nos 260, 259, 258), as well as an example previously unidentified in print (associated with Anglo-Saxon imports) from Borg in the Lofoten Islands of Norway (Munch 1987, 161, fig 11). The latter is decorated with filigree only and has no extant granulation. A 7th-century Anglo-Saxon stick pin from Wingham, Kent, though it hardly doubled as a stylus, has a flat, fan-shaped head set with gold granules and garnet (Smith 1923, 57, fig 63). 9 Reeves observed of the styli attributed to the saints that they 'seemed to answer a double purpose' (1857, 359, n k). Some 11th-century bone points from York may have been stylus-pins (Waterman 1959, 82-3, figs 12. 6, 10, 11; 14.1, 2; but cf. Wilson 1983).

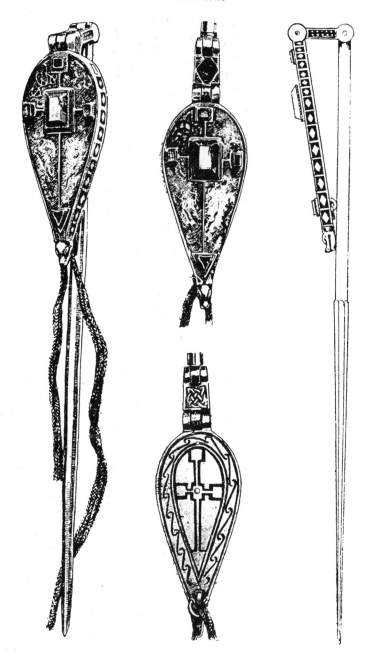

Figure 2   Kite brooch, Clonmacnoise, Co Offaly (after Macalister 1909).

Figure 3   Head of unprovenanced kite brooch.

such an object is denoted by the term *delg graiph*, 'pin of writing', in the story of Brandub's birth. While, in isolation, *delg* (lit 'thorn': *DIL* sv) might mean either 'pin' or 'brooch', the *Delg Aidechta* was probably a *pin* – given its apparent equation with Columba's stylus – as opposed to a penannular (or pseudo-penannular) brooch. It is assumed for our purposes that an insular, Irish type must be in question (despite the story of its origin), although it is not denied that a continental exotic could have graced the Columban treasury. Neither is it denied (bearing the story in mind) that the *Delg Aidechta* might have been one of the *aestel*s associated in 9th-century England with Pope Gregory's name.

A form of dress-fastener somewhat reminiscent of a stylus is the kite 'brooch', in effect a pin with hinged, pendant head. While the head of a kite brooch could have no role in making erasures in wax, *ad hoc* scribing would be possible with the pin (in the case of smaller examples), and the heads of some 9th- or 10th-century kite brooches – one (now lost) from Clonmacnoise (Fig 2), another (unprovenanced) with silver granulation (Fig 3) – have been compared independently with the Alfred Jewel (Cochrane 1891, 319; Macalister 1909, 155; Henry 1965, 130; Ryan 1983, no 70). Conceivably, therefore, the more accomplished kite brooches and the Anglo-Saxon terminals are both obliquely reflected in the Irish literary evidence. The two series may be related to a strictly functional but hardly less elaborate stylus-pin.

Figure 4 The Hunterston brooch, Hunterston, Ayrshire.

Granulation and filigree adorn the pseudo-penannular brooch from Hunterston, Ayrshire (Fig 4), in which Stevenson has seen both Christian iconography and a subsidiary skeuomorph of a continental disc brooch of the 7th century (1974; 1983). The Hunterston brooch and the *Delg Aidechta* might almost be variations on a theme. The former can be compared with the book-covers, vessels and reliquaries of continental treasuries which sometimes physically incorporate antique elements, and the cells between its 'terminals' form a cross 'such as might have covered a relic on the hypothetical ... prototype' (Stevenson 1983, 469). The evidence, however oblique, has allowed us to identify the *Delg Aidechta* as a kite brooch, but whether it was also a skeuomorph or a functional reliquary must remain unknown. The finest of the kite brooches, that from Clonmacnoise, Co. Offaly (Fig 2), is known today only from drawings and photographs; prominent crosses on both faces of the head resemble those on certain Clonmacnoise slabs (e.g. Macalister 1949, no 747) and suggest an ecclesiastical context. It is not impossible that the Clonmacnoise brooch was itself a reliquary, if a relic was housed beneath the stud at the centre of the principal face.[10]

10 The central (?glass) stud on the head of the Clonmacnoise kite brooch, in projecting from its setting and having bevelled edges, is exceptional in an Irish context, but the rock crystal of the Alfred Jewel is similarly treated; the iconography of the jewel also has Irish connections (Henry 1967, 165-6, n 4; 1974, 190-91). That the head of the kite brooch owes something to Anglo-Saxon models is suggested as well by a bronze key

The existence of an elaborate dress-fastener in ecclesiastical hands need not occasion surprise. The Ardagh, Co. Limerick, hoard, deposited in the late 9th or early 10th century, included four brooches, besides the silver chalice and a lesser chalice of bronze. Bosses on the 8th- or 9th-century Londesborough brooch have been likened to shrine fittings, inspiring the suggestion that it was made 'as part of a suite of metalwork for a senior cleric' (Youngs 1989, no 71), and brooches fasten the clothing of Christ and the Virgin in contemporary carvings (Nieke 1993, 132-3). A bell attributed to Máedóc and associated with Drumlane, Co. Cavan, was termed *Clocc an Deilce*, the 'bell of the brooch', through being carried beneath the saint's cloak (*bhíos fom brot ar gach en leirg*, 'which is under my mantle on every path': Plummer 1922 I, 270; II, 262, §241).[11]

If not commissioned by a coarb of Columba for his own use, the *Delg Aidechta* might have been the gift of a king or wealthy pilgrim. The life of Columba compiled from earlier sources by Maghnas Ó Domhnaill in 1532 refers to a gold brooch, *delg óir*, given to Columba by Scandlán, newly installed king of Osraige (*BCC* §349).[12] A sword decorated with ivory which, according to Adomnán (*VC* ii. 39), Columba gave to Librán further exemplifies the kind of gift which the saint might have received from lay patrons (Doherty 1980, 75).

If the *Delg Aidechta* was a 9th- or 10th-century kite brooch it probably pertained not to Iona but to Kells, which was founded in the early 9th century and assumed headship of the Columban *familia* in the first half of the 10th (Herbert 1988, 68-70, 79).[13] The known corpus of kite brooches numbers only thirteen (Somerville 1993; Whitfield forthcoming); their distribution is confined to Ireland and the granulation of the only example with such decoration may reflect Scandinavian taste (Ryan 1983, no 70) (Fig 3). Scandinavian influence at Kells at the end of the 11th century is manifest in the shrine of the *Cathach* and in the name of its maker, Sittriuc (Sitric) mac

from Brandon, Suffolk (Webster & Backhouse 1991, no 66 q), the openwork bow of which is likewise almond-shaped and subdivided by a cross. Several styli are known from the same site (ibid., nos 66 r, s, t). 11 It is appropriate to note that McRoberts believed it to be 'not impossible' that the hoard from St Ninian's Isle, Shetland, might include the *delg aidechta* of the local abbots (1961, 305). But the hoard is unlikely to be ecclesiastical (Wilson 1973, 103-5, 145-6), and there is no evidence that a *delg aidechta* formally recognised as such existed other than in the Columban *familia*. Both McRoberts (1961, 305) and Carney (1961, 121, n 1) thought that the *Delg Aidechta* was habitually *worn* by the coarbs of Columba; it may well have been, but is as likely to have been set apart in the context of a formal treasury. 12 Ó Domhnaill also records Columba's exchange with Gregory, but without using the term *Delg Aidechta*; he says nothing of Columba's stylus and attributes a *delg* to both parties (*BCC* §219). 13 Ó Domhnaill's statement that Columba returned with the dress-fastener to Iona (*BCC* §219) appears to be supposition, and the primary account refers neither to Iona nor to Kells. By the 16th century the *Delg Aidechta* may have been long since lost.

Meic Áeda (Henry 1970, 89). Conceivably the ornament which came to be known as the *Delg Aidechta* was created earlier in the same milieu, and the death of the Christian king of Viking Dublin, Amlaíb (Olaf) Cúarán, on pilgrimage in Iona in 979 (*recte* 980) *AFM* II is consonant with such a possibility. The same king was associated with the church of Scrín Coluim Cille (Skreen, Co. Meath), the repository of a Columban shrine (Bhreathnach 1996).

There can be no doubt that fine dress-fasteners were sometimes owned by senior clerics. One such, the *Delg Aidechta*, perhaps a kite brooch of 9th- or 10th-century date and of insular workmanship, had intrinsic and associative value for the *familia* of Columba and perhaps specifically for the community of Kells. It was believed, ultimately, to have been conferred on his coarbs by the saint's bequest and was accordingly distinguished by its name.

ACKNOWLEDGEMENTS

I am grateful to Kaarina Hollo for suggesting the date of the two Brandub stories, to Conor Newman for bringing the Dublin stylus-pin to my attention and to Arthur MacGregor for informing me about it, as well as to Edel Bhreathnach, Sally Foster, Niamh Whitfield and Susan Youngs for their comments and advice.

The Columban Onomastic Legacy

Nollaig Ó Muraíle

At first sight, Columba would appear to be one of the best-documented and most celebrated of early Irish saints of Irish birth. But, on closer examination, much of the documentation is seen to be rather unsatisfactory from a modern historiographical standpoint. As Herbert has remarked (1988, 9), 'the view that Colum Cille is an accessible historical figure' is due in no small measure to his biographer Adomnán,[1] the ninth abbot of Iona, who has left us a classic of the Irish hagiographical genre in his *Vita Columbae* (*VC*), compiled towards the end of the 7th century – just under a century after its subject's death. Whatever the historical uncertainties, however, it is undeniable that the saint and his cult had enormous influence on various aspects of Gaelic culture, both in Ireland and Scotland, throughout the middle ages and on down almost to our own day. Nowhere is this influence more noticeable than in the onomastic sphere – in relation to personal names, family-names and place-names.

The name *Columba* ('dove') is, of course, of Latin origin, and was gaelicized at an early stage (perhaps by the middle of the 6th century, at the latest) as *Columb*, later *Colum*. According to a late medieval commentary on the 9th-century *Félire Óengusso* (Stokes 1905, 144-6), this name (at least in relation to the saint who died on Iona in AD 597) was originally a nickname, the name it replaced being the common early Irish personal name *Crimthann*. However, Adomnán insists (*VC* second Preface) that it was his earliest, God-given, name: 'So great a name cannot have been given to the man of God but by divine providence ... From the days of his infancy, our abbot was enriched with this appropriate name by God's gift' (Sharpe 1995, 104). Whether or

---

1 Inevitably, in a work such as this, using sources which range from the Old Irish to the Modern Irish periods, it is well-nigh impossible to achieve complete consistency and uniformity in the orthography of names. By and large, early Irish names in the body of the text are given in Old Irish form, but in the gazetteer lists Irish-language names are generally given in Modern Irish form (sometimes in conformity with the present-day standard or *caighdeán*, sometimes in a 'classical' form such as that found in *FGB*); as one might expect, many of the Scottish names conform to a greater or lesser degree to Scots Gaelic norms. The following are random examples of unavoidable orthographic variation: *Adomnán, Leaba Adhamhnáin* and *Muileann Eódhnain, Í Coluimb Chille, Buaile Cholm Cille, Cros Choluim Chille* and *Salen Dubh Challum Chille*.

not it was the case that the son of parents said to have borne the native names
Fedelmid mac Ferguso and Eithne (daughter of Mac Naue or, alternatively,
of Dímma mac Noí: Ó Riain 1985, §§ 397, 651, 691, 722.23) – as stated by
Adomnán (*VC* second Preface) – was indeed conferred with the Latin name
Columba shortly after birth, it should be noted that there were several other
early bearers of the name: there are more than a score of examples in the pre-
Norman Irish secular genealogies (O'Brien 1962), as well as approximately
sixty in the saints' genealogies (Ó Riain 1985). (In the secular genealogies
Columb also occurs once as a female name, while of the sixty or so instances
in the genealogies of the saints no fewer than twenty-one are borne by
females.)

Our Columba does not seem to have been the first Irish ecclesiastic to
bear the name: one especially notable homonymous saint was Colum Tíre Dá
Glas (of Terryglass, Co. Tipperary), whose death is recorded in 552 *AI*, and
who seems to be identical with *Colaim nepos Craumhthainan* whose death is
recorded in a list of those who died in the 'great mortality' of 549 (549.3 *AU*;
548 *AFM* I, p 186). Another early instance of the name occurs at the end of
the same list, *Columbe Inse Celtrae*. The two examples just quoted occur
almost half a century earlier than the death of the great abbot of Iona. There
are also several early occurrences of the diminutive form *Colmán* in *AU*:
555.2, 558.1, 563.3 (Colman Mar mc. Diarmata Derg), 568, 586.1, 587.1,
593.3 (Colman mBec m. nDiarmato), 573.1 (Colman Modicus filius Diarmado).

It should be noted, of course, that while the only name-form which
occurs in a Latin context in relation to the saint of Iona is Columba, in an
Irish-language context he is generally, if not invariably, referred to as *Columb
Cille*, 'dove of [the] church'. (The more common later form is *Colum Cille*,
while the spelling in standardized Modern Irish is *Colm Cille*, and in Scots
Gaelic *Calum Cille*.)[2] This fuller form of the name dates right back to the
saint's own lifetime: it occurs in the canonical text of the poem *Amra Coluim
Cille* which the poet Dallán Forgaill is said to have composed on Columba's
death and which scholars, on linguistic grounds, are happy to date to about
the year 600 (Herbert 1988, 9-10; 1989, 68). See ... *cech ndiruais ro- Columb
ó Chille -cúalammar*, '... all the rest which we have heard from Colum Cille'
(Clancy & Márkus 1995, 108-9, v. 15-16), and the reference, involving a play
on words, to *Columb cen beith, cen chill*, 'Colum, lifeless, churchless' (ibid.,104-
5, i. 5). Hybrid forms occur, in the genitive, as *Columbae Cille* and *Coluimb
Cillae*, in Tírechán's work on St Patrick from the later 7th century (Bieler

2 'The name Columba was a Latin one, adopted for monastic use. In Irish, Columb or
Colum was the name of a few men before Columba, and continued to be the name of
many others after him; and so he was distinguished in retrospect by the designation
Colum(m)-cille, 'church-pigeon'' (Anderson & Anderson 1961, 67).

1979, 140.28 and 164.29 respectively), while the correct Irish form, *Colomb Cille* (in the nominative), occurs in the same work (ibid., 164.26).

An early diminutive form of *Colum(b)* is *Columbán* (latinized *Columbanus*), but the later and much more common diminutive form is the further reduced one mentioned above, *Colmán*. This last is one of the commonest of early Irish saints' names: there are more than 260 instances in the saints' genealogies, while the secular genealogies have over seventy bearers of the name. It is interesting to note that Columba's slightly younger and almost equally celebrated contemporary, the Leinster monk Columbanus, who died at Bobbio in northern Italy in 615, preferred the form *Columba* to the name by which he is best known (Sharpe 1995, 243). Several individuals named *Columbanus* are mentioned in association with Columba by Adomnán (*VC* i. 5, 14; ii. 15, 16, 21, 22, 43; iii. 12). (The form *Colmanus* is also found: i. 11; in the listed headings of i. 5, 43 and the text heading of i. 5; and *Colman*, i. 43.)

There are at least three other personal names deriving directly from *Colum*: *Giolla Coluim*, *Mac Coluim* and *Máel Coluim*, while among those which come more indirectly from it are the hypocoristics (or pet-forms) *Mo-Cholmóc* and *Mo-Chumma*, or *Do-Chumma*, *Mo-Chonna*, *Do-Chonna*, *Mo-Chonóc*, *Do-Chaineóc* and even *Cainnech* (Ó Riain 1983; O'Brien 1973, 220),[3] and at a still further remove are forms such as *Giolla Colmáin*, *Giolla Mo-Cholmóg*, *Giolla Mo-Chonna*, and so on. The two names *Giolla Coluim* and *Máel Coluim* belong to a significant category of early Irish nomenclature deriving from saints' names. There appears to have been a hesitancy in early Ireland about the use of saints' names as personal names. In the words of Ó Cuív (1986, 16): 'in the pre-Norman period we find saints' names ... commonly used as first names [only] in the form of loose compounds'. Thus, for example, the name *Pátraic*, Patrick, did not come to be used as a personal name until the Norman period (when John de Courcy promoted the Patrician cult in east Ulster) – see again Ó Cuív's statement (1986, 17) on 'the practice ... of using saints' names as baptismal names'. Prior to that one gets compound forms such as *Gilla Pátraic* and *Máel Pátraic* – just as, in relation to the yet more sacred names *Ísa* and *Maire* (modern *Muire*), one gets *Gilla Ísa* and *Máel Ísa*, *Gilla Maire* and *Máel Maire*. Ó Cuív also notes (1986, 16, n 30):

> There is no example of *Maél Coluim* in [O'Brien 1962] ... There is one of *Gilla Coluim* ... in a northern family, that of Mág Uidir. However, there is annalistic evidence of the use of both names. Thus among the descendants of Canannán of Cenél Conaill we find *Maél Coluim* (*AFM* 955 [also 955.3 *AU*]) and *Gilla Coluim* (id. 974 [also 977.3 *AU*]).

3 For a useful discussion of the forms *Mo Chummae*, *Mo Chomma*, *To Cummi* and *Do Chumma*, see Kelly 1973, 25.

In the index to the same collection of pre-Norman genealogies to which Ó Cuív refers (O'Brien 1962) there are, however, four instances of *Máel Coluim*, all of them in a Scottish context. The four in fact boil down to three (as will be explained presently),[4] and all three were actually kings of Scotland: Máel Coluim mac Donnchada (also known as Malcolm III who died in 1093.5 *AU*; 1093.13 *AI* (see also 1058.2 (and .6), 1085.2, 1094.7, 1118.5, 1124.5 *AU*), his great-grandfather, Máel Coluim mac Cinaeda (alias Malcolm II, who died in 1034 – 1033.7, 1034.1 *AU*; 1034.9 *AI*), and the latter's grandfather, Máel Coluim mac Domnaill (alias Malcolm I, who died in 954.2 *AU*; see also 967.1 and 995.1).[5] Macalister's reading of the name *Giolla Coluim* on a slab on Iona (1949, no 1072) has been shown to be without foundation (RCAHMS 1982, 189–90).

In addition to the two individuals named *Giolla Coluim* and *Máel Coluim* who, as mentioned by Ó Cuív, appear in the 10th-century annals, and to the three Scottish kings aforementioned named 'Malcolm', there are several bearers of the name *Máel Coluim* in various pre-Norman annals: Máel Coluim, king of Caenraige, slain in 1031 (1031.6 *AU*; 1031.7 *AI*; *AFM* II, p 822) – see also a reference at 1013 *AFM* II (p 770) to Maolcolaim Caonraigheach – Máel Coluim mac Domnaill, king of the northern Britons (997.5 *AU*), Máel Coluim mac Maíl Brigte meic Ruaidrí (1029.7 *AU*; 1029 *AFM* II, p 818 – king of Scotland according to *ATig*), and Máel Coluim Cennmór mac Énríg (Malcolm IV, known as 'The Maiden'), king of Scotland (1165 *AU¹*).

Of the three personal names derived directly from *Colum*, two (*Giolla Coluim* and *Máel Coluim*) apparently gave rise to a number of surnames: *Mac Giolla Choluim*, *Mac Maoil Choluim* and *Ó Maoil Choluim*. In relation to the first of these, Black (1946, 303), having described 'Gillecallum' as 'a very popular personal name in the twelfth and thirteenth centuries', states that 'Gillyecallom was the name of an early Sutherland family.' MacLysaght (1982, 132–3), in dealing with the name in the anglicized form MacIlholm, corrects Woulfe's statement (1923, 371) that 'Mac Giolla Cholm, Mac Giolla Choluim ... MacElholm' was 'a very rare and scattered surname'; instead he declares that 'in fact it is associated with a definite and limited area, viz. the country between Enniskillen and Castlederg'; he goes on to cite a reference from the Elizabethan Fiants to a soldier named 'Donogh duff Mac Gillacollum' (*Fiants* no 6549) who is mentioned in a Co. Cavan context. However, MacLysaght suggests elsewhere (1980, 166) that the surname represents, not *Mac Giolla Choluim* but rather *Mac Giolla Chalma*, a form which occurs in the annals.

4 See next note. 5 The example of the name which occurs in the Book of Leinster genealogical recension, Máel Coluim mac Domnaill meic Cináeda, is a mistake for Máel Coluim mac Domnaill *meic Causantín* meic Cináeda – 'Malcolm I'. (Note, incidentally, the statement in *BCC* §93 that *Clann Mhaoil Choluim meic Donnchadha* – the descendants of Malcolm III – were kings of Scotland for a long time.)

(We may also note a reference in another Fiant (no 6533) to one 'John Mully M'Gillecallym' – in a Co. Tipperary context.)

Woulfe has a brief entry (1923, 605) under the heading *Ó Maolcholm, Ó Maolcholuim*, with such anglicized forms as *Malcolm, Mulholm, Mulhollum*,[6] *Maholm, Mahollum*; he describes it as 'an Antrim surname' and goes on to cite an entry at 1061 *AFM* II (p 878) recording the death of Muireadhach Ua Maolcholuim, erenagh of Derry. By contrast, Black's entries on the names *Malcolm* and *Malcolmson* (1946, 576-7) are lengthy and detailed. Remarking that four kings of Scotland bore the name *Maol Coluim*, he goes on to cite numerous instances from medieval Scottish records. He also mentions that 'in the Orkneyinga Saga the name of Scottish kings is spelled Melkolmr, and Melkolfr was the name of two thralls in Iceland' mentioned in 13th-century sagas. He also states that 'the full form Maolchaluim ... was in use till the seventeenth century, but eventually gave way to Gillecaluim and both now appear as Calum and Callum ... In the form Maiklum it was an old surname in Strathblane, and in the Lowlands it has become Maecom.' Moving on to *Malcolmson*, 'son of Malcolm', he remarks that it 'is found early', and cites one Symon Malcomesson of Berwickshire who appears in a document dated 1296.

There are also surnames deriving from some of the personal names which come indirectly from *Colum*, notably *Mo-Cholmóg* and *Cainneach*. From the first of these names comes the surname *Mac Giolla Mo-Cholmóg*, which was borne by one of the principal families of the north Leinster dynasty of Uí Dúnchada at the time of the Norman invasion in the later 12th century (Smyth 1982, 44) – the chieftain *Domnall mcgellmochomoc* witnessed Strongbow's Glendalough Charter about the year 1173 (Price 1967, xxxiv). The surname would seem to be no longer extant. From *Cainneach* come the surnames *Mac Coinnigh* (anglicized *MacKinney* and *MacKenzie*) and *Mac Giolla Choinnigh* (variously anglicized as *MacElhenny, MacLehinney, Kilkenny*, etc).

When we move on to look at the commemoration of Columba in placenames both in Ireland and in Scotland, we find that the most unambiguous examples are those which specifically call the saint by his traditional Irish name *Colum Cille*. (Those which simply mention *Colum* are more difficult to assess: some, or even most, undoubtedly relate to our saint – especially when located in Scotland – but others very likely refer to one or other of the many early saints of the same name.) Of the numerous place-names in both countries which derive from the career and, later, the cult of Columba, the most

6 Not to be confused with the Ulster surname generally anglicized *Mulholland*; this represents *Ó Maoil Challainn*, and is derived from the personal name *Máel Callann* (meaning, apparently, 'servant of [the] kalends'). This surname was also found in medieval times in Cos Limerick and Meath (Dobbs 1938).

celebrated are no doubt Derry and Iona. The former, the 'oak-grove', is referred to on innumerable occasions in all the early annalistic collections, beginning with the bare (retrospective) announcement in 546 *AU*: *Daire Coluim Cille fundata est*. The place continues to be mentioned in the annals down through the centuries – to the early 17th century in the case of the Four Masters. These latter are the most diligent recorders of every incident in the history of the great Columban foundation – in all, there are more than a hundred references to the place between AD 535 and 1608. What is also interesting is that this collection more than any other preserves what was said to be the original name, *Daire Calgaich* (?'Calgach's oak-grove'), rather than the form *Doire Coluim Chille* which – along with plain *Doire* – is the one found most commonly in other sources (Reeves 1857, 277-8, §2; Gwynn & Hadcock 1970, 33, 67, 168, 224, 278, 304, 316).

The most detailed study of the name of Iona (Í Choluim Chille) is that by Watson (1926, 87-90, 147, etc). The name is also discussed by Anderson (1973 282-3, n 106) and, at greater length, by Sharpe (1995, 257-9), who recounts both scholarly opinions of the subject and more fanciful and even bogus 'explanations'. He points out that the form *Iona* 'is relatively modern, being found in manuscripts of the fourteenth century and later'; it seems to have arisen through a misreading of *Ioua insula*, and to have come into common use only in the later 18th century (perhaps under the influence of Dr Samuel Johnson). An interesting coincidence which may also have encouraged the adoption of this form is that *Iona* (or *Jona*) is the Hebrew word for *dove* (i.e. *columba*)! Remarking that an exhaustive collection of name-forms has been given by Reeves (1857, 258-62), Sharpe paraphrases Watson's explanation of *Í Coluimb Chille*, which 'from the ninth century for nearly a thousand years' was the name by which the place was generally called: the name-forms were divided into two series, both of which, it is suggested, are most likely to derive from **iuo*, related to Old Irish *éo*, 'stem, trunk', which in Middle Irish 'was chiefly used of yew-trees' (as in the name *Mag nÉo*, modern Mayo).[7]

A point worth remarking in relation to the topography of Iona is the striking dearth of place-names on the island which refer to either Columba or Adomnán (Map 5 and frontispiece) (see Reeves 1857, 413-33, especially the list, 425-31) – unless we deem such names as *Cill-Chainnich, Kilchainnich, Cladh Chaoinich, Inch Kenneth*, etc (ibid., 417, 418, 426, 432, respectively), to involve a hypocoristic form of Columba's name (as has been argued by Ó Riain 1983 – see above).

Here follows a selection of place-names, in Ireland and Scotland, which

---

7 There is a further brief note on the place in Gwynn and Hadcock 1970, 38; see also MacBain 1922, 69; Mackenzie 1931, 139-41, Johnston 1934, 211; MacArthur 1995, 4.

include the saint's name in its fuller Irish form.[8] (Those names, particularly in Ireland, for which modern equivalents are not given – e.g. *Cédimtheacht Coluim Chille*, no 2, below – may, by and large, be deemed obsolete.)

LIST I, IRELAND (Map 5)

1 *Buaile Cholm Cille*. Boley. A minor place-name in the townland of Tullybrick, parish of Ballynascreen, barony of Loughinsholin, Co. Derry. There is a local tradition that Columba's cow, the mythical animal known as the *Glas Ghaibhleann*, was tethered to a standing stone in the vicinity called *Breacán na Glaise*, or *Breacán Ghlas Ghaibhleann* (Toner 1996, 44-5; also 39).

2 *Cédimtheacht Coluim Chille*. A *reilec* or churchyard in the townland of Templedouglas (Tulach Dubhghlaise), near the townland of Gartan, in the parish of Conwal, barony of Kilmacrenan, Co. Donegal. The only mention of the place appears to be in Maghnas Ó Domhnaill's great 16th-century *Betha Colaim Cille* (*BCC* §§55-6; R 281, §15).

3 *Cnoc Choluim Chille*. Knock. A townland in the parish of Knockbreda, baronies of Lower and Upper Castlereagh, Co. Down. The name is carefully documented by Flanagan (1982, 62; cf. R 283, §25).

4 *Columbkille*. Paróiste Coluim Chille. A parish in the barony of Granard, Co. Longford. It is called *Colomkill* on the Down Survey barony-map from the 1650s; *p[aráiste] Colaim Chille* in a pencilled note in the *OSNB* (sn),[9] where there is also record of *Teampall Cholum-cille* (see no 34, below) and *Reilig Ch. c.* The parish had its origins in the monastery of Inchmore on Lough Gowna (R 282, §21; G & H 179).

5 *Columbkille*. Cill Cholm Cille. A parish in the barony of Gowran, Co. Kilkenny. The place is called *Colmekyll Chapel* in a document dated 1303 (in the calendar of the *Liber Ruber Kilkenniensis*, the Red Book of Kilkenny), *Kylcolmkylle* in a document in the same collection dated c 1480, and *Paráiste Cholaim Chille* in the *OSNB* (sn) (R 284, §28; see also the very brief note in G & H 378).

6 *Columbkille Point*. A tiny peninsula on the southern shore of Lough Neagh, in the townland of Derrylard, parish of Tartaraghan, barony of Oneilland West, Co. Armagh.

---

8 For the sake of consistency, the genitive form *Coluim Chille* is generally used in the lemmata below, in preference to, say, *Colaim Chille* – even where the latter is the form cited by, for example, Reeves. References cited repeatedly in the lists are abbreviated as follows: G & H = Gwynn & Hadcock 1970; R = Reeves 1857; W = Watson 1926. (See also abbreviations cited in the Bibliography: *AFM, ALC, AU, CS, LL, LU, OSNB*, etc.) 9 The abbreviation 'sn' (*sub nomine*) refers to information under a given headword in the source cited.

7 *Cros Choluim Chille.* In medieval Armagh. This cross is mentioned in 1166 *AU[1]* and *AFM* II (p 1157), where it is reported that Armagh was burned 'from the cross of Colum Cille', *ó chrois Cholaim Chille.*

8 *Cros Choluim Chille.* In the townland and parish of Clonmacnoise, barony of Garrycastle, Co. Offaly. This is mentioned in the prose *Dinnshenchas* of Mag nÚra (Gwynn 1924, 276).

9 *Cros Mhór Choluim Chille.* On Tory Island (*BCC* §215: *an cross mor C. C.*).

10 *Disiurt Choluim Chille hi Cenunnus cona lubgortán.* In Kells, Co. Meath. This 'hermitage' is recorded in one of the charters preserved in the Book of Kells (O'Donovan 1846a, 130; Mac Niocaill 1961, 14.6-7).

11 *Doire Coluim Chille.* Derry. Discussed above.

12 *Druim Coluim Chille.* Drumcolumb. A townland and parish in the barony of Tirerrill, Co. Sligo. The Irish name as given here (it means 'Colum Cille's ridge') occurs in *BCC* §154, where its former name is said to have been *Druim na Macraidhe* (see also R 282, §20, and a brief note in G & H 381).

13 *Duib-Recles Coluim Chille.* In Derry. This 'black oratory' is referred to in 1166 *AFM* II (p 1156): Doire is said to have been burnt *gus an Duibh reccles*; 1173 *ALC* I (p 148): *a nduib reigles Coluim Cille a nDoire* (cf. R 284, §30).

14 *Ecclas Choluim Chille hi cCeanannus.* In Kells, Co. Meath. This church is mentioned in 802 *AFM* I (p 412).

15 *Gleann Choluim Chille.* Glencolumbkille. A parish in the barony of Banagh, Co. Donegal. It features in the annals (1583 *AFM* VI, p 1890; 1530 *ALC* II, p 274 – *a nGlionn Cille[10]*) and in Maghnas Ó Domhnaill's work (*BCC* §42: *ag abuind t-Senglenda ... ris a raiter Glend Colaim cilli aniug*; see also §132: *Senglend C. C.*; §133: *Senglend*) (cf. R 281, §14; G & H 385).

16 *Gleann Choluim Chille.* Glencolumbkille, North and South. A double townland in the parish of Carran, barony of Burren, Co. Clare. It seems to be first attested in the early 17th-century life of Aodh Ruadh Ó Domhnaill (Walsh 1948, 202: *co Gleann Colaimb Cille* = 1599 *AFM* VI, p 2100); while an abridged form, *Glann*, occurs in the so-called 'Census' of 1659 (Pender 1939, 186; cf. G & H 385).

17 *Leac Choluimb Chille.* A flagstone in the townland of Churchfield, parish of Oughaval, barony of Murrisk, Co. Mayo, beside the ancient parish church, said to have been built by Columba; there is also 'a holy well blessed by that saint, lying close to the church' (*OSLM* I, 431; cf. Logan 1980,111) – *St Columbkille's Well* (no 25, below).

18 *Loch Coluim Chille.* Three in Co. Donegal and (at least) three in Scotland:
    i Columbkille Lough, in the parish of Tullyfern, barony of Kilmacrenan

10 Hennessy, editor of *ALC*, emends *Glenn-Cille* to *Glenn-Coluim-Cille* (*ALC* II, 274, n 1).

(OS 36[11]); ii Columbkille Lough, in the parish of Kilbarron, barony of Tirhugh (OS 108); iii Columbkille's Lough, in the parish of Clondahorky, barony of Kilmacrenan (OS 25).

19 *Maon / Maén / Móen Coluim Chille.* The townland and parish of Moone, barony of Kilkea and Moone, Co. Kildare. The name is thoroughly documented by de hÓir (1968, 55-7), who suggests that it means 'the wealth, or property of Colum Cille'. The earliest reference to the place cited by de hÓir is that in 1005.1 *AU,* but it already occurs – possibly a century or more earlier – in the *Tripartite Life* of St Patrick (Mulchrone 1939, 114, line 2200 – see MacNeill, 1930, 33; cf. R 280, §10; G & H 280, 367, 399).

20 *Oileán Coluim Chille.* Illan Columbkille. An island of just under two acres at the north-eastern end of Lough Mask, about midway between the townlands of Ballygarry and Derrymore, in the parish of Ballyovey, barony of Carra, Co. Mayo. The OS 6-inch map shows 'Church (in ruins)' on the island. In Ballygarry is a holy well called *Tobercolumbkille* (no 40, below).

21 *Proinnteach Coluim Chille.* In Co. Tyrone. According to Hogan (1910, 565) this 'refectory' is mentioned in the so-called *Dublin Annals of Inisfallen* (p 49a). (See the reference to *Proinnteach Cruimthir Choluim* from *MIA* in List III, no 24, below.)

22 *Recles Coluim Chille.* See *Duib-Recles Coluim Chille* (no 13, above).

23 *St Columbkille's Bed.* A minor place-name in the townland of Carrickmore, parish of Termonmaguirk, barony of Omagh East, Co. Tyrone.

24 *St Columbkille's Stone.* A minor place-name in the townland of Ballynameen, parish of Desertoghill, barony of Coleraine, Co. Derry.

25 *St Columbkille's Well.* In the townland of Churchfield, parish of Oughaval, barony of Murrisk, Co. Mayo. (See no 17, above.)

26 *St Columcille's Holly.* In the parish of Glencolumbkille, Co. Donegal (no 15, above) (Logan 1980, 93).

27 *St Columcille's Well.* Nine wells of this name are listed by Logan (1980, 40-41, 127, etc): in (a) Ardcolm, Co. Wexford (List III, no 3, below), (b) Clonmany, Co. Donegal (List III, no 11, below), (c) Durrow, Co. Westmeath (see below), (d) Glencolumbkille, Co. Donegal (no 15, above), (e) Inishkea North, Co. Mayo (see no 35, below), (f) Kilconickny, Co. Galway (no 39, below), (g) near Lough Columcille, Co. Donegal (which of the three lakes of this name in the county is not specified – see no 18 i-iii, above), (h) Oughaval, Co. Mayo (no 25, above), (i) Sandyford, Co. Carlow.[12]

---

11 In the case of Irish place-names, 'OS' followed thus by a number represents the appropriate Ordnance Survey map-sheet on a scale of six inches to one mile. The numbers begin at '1' for each county. 12 I do not know of any place named *Sandyford* in Co.

28 *St Columkille's Stone*. A minor place-name in the townland of Ballinloughan, parish of Culfeightrin, barony of Cary, Co. Antrim.

29 *Scrín Choluim Chille*. The townland, parish and barony of Skreen, Co. Meath. The first reference to 'Columba's shrine' occurs in the annals in 818 *CS*; in 878.9 *AU* (cf. 875 *AFM* I, p 522) it is reported that 'the shrine of Colum Cille and his other halidoms arrived in Ireland, having been taken in flight to escape the foreigners [i.e. Vikings]'. In this case, however, the entry denotes an actual shrine rather than the place-name; the first unequivocal mention of the place-name is at 974 (*recte* 976) *CS*: *Scrín Coluim Cille*; it occurs again at 986 and 1035 *CS*: *Scrin Coluim Cille*, and in 1027 *AFM* II (p 814), 1037 (p 832), 1058 (p 874) and 1152 (p 1102): *Scrín C(h)olaim Chille*. (See also 1176.10 *MIA*: *Sgrín Coluim Cilli*.) It is also mentioned in the noted Irish manuscript *Lebor na hUidre*, written about the year 1100: 50b (in the text called *Senchas na Relec* – *LU* line 4055n: *Scrín Choluim Cille*); 53b (in the text *Tucait innarba na nDessi* – ibid., line 4378n: *Scrín Cholaim Cille*). (R 282, §17; for a summary of the site's history see G & H 44; Bhreathnach 1996.)[13]

The element *scrín* (from Latin *scrinium*, 'a shrine, i.e. an ornamented casket or box, containing the relics of a saint' (Joyce 1869, 321)) occurs in a small number of Irish (but, interestingly enough, in no Scottish) place-names; about a dozen of these are cited in medieval Irish sources: three associated with Columba himself (this and the following name, as well as Scrín in Arda[14]), two with Adomnán (Columba's biographer), two associated with Ciarán of Clonmacnoise, and one each with Do-Chonna (a hypocoristic form of the name *Colum*), Do-Chuailén, Manchán, Mo-Cholmóg (another hypocoristic form of *Colum*) and Patrick. The word also occurs in the parish-name Skreen in the baronies of Ballaghkeen and Shelmaliere East, Co. Wexford,[15] and in such townland-names as Skreen, parish of Drumhome, Co. Donegal; parish of Cleenish and parish of Killesher, Co. Fermanagh; parish of Donacavey, Co. Tyrone; Skreen, Lower and Upper; parish of Kilmacrenan, Co. Donegal; Skreeny and Skreeny Little, parish of Cloonclare, and Skreeny, parish of Killasnet, Co. Leitrim; Skrine, parish of Kilmeane, Co. Roscommon, and perhaps Skrinny, parish of Drumkeeran, Co. Fermanagh. The word occurs as a final element in a number of other townland-names: Ballynaskreena, parish of Killury, Co. Kerry; Castleskreen, parish of Bright, Co. Down; Eshnascreen, parish of Aghalurcher, Co. Fermanagh; Gortnascreeny, parish of Caheragh,

Carlow. 13 I have failed to locate the reference which is given as 'Lu [=LU] 41b' by Hogan (1910, 593). 14 See *BCC* §146; this place was in the parish of Tamlaghtard, Co. Derry. 15 This place does not seem to be attested prior to the 16th century. It has been tentatively suggested (Ranson 1949, 166) that the name in its fuller form was *Scrín Maoil Ruain*.

Co. Cork, and parish of Clonrush, Co. Clare (formerly Co. Galway); Reanascreena North and South, Co. Cork; Tullanascreen, parish of Conwal, Co. Donegal; Tullynascreen, parish of Killanummery, Co. Leitrim.[16] (I have omitted from the foregoing lists the townland and parish of Skreen, Co. Meath, whose name is being discussed here, and the parish of Ballynascreen, Co. Derry, the subject of the next entry.) In relation to such names, Flanagan – who noted the strong northern bias in their distribution – has stated that 'Skreen names [derive] from a reliquary held by the named monastery, presumably a place of pilgrimage and devotional ritual ... The probability is that some, if not all of them refer to pre-Reform [i.e. the 12th-century reform of the Irish church] sites, distinguished by their possession of a venerated shrine' (Flanagan 1982, 73). (See also Flanagan & Flanagan 1994, 140; also 141 for an interesting distribution-map of '*Scrín* as sole or first element in the names of parishes and townlands.')

In addition to the examples just listed, the word *scrín* occurs as a constituent element in a number of minor place-names; two instances which may be cited are *Fearann na Scríne* on Rathlin Island (Holmer 1942, 194)[17] and Cross Skreen (*Cros Scríne*) in the townland of Ballyteerim, parish of Culfeightrin, barony of Cary, Co. Antrim. The latter place – which appears to be first attested as *Skrine* in 1661 – is said to be where Shane O'Neill (Seán an Díomais) was buried following his death at the hands of the MacDonnells of Antrim in 1567.

---

16 It must be emphasised that the names in this list have been selected on the basis of their anglicized forms alone – a hazardous procedure at the best of times which can all too easily lead one into error. For example, a random check on just one of the townland-names listed, Castleskreen, reveals that the second 's' is a later intrusion which first appeared in the 17th century; earlier evidence includes forms such as 'Castlecreen', so the supposed link with *scrín* dissolves before our eyes. In this case there is a fairly good spread of evidence, but another name on the list, Eshnascreen, seems to be quite unattested prior to the early 19th century. Therefore, any attempt at a definitive statement about the element *scrín* in Irish place-names must await a thorough gathering and sifting of all the available evidence. 17 We may note the entry at 790 (*recte* 795) *AFM* I (p 396): 'The burning of Reachrainn by plunderers; and its shrines (*a Scrríne*) were broken and plundered.' One wonders if *Fearann na Scríne* might not preserve a tradition of one such shrine. Admittedly, there is a degree of uncertainty about the precise identity of the Vikings' first Irish target since the name Rechru (later Reachra and Reachrainn) was borne both by Rathlin, Co. Antrim, and by Lambay, Co. Dublin. O'Donovan, in his note to the entry in *AFM*, opined that the latter was 'probably the place here referred to'. He was followed in this by Ó Corráin (1972, 81) who, however, changed his mind later and opted for Rathlin (1986, 32; 1989, 31) – as did Smyth (1984, 145). Perhaps the very existence of the microtoponym *Fearann na Scríne* might serve to tilt the balance ever so slightly further in Rathlin's favour! Within three years, though, the Vikings were certainly in the vicinity of Lambay: in 798.2 *AU* they burned Inis Pátraic, near Skerries, and 'broke the shrine of Do-Chonna' (*scrín Do-Chonna*) – *AFM* I 793 (*recte* 798) (p 400) says that 'they bore away the shrine'.

30 *Scrín Choluim Chille.* The parish of Ballynascreen, barony of Loughinsholin, Co. Derry. This is treated of in a most comprehensive fashion by Toner in his recently published study of the place-names of the Moyola Valley (1996, 6-9; cf. R 282, §18; brief note in G & H 374).

31 *Sord Coluim Chille.* A parish in the barony of Nethercross, Co. Dublin (two of whose townlands are called Swords Demesne and Swords Glebe). The name is discussed briefly by de hÓir (1975, 132), who cites without comment the statement in *BCC* §103 that *Sord* was the name of a well and that it meant 'clean' (*Glan*).[18] The place is first mentioned in the early 9th-century *Martyrology of Tallaght*, simply as *Suird* (genitive of *Sord* – Best & Lawlor 1931, 24: 16 March): *Finani loboir Suird* – repeated in the 12th-century *Martyrology of Gorman* (Stokes 1895, 56: 16 March; see also ibid., 132: 9 July), and this simple form (either in the genitive or the dative) also occurs in 965 *AFM* II (p 688), 1020 (p 796), 1028 (p 816), etc, as well as in 1056.9 and 1060.5 *AU*. It is first mentioned in relation to Columba in 994.3 *AU* (and again in 1014.2, 1020.1, 1035.6, etc): *Sord Coluim Cille;* and in 1013 *AFM* II (p 778), 1023 (p 804), 1035 (p 830), 1060 (p 878), etc: *Sord C(h)olaim Chille.* It occurs in the *Martyrology of Gorman* (Stokes 1895, 64, n: 29 March – *i taebh Suird Choluim cille*) and in the Uí Bhriain propaganda tract *Cocad Gaedel re Gallaib*, from about the same period (Todd 1867, 18: *Sord Coluim Cilli*; 200: *co Sord*; 224: *Sord Coluimcille* [*LL*]) (cf. R 279, §6; G & H 44).

32 *Suidhe Coluim Chille.* Near Cúil Dreimne, in the parish of Drumcliff, barony of Carbury, Co. Sligo. *BCC* §175: *Suidhe C. C.*

33 *Teach Choluim Cille i cCill mic Nénain.* In the townland of Kilmacrenan, in the parish and barony of the same name, Co. Donegal. This 'house' is mentioned in 1129 *AFM* II (p 1030).

34 *Teampall Coluim Chille.* On Inchmore in Lough Gowna, barony of Granard, Co. Longford. In 1415 *AFM* IV (p 820, n) an old church called *Teampull Coluim Cille*, parish of Columbkille (no 4, above) (R 282, §21).

35 *Teampall Coluim Chille.* On the island of Inishkea North, parish of Kilmore, barony of Erris, Co. Mayo. It is described by O'Donovan (1844, 498) as 'a small church dedicated to St. Columbkille' (cf. *OSLM* I, 207; R 462).

36 *Teampall Coluim Chille.* On Inishturk, parish of Kilgeever, barony of Murrisk, Co. Mayo. It is described by O'Donovan (1844, 498) as 'a Kill dedicated to St. Columb' (cf. *OSLM* I, 476; R 462).

37 *Tobar Coluim Chille.* In Derry (*BCC* §86: *tobar C. C.*).

---

18 A possible alternative interpretation would be that 'the well of Sord' was called *Glan* – *do bendaigh tobar Suird .i. Glan a ainm.*

38 *Tobar Coluim Chille*. In the Fanad peninsula, parish of Clondavaddog, barony of Kilmacrenan, Co. Donegal (*BCC* §163: *Tobar C. C.*).

39 *Tobar Coluim Chille*. 'In the townland of Boherduff, Bóthar Dubh [parish of Kilconickny, barony of Dunkellin, Co. Galway], are three wells called St. Columbkill's Wells. The name in Irish, however, is Tobar Choluim Cille ...' (*OSLG* I, 474). 'At some one of these a stone lies in which is visible the impression, it is said, of St. Columbkille's knees ...' (ibid., 475).

40 *Tobercolumbkille*. In the townland of Ballygarry, parish of Ballyovey, barony of Carra, Co. Mayo. (See no 20, above.)

41 *Tobercolumbkille*. In the townland of Kintogher, parish of Drumcliff, barony of Carbury, Co. Sligo.

Finally, we may note Hogan's reference (1910, 30) to one other place-name which includes the name *Colum Cille*. It has been read as *Améd Coluim Chille 7 Inis Muireoc*, but the initial element of the 'name' is in fact a ghost-word, being based on a mistranscription in an Irish manuscript. The text in which it occurs, in TCD MS H.2.17, page 353, is a copy of the early 12th-century Munster propaganda tract *Cocad Gaedel re Gallaib*; but the reading in Todd's edition of the text (1867, 16) is: *ro hinred leo am I Coluim Cilli, ocus Inis Muireoc, ocus Daminis ...*

LIST II, SCOTLAND (Map 6)

1 *Cill Chaluim Chille*. At Tarbert on the east side of Jura (RCAHMS 1984, 162).

2 *Cill Choluim Chille*. Kilcholmkill. In the parish of Sand, North Uist (R 291, §12; W 280).

3 *Cill Choluim Chille*. Kilcholambkille. On Benbecula. 'The Church of St. Columba in Beandmoyll' (R 291, §13; cf. W 280).

4 *Cill Choluim Chille*. At Snizort on Skye. 'Formerly Kilcolmkill or St. Colme's Kirk in Snesford' (R 291, §6; cf. W 280).

5 *Cill Choluim Chille*. Killchallumkill. Now Keil at Duror in Appin, on Loch Linnhe, Argyllshire (R 292, §18; W 280). (The statement by Reeves that it is 'opposite Lismore' relates to the next name, no 6.)

6 *Cill Choluim Chille*. Kilcolmkill. Now Kiel Crofts in Ardchattan, in Benderloch, on Ardmucknish Bay, Argyllshire. 'St. Colme's Chappell' (R 292, §19; cf. W 280).

7 *Cill Choluim Chille*. 'St. Columba's in Kinelvadon or in Morwarne.' Kiel on Loch Aline in Morvern, to the west of Loch Linnhe, Argyllshire (R 292-3, §20; cf. W 280).

8 *Cill Choluim Chille*. Kilcollumkill. An old parish in Mull (R 293, §21; W 280).

9 *Cill Choluim Chille*. Kilcholmkill. In the parish of Kildalton in eastern Islay (R 294, §24; W 280).

10 *Cill Choluim Chille*. Kilcholmkill. In the parish of Kilarrow in Islay. 'St. Columba's or Portesock' (R 294, §25; cf. W 280).

11 *Cill Choluim Chille*. Kilcolumkill. In the parish of Southend, Kintyre, Argyllshire (R 294, §27; W 280).

12 *Cill Choluim Chille*. Killcolmkill. In Strabruraich, or 'Srath of Brora'. East of Loch Brora, eastern Sutherland (R 295, §6; cf. W 280).

13 *Í Choluim Chille*. Iona. Discussed above.

14 *Loch Colmkille*. On the eastern side of Lewis (R 291, §10).

15 *Loch Coluimcille*. On Skye (ancient name of Portree Bay) (R 139, n a, 291, §7).

16 *Loch Columkille*. In the north-east of Skye (now drained) (R 138, n a, 290, §3).

17 *Oileán Coluim Chille*. Eilean Coluimcille. In Portree Bay, eastern Skye (R 291, §7).

18 *Oileán Coluim Chille*. Island Columbkill. At the head of Loch Arkaig in south-western Inverness-shire (R 292, §17).

19 *Salen Dubh Challum Chille*. In the parish of Torosay in north-eastern Mull (R 293, §22).

LIST III, IRELAND (Map 7)

There are numerous places in both Ireland and Scotland apparently named after a person called Colum or Columba; as mentioned above, these would appear mostly to represent our saint (particularly those occurring in Scotland), but perhaps not in all cases. There are even two or three which, despite their anglicized forms, appear not to reflect the name Colum at all (e.g. nos 4 and 14, and perhaps 2, below). There are also some places associated with Columba but not named from him; in such cases, i.e. where the saint's name does not appear to form part of a place-name, the location is used – in square brackets – as a headword.

1 *Aghacolumb*. A townland in the parish of Arboe, barony of Dungannon Upper, Co. Tyrone. The earliest attestation appears to be in the Civil Survey from the 1650s where the name occurs as *Aghicolum* (Simington 1937, 303).

2 *Ardcollum*. A townland in the parish of Kilronan, barony of Boyle, Co. Roscommon. The forms in the early 17th-century Chancery Inquisitions

(unpublished), *Ardechallen* and *Ardkallen*, and that in Edgeworth's Grand Jury Map of 1817 (Rodger 1972, 44, no 801), *Arcolan*, would suggest that the second element in the name is something other than *Coluim*. (As against that, there is the Irish form written in pencil in the *OSNB* (sn), *ard collam*, but this can scarcely be regarded as overwhelming support for our saint's name; see no 14, below.)

3 *Ardcolm.* A parish in the barony of Shelmaliere East, Co. Wexford. The name occurs as *airdne coluim* in 890 *AFM* I (p 544) and also in the 12th-century *Martyrology of Gorman* (Stokes 1895, 214; cf. R 284, §29).

4 *Ardcolum.* A townland in the parish of Kiltoghert, barony of Leitrim, Co. Leitrim. Although the Irish form recorded in the *OSNB* (sn) is *ard cailm*, O'Donovan suggests that the name's meaning is 'Altitudo Columbae, Columb's hill or height'. The earliest attested form seems to be that on Larkin's Grand Jury Map of 1819 (Rodger 1972, 42, no 775), *Ardcollon*. In the light of this admittedly rather tenuous evidence, the link with someone named Colum, still less our Columba, must be deemed dubious, to say the least.

5 *[Ballymagrorty.]* B Irish and B Scotch. A double townland in the parish of Drumhome, barony of Tirhugh, Co. Donegal. The remains of an old chapel, which formerly bore the name of St Columba (R 284-5, §35).

6 *Caílle Coluim.* In Laígis of Leinster. This name occurs in the midst of the Laígis genealogies, Rawlinson B 502, 127a6, *LL* 318ab, etc (= O'Brien 1962, 89; *LL* VI, line 40939).

7 *Castlecolumb.* Caisleán Chill Cholm. A townland in the parish and barony of Knocktopher, Co. Kilkenny. The place is mentioned as *Kilcolm* in a document dated 1272 (White 1943, 304). The form *Caisleán Tigh Cholaim* which occurs in the *OSNB* (sn) probably represents a misunderstanding of *Caisleán Chill Cholaim*.

8 *Cell Collumbae.* Colum of Cell Columbae (*Colum Cilli Columbae*), in the tract on the Holy Virgins of Ireland (*Comanmand naebúag Hérenn*) (*LL* 369b: VI, line 51378; Ó Riain 1985, 155, line 86).

9 *Cenél Coluim.* TCD MS H.2.7, 109a: *Cland Indercaig: Dimma mc Cairnain mc Concertaig mc M. Lasrida mc Indercaig mc Beccanaig. Da mcc m. Lasri .i. Conchertach 7 Colum, a quo Cenel Coluim* ('The family of Indercach: Dímma son of Carnán son of Conchertach son of Mac Laisre son of Indercach son of Beccánach. Two sons of Mac Laisre, i.e. Conchertach and Colum, from whom [are descended] Cenél Coluim').

10 *[Cloghmore.]* C North and South, townlands in the parish of Killannin, barony of Moycullen, Co. Galway. *Altar of St Columb-Kille* – cited in Roderick O'Flaherty's account of Iar Chonnacht, 1684 (Hardiman 1846, 63; see, too, *OSLG* III, 149, where mention is also made of 'a burial

ground called after St. Columbkille in the north-west of the townland';
cf. R 283-4, §27).

11 *[Clonmany.]* A parish in the barony of Inishowen East, Co. Donegal. St
Columba was patron (R 284, §33).

12 *Clonmore.* A parish in the barony of Ferrard, Co. Louth. Styled *Ecclesia S
Columbae de Clonmore* in the early 15th-century Register of Archbishop
Fleming (R 280-81, §11).

13 *Coenobium S Columbae de Inistiock.* The townland and parish of Inistioge,
barony of Gowran, Co. Kilkenny (R 462; G & H 179-80, 388).

14 *Collum.* A townland in the parish of Cashel, barony of Rathcline, Co.
Longford. The form of the name which occurs in the *OSNB* (sn) is
calaim, which O'Donovan rationalizes as 'callaim, bare land, q[uod] d[icitur]
caladh lom, bare callow'. (The present anglicized form occurs on
Edgeworth's Grand Jury Map of Longford of 1814: Rodger 1972, 43, no
784.) While O'Donovan's interpretation may be deemed rather unlikely, it
does at least suggest that the place-name has nothing to do with a person
called Colum. (We may note that there is also a minor place-name, Collum
Point, in the west end of this townland, close to the shore of Lough Ree.)

15 *Derrycolumb.* A townland in the parish of Cashel, barony of Rathcline,
Co. Longford. The Irish form *doire Choilm* occurs in the *OSNB* (sn).

16 *[Desertegny.]* A parish in the barony of Inishowen West, Co. Donegal. St
Columba was patron (R 284, §32).

17 *[Desertoghill.]* A parish in the barony of Coleraine, Co. Derry. St Columba
was patron (R 284, §34).

18 *Kilcolumb.* A townland in the parish of Kilmaley, barony of Islands, Co.
Clare. The earliest attestation of the name is in 1621 as *Kilcolman* (*CPR*
494), but the form *Killcolome* occurs in the Chancery Inquisitions in 1624
(2.28: unpublished), while the *OSNB* (sn) has *cill choloim*.

19 *Kilcolumb.* Cill Cholma. A townland in the parish of Ballynakill, barony of
Ballymoe, Co. Galway. The form which occurs in the late 17th-century
Book of Survey and Distribution (Mac Giolla Choille 1962, 166), *Killcollmay*,
indicates by its declension that this is an instance of *Colum* as a female
name.

20 *Kilcolumb.* A parish in the barony of Ida, Co. Kilkenny (R 283, §24).

21 *Lettercollum.* A townland in the parish of Timoleague, barony of Ibane
and Barryroe, Co. Cork. The name occurs in its present-day form in the
late 17th-century Book of Survey and Distribution (unpublished).

22 *[Mornington.]* In the parish of Colp, barony of Lower Duleek, Co. Meath.
Ecclesia S Columbae (R 284, §3).

23 *Petra Columbae.* On the Shannon, below Limerick (Heist 1965, 230, §21).

24 *Proinnteach Cruimthir Choluim.* In Co. Tyrone? (1195.2 *MIA*). See List I,
no 21.

25 *St Columba's Spring.* In the townland of Coolessan, parish of Drumachose, barony of Keenaght, Co. Derry. (Note the occurrence in the same townland of *St Canice's Graveyard.*)

26 *St Columb's Point.* In the townland of Londonderry, parish of Templemore, Co. Derry.

27 *Tech Inghean Coluim.* In Cremthanna – on the borders of Cos Louth, Meath and Monaghan. This name occurs in the *Martyrology of Gorman* at 13 September (Stokes 1895, 176) and, in Latin form, as *Domus filiarum Columbe* in a life of St Daig mac Cairill (Heist 1965, 392, §15).

28 *Tobar Naomh Choluim.* Tobar na gColumb in the parish of Kilcolumb, barony of Ida, Co. Kilkenny.

LIST IV, SCOTLAND (Map 8)

1 *[Auldearn.]* A parish in Nairn. *Church of St Columba; St Colm's Market* (R 295, §7; W 280).

2 *[Belhelvie.]* A parish near Aberdeen. St Colm its tutelary. *St Colm's Fair* (R 296, §14; W 280).

3 *[Berneray.]* An island in the parish of Harris, near North Uist. Ancient chapel named after St Columba (R 291, §11).

4 *[Burness.]* A parish in Sanday, one of the principal islands of Orkney. Formerly *St Colm's* (R 295, §1; W 280).

5 *Caer Coluim.* One of chief cities of Britain (*Inis Breatan*). The name takes this form in the copy of *Lebor Bretnach* in the Book of Uí Mhaine (*UM* 91vb20); the form in the critical edition of the text, however, is *Caer Colun* (Van Hamel 1932, 3).

6 *[Canna.]* An island to the south-west of Skye. Church dedicated to St Columbus (R 292, §16; W 280).

7 *Columbus's Church.* At Howmore in South Uist (R 292, §14; W 280).

8 *[Cortachy.]* A parish in Angus (formerly Forfarshire). *St Colm's Fair* (R 296, §16).

9 *[Cove.]* In the parish of North Knapdale in Argyllshire. A chapel of St Columba (R 294, §26); also *St Columba's Cave,* Ellary (RCAHMS 1988, 35-6).

10 *[Daviot.]* A parish in Aberdeenshire. St Columba was patron. *St Colm's Fair* (R 296, §13; W 280).

11 *[Dirlet.]* In the parish of Halkirk in Caithness. There was a chapel of St Columba at this place (R 295, §4).

12 *[Drymen.]* A parish in Lennox in west Stirlingshire. *Church of St Columba; St Colm's Fair* (R 298, §21).

13 *[Dunkeld.]* In Perthshire. Columba was patron (R 296-8, §18; W 280).

14 *[Fladda-Chuain.]* A tiny island to the north-west of the northernmost point of Skye. A chapel dedicated to St Columbus (R 290, §4).

15 *[Hoy.]* The second-largest of the Orkney Islands. *Chapel of Columkill* (R 295, §2; W 280).

16 *Inchcolm.* An island in the Firth of Forth, in Fife (R 298, §19; W 152).

17 *Kilmacolm.* A parish in Renfrewshire (R 294, §29; see also Johnston 1934, 67, 220; the name is given as *Cell Mo-Choluim* by Hogan (1910, 202), one of the sources cited being Johnston[19]). Hogan also has as a headword *Cell Maeil Choluim*, which is identified as 'Kelmalcolme, Scotland', the source cited being Theiner's *Vetera Monumenta Hibernorum et Scotorum*, 24, an[no] 1226, while W 193 cites *Kilmalcolm* and *Kilmacolme*, adding that they 'may commemorate Colum Cille or some other Colum'.

18 *[Kincardine.]* In Perthshire, on the Forth (now in Fife). *Croft land of St Colme* (R 298, §20).

19 *[Kingussie.]* A parish in Badenoch in south-east Inverness-shire. St Columba was patron (R 295, §9; W 280).

20 *Kirkcolm.* A parish in Wigtownshire, on the shores of Loch Ryan (R 294, §31; W 165).

21 *[Largs.]* In northern Ayrshire. Church dedicated to St Columba (R 294, §30).

22 *[Oronsay.]* An island partly attached to Colonsay. Church dedicated to St Columbus (R 293, §23).

23 *St Collum's in Ui.* At Eye on the north-east side of Lewis (R 291, §9; W 280).

24 *St Colm.* Name of a fountain at Tannadice, Angus (formerly Forfarshire) (R 296, §17).

25 *St Colm.* Former name of the parish of Lonmay, Aberdeenshire (R 296, §12).

26 *St Colm's.* Former name of Monycabo, or New Machar, a parish ten miles north of Aberdeen (R 296, §15).

27 *St Colm's.* A chapel at Aird, in the parish of Fordyce, Banffshire (R 295, §10).

28 *St Colm's Church.* At Garien in the parish of Stornoway in Lewis (R 291, §8).

29 *St Colm's Isle.* In Loch Erisort, in the parish of Loch, on the east side of Lewis. Here stood *St Columba's Church.* North of this was the bay called *Loch Colmkille* (List II, no 14, above) (R 291, §10; W 280).

30 *St Colm's Well.* In the parish of Alvah, Banffshire (R 296, §11).

---

19 Johnston's work first appeared in 1892; either this or the second edition of 1903 was used by Hogan. The latter also cites another source, 'Max.', but there is no key to such an abbreviation in the list of sources prefixed to the book (1910, xi-xiv).

31 *St Colomb's*. A chapel of the parish of Rothesay in Bute, Argyllshire (R 294, §28).

32 *St Columba de Petyn, Vicarage of.* In the parish of Pettie, Inverness-shire (R 295, §8; W 280).

33 *St Columba's*. An ancient chapel on Hirt, St Kilda (forty miles west of North Uist) (R 292, §15; W 280).

34 *St Columba's Burying Ground*. In the parish of Glenmoriston in Inverness-shire – about two hundred yards on the north side of Loch Ness (R 462).

35 *St Columba's Chapel*. In the parish of Caerlaverock, Dumfriesshire (R 294, §32; W 165).

36 *St Columba's Chapel*. In Skipness Castle, Argyllshire (RCAHMS 1971, 178).

37 *St Columba's Well*. On Elachnave (Eileach an Naoimh), one of the Garvellach Islands at the mouth of the Firth of Lorn (R 289-90, §2).

38 *St Columba's Well*. In the parish of Caerlaverock, Dumfriesshire (W 165).

39 *St Columba's Well*. In the parish of Cramond, Midlothian (formerly Edinburghshire). 'A mensal church ... with two altars; the one dedicated to St. Columba' (R 462; cf. W 152).

40 *St Columba's Well*. In the parish of Glenmoriston, Inverness-shire – a little more than half a mile north of Loch Ness (R 462).

41 *St Columba's Well*. In the parish of Kirkcolm in Wigtownshire – see Kirkcolm, no 20, above (W 165).

42 *St Comb's*. In the parish of Olrick in Caithness. *St Coomb's Kirk* (R 295, §3; W 280).

43 *St Com's Well*. In the parish of Birse, south of the Dee, in southern Aberdeenshire: 'a well ... in honour, probably, of the celebrated saint of Icolumkill' (R 462).

44 *[Trodda.]* A tiny island off the north of Skye. Had a chapel dedicated to St Columbus (R 291, §5).

Watson remarks (1926, 280) that Columba 'was [also] commemorated in Iceland', while in Scotland 'he was [also] the patron of Arryngrosk, now Arngask [Perthshire], and of Dollar [Clackmannanshire] ... The lands of Forglen in Aberdeenshire [*recte* Banffshire] were ... held ... by the immediate custodians of the reliquary of Columba called the Bracbennach ...'

There are some further relevant place-names to be found on John Speed's map of 'The Kingdome of Scotland' in his atlas, *The Theatre of the Empire of Great Britaine* (1611-12: see Nicolson 1988, 266-7). The most noted example is of course *Colmkil or Iona Ile*, while other instances include: *S Columban* and *S Columbanus* in northern Lewis (the second of these near *Stornwaye*), *S*

Columbanus in South Uist, *Colmekil* in or near northern Jura and *S Colme's* (?) in the Firth of Forth.

Some names closely associated with Columba, or sites of Columban churches, do not refer explicitly to the saint.

Cúil Dreimne (Cúl Drebene). The site of the battle of 561 is named by Adomnán as *Culedrebina* and *Cuil Drebene* (genitive forms: *Culedrebinae* and *Cule Drebene*, R 9 and 31 respectively); it occurs in 560.3 and 561.1, 2 *AU* as *Cuile Dreimne* (gen) and a virtually identical form occurs in the commentary to *Amra Coluim Cille* in *Lebor na hUidre* and also in the *Liber Hymnorum*, both from about the year 1100, and in the Book of Leinster from later in the same century. In the edition of the Middle Irish work known as *Agallamh na Seanórach* (O'Grady 1892) there are some references, direct and indirect, to the name, including an attempt to explain it (79.14: *cúil sibrinne .i. a ngar do dreimne*; .33-5: *fri féine ndremain ... .i. cúil dremne nó dreimféne*; .41: *carnn dreimni*). There are about half a dozen instances of the name in *BCC* (§§139, 159, 172, 176-7, 179, 182), and in conjunction with one of these is the explicit statement that the place was located between Sligo and Drumcliff (§172: *Cuil Dremhne a Connachtuib aniugh iter Sligech ocus Druimcliab*). This famous, or infamous, place was identified by Mac Airt (*AI* p 529) as the present townlands of Cooldrumman, Lower and Upper, parish of Drumcliff, barony of Carbury, Co. Sligo. This identification has been repeated in the *AA Road Book* (1963, 130) and in various popular historical works. There seems to be little basis for the equation, other than a slight coincidence in form. There is the additional difficulty that the double townland of Cooldrumman does not lie between Sligo and Drumcliff; instead, it is situated a mile or so to the north-west of the various townlands whose names include the toponym Drumcliff (see below). The earliest attestations of the townland-name do not appear to antedate the early 17th century. In documents relating to the so-called 'Strafford Inquisition', 1635, it appears as *Colladrommanoghta* (Wood-Martin 1889, 148) (= Cúil Dromann Uachtair) and *Culladrammaneghter* (ibid., 181) (= Cúil Dromann Íochtair), as *Culadruman* in the 'Census' of 1659 (Pender 1939, 597), and as *Culedroman* and *Cooldrumman* in the Hearth Money Roll for Co. Sligo, c 1663 (MacLysaght 1967, 46, 50, 58, 65, 68).

Dairmag. The parish of Durrow, mainly in the barony of Ballycowan, Co. Offaly, and partly in the barony of Moycashel, Co. Westmeath; there is in the parish (in the Co. Offaly portion) a townland called Durrow Demesne. (On the foundation of this important monastery (the place-name means 'oak-plain') – perhaps c 590 – see Herbert 1988, 32-3; cf. R 276-7, §1; G & H 174-5, 317.) The name also occurs as *Dayrmag* (Heist 1965, 371, §20).

Druim Cet. This, the scene of the famous 6th-century *mórdál* or 'convention', is generally held (e.g. Hogan 1910, 359-60; R 37, n b) to be represented by Daisy Hill, a minor place-name in the townland of Mullagh, near Newtown Limavady (the well-known town of Limavady), parish of Tamlaght Finlagan, barony of Keenaght, Co. Derry. There are numerous references to the place in *BCC* (§§95, 143, 322, 330: *Druim Cet (a Cianachta Glinde Gemhin)*; 136, 142, 157, 197, 315, 316, 317, 321, 340, 350, 352: *m. Droma Cet*; 315, 333, 335: *a nDruim Ceta*; 315: *m. Droma Céta*). (For a modern discussion of the significance of the convention, see Bannerman 1974, 157-70; also Sharpe, 1995, 312-14, where it is argued that the annalistic date, given in 575.1 *AU*, may be about fifteen years too early.)

Druim Cliab. The four townlands of Drumcliff Glebe and Drumcliff North, South and West, parish of Drumcliff, barony of Carbury, Co. Sligo. The monastery is first mentioned in the annals in the early 10th century (923.1 *AU*). There is also a reference in the *Tripartite Life* of Patrick (Mulchrone 1939, 89, line 1689), a work with roots in the 9th century, but containing later accretions. There is also an attempt to explain the origin of the name – it means 'ridge of [the] baskets' - in the *Dinnshenchas* (Gwynn 1924, 8-10) (cf. R 279, §5; G & H 34-5, 349; see also *BCC* §§94, 172, 279).

Gartán. The parish of Gartan, barony of Kilmacrenan, Co. Donegal; in the parish are two townlands called respectively Gartan or Bellville and Gartan Mountain. The place is referred to on numerous occasions in *BCC* (§§44, 51-2, 54, 57-8, 108-10, 159). Sharpe remarks (1995, 9): 'Gartan ... is celebrated as the place of his birth, but this depends on a tradition that cannot be traced earlier than the Middle Irish homily in the twelfth century ... Gartan lies outside the territory ruled directly by Cenél Conaill.' The name appears to represent a diminutive of *gart*, a variant of *gort*, 'a field (of arable or pasture land)'. (See also Gwynn & Hadcock 1970, 385.)

When we look back over the names listed above, about 140 in all, of varying age and with varying degrees of documentation, it is interesting to note that they appear to be divided remarkably evenly between Ireland and Scotland. (Ireland has a slight preponderance – at a proportion of about four to three – over Scotland, and within Ireland there is, as might be expected, a heavy preponderance of names – more than four to one – in the northern half of the island.) These figures, it should be emphasized, are not quite definitive. While the principal sources – Reeves (1857), Hogan (1910), the *Townland Index* (*TI*) and the like – were searched fairly thoroughly, and other lesser sources cropped up from time to time, I feel that I am bound to have missed many other names deriving from *Colum Cille/Columba* (particularly in the microtoponymical category) which might be brought to light if one were to scour the large-scale maps of both Ireland and Scotland. For instance, I am quite convinced that there must be – at a conservative estimate – dozens of holy wells dedicated to Columba throughout Ireland and Scotland. But the kind of exhaustive search which would be needed to locate and catalogue them is a task for another occasion.

The distribution of the names from Lists I – IV is of some interest. The concentration in north and especially north-west Ulster is unsurprising, but some of the outriders – the List I names in south-west Mayo and the List III names in south Leinster and, in one instance, in south-west Cork – are quite intriguing. However, it is the Scottish distribution which is particularly striking, the List II names being confined, with one exception, to the western Highlands and Islands, while the List IV names are widely spread throughout eastern and southern Scotland, albeit with several instances also in the Western Isles and a couple in Argyll.

This article makes no pretence to being a comprehensive coverage of the multifarious reflexes of the celebrated saint of Gartan, Derry and Iona (and elsewhere) on the insular onomastic corpus, either in relation to people or to places. Such a coverage would require quite a substantial dissertation. It would indeed be gratifying if the present very preliminary, inadequate and frequently uneven survey were to inspire someone – with the requisite qualifications – to undertake such a task.[20] Another urgent desideratum is a somewhat similar survey of the onomastic legacy of those other blazing stars in the early Irish Christian firmament, Patrick and Brigid. A study of the distribution of places named from the three 'national patrons', whether these be purported foundations or simply cult-sites, should prove illuminating. Pending the completion of such studies, however, I feel it wise to refrain from drawing any firm conclusions from the evidence presented here.

ADDENDUM I
People and places named from Columba's biographer, Adomnán

It would be just as feasible to do a study similar to the foregoing of the occurrence of Adomnán's name as a component of personal names, surnames and place-names, both in Ireland and Scotland. The following is merely a brief summary of what we might find.

Personal name: Giolla Adomnáin.
As discussed by Herbert (1988, 101), Gilla Adomnáin Ua Coirthén was a

20 I am already fairly confident that the spate of conferences and publications which have been planned to mark this 'Columban Year' will give rise to some worthwhile contributions in this field.

priest of Durrow and an abbot of Kells in the early 12th century. I have (following a search which was far from exhaustive) found just one additional instance in the annals, 1328 *AFM* III (p 538), where there is record of the death of Giolla Adhamhnáin Ó Firghil, coarb of Adomnán, whom O'Donovan associates with Ráth Bhoth/Raphoe, Co. Donegal. The name, and quite possibly the very same individual, is also to be found in the Ó Firghil genealogies in Dubhaltach Mac Fhirbhisigh's great 17th-century Book of Genealogies (*Leabhar na nGenealach*, UCD Add Ir MS 14), page 152. The name occurs at least twice in the same work among the genealogies of Clann Domhnaill na hAlban, the MacDonnells/MacDonalds: page 341, Giolla Adhamhnáin mac Soloimh, the great-great-grandfather of Domhnall, eponymous ancestor of Clann Domhnaill;[21] page 345, Giolla Adhamhnáin mac Alusdrainn Óig, a great-grandson of that same Domhnall. Black (1946, 305), under the lemma *Gilleonain*, states : 'It was a favorite name in the Macdonald family, and subsequently passed into the family of Macneil of Barra.' He goes on to give numerous instances of the name from a variety of Scottish sources ranging in date from the early 13th to the late 17th century.

Surname: Mac Giolla Adhamhnáin

The only annalistic reference to the name appears to be that to Somhairle Mac Gille-Adhamhnain in *AU[1]* 1164. Woulfe (1923, 366-7) describes the name (anglicized *MacAlonan*, *MacLennan* and *MacLennan*, together with the earlier anglicization *M'Eleownan(e)*) as 'a Co. Down surname; also a Scottish surname, said to be the origin of Mac Lennan of Rosshire.' MacLysaght (1980, 5) locates the surname *Mac Alonan* in Cos Antrim and Derry, declaring that it derives 'from a famous Christian name in the diocese of Raphoe.'

Place-names: List V, Ireland (Map 9)

1 *Aireagal Adhamhnáin*. Errigal. A parish in Co. Derry whose Irish form is given by O'Donovan (*OSLL* 29) as *Airegal Ónáin*. (For further details of the cult of Adomnán in the county see *OSLL* 67, 69, 73-4.) O'Donovan also mentions a feature in the parish known as *Onan's Cap*; its Irish form, as recorded in a manuscript note by Séamus Ó Ceallaigh in the Placenames Office, Ordnance Survey, Dublin, was apparently *Carraig Adhamhnáin*.

2 *Cros Adhamhnáin*. At Tara, in the parish of Tara, barony of Skreen, Co. Meath. In the text *Dindgnai Temrach: LL* 30b: VI, line 3835 – *Adomna(i)n ... a cross ara belaib*; line 3838 – *o chroiss Adomnain*; also *BB* 188b and *UM* 143b1.

21 The name also occurs in other 17th-century genealogical compilations such as the O Clery Book of Genealogies (Pender 1951, §§301, 1698, 1706) and *Leabhar Cloinne Aodha Buidhe* (Ó Donnchadha 1931, 52).

3 *Droichead Adhamhnáin*. In the parish of Skreen, barony of Tireragh, Co. Sligo. R lxii – *Drehid Awnaun* (? = *Leic Adamhnáin*: Hennessy & Kelly 1875, 410.8; see no 7, below).

4 *Droichead Adhamhnáin*. The townland of Ballindrait, parish of Clonleigh, barony of Raphoe, Co. Donegal. Identified with *Pons Adamnani* cited in the early 17th-century *Collectanea Sacra* of the Franciscan, Patrick Fleming (1599-1631) (R lxiv; Hogan 1910, 355).

5 *Lathrach pupaill Adomnáin*. At Tara, Co. Meath (see *Cros Adhamhnáin*, no 2, above). (In the text *Dindgnai Temrach* – LL 30b: VI, line 3835.)

6 *Leaba Adhamhnáin*. In the parish and barony of Raphoe (townland of Raphoe Demesne?), Co. Donegal. (R lxii: 'St. Adomnán's bed'.)

7 *Leic Adhamhnáin*. Perhaps to be identified with *Droichead Adhamhnáin* in the parish of Skreen, barony of Tireragh, Co. Sligo – see no 3, above (Hennessy & Kelly 1875, 410.8).

8 *St Adamnán's Well*. In the townland of Templemoyle, parish of Clonca, barony of Inishowen East, Co. Donegal (Logan 1980, 102).

9 *Scrín Adhamhnáin*. The townlands of Skreen, Beg and More, parish of Skreen, barony of Tireragh, Co. Sligo. The place is first mentioned in 976 (*recte* 978) *CS*, an entry which is pretty bare of contextual detail, merely stating that *Scrín Adamnáin* had been burnt by Domnall ua Néill (the high-king); see also 1022 *AFM* II (p 802), 1030 (p 820); 1395 *AFM* IV (p 734). There is a very detailed note on the name and the place by O'Donovan (1844, 267-8, n); see also Plummer (1907, 4, cap 6): *Tulach na Maoile, risan abarthar Sccrin Adhamnain aniu*.

10 *Scrín Adhamhnáin*. At Donaghmoyne, a townland and parish in the barony of Farney, Co. Monaghan. An entry at 830 *AFM* I (p 444) records that 'the shrine of Adomnán was carried off from Domhnach-Maighen by the Foreigners [i.e. the Vikings].' The reference here is clearly to an actual shrine or reliquary rather than to a place-name.

11 *Suidhe Adhamhnáin*. At Tara, Co. Meath (south of *Cros Adhamhnáin* – see no 2, above). In the text *Dindgnai Temrach*, LL 30b: VI, line 3836 – *Adomna(i)n ... a shuide fri croiss andess*; see also *BB* 188b.

12 *Suidhe Adhamhnáin*. The townland of Syonan in the parish of Ardnurcher or Horseleap, barony of Moycashel, Co. Westmeath (R lxv; O'Donovan 1846b, 196, 197, n) – *a Suidhe Adhamnáin*.

13 *Tiobraid Adhamhnáin*. In Derry. At 1203 *AFM* III (p 134) is a record that Doire Colaim Chille was burned from Relecc Martain (the cemetery of St Martin) to *Tioprait Adhamhnain*.

14 *Tobar Adhamhnáin*. St Adomnán's well, in the townland of Toberawnaun, parish of Skreen, barony of Tireragh, Co. Sligo (R lxii).

List VI, Scotland (Map 10)

1 *Ard-Eódhnaig.* Ardeonaig. On the south side of Loch Tay, in north-eastern Stirlingshire. *Ardewnan* in 1494 (W 270).

2 *Craig Euny.* In Glen Lyon, Perthshire (Anderson 1881, 179).

3 *Croft of St Adampnan.* In Glen Urquhart, Inverness-shire, in 1556 (W 271).

4 *Crois Adhamhnáin.* In North Uist, near Dun Rosail; it is also called *Clach na h-Ulaidh*, 'stone of the grave' or 'stone of the praying-station' (W 270).

5 *Crois Adhamnáin.* Adomnán's cross, on Iona (R 427).

6 *Croit Eódhnain.* Adomnán's croft in Glenfalloch, at the southern end of Loch Lomond, Dunbartonshire (W 270).

7 *[Dalmeny.]* In West Lothian (about ten miles north-west of Edinburgh). A chapter and altar of Adomnán (W 271).

8 *[Dull.]* In Perthshire (north-east of Loch Tay). Adomnán is the patron (W 270).

9 *Fuaran Eódhrain* (for *F Eódhnain*). Near Grantully in Strath Tay, Perthshire (south of Pitlochry) (W 270).

10 *Killeonan.* Cill Eódhnain. Near Campbelltown in Kintyre, Argyllshire. *Killewnane* in 1481 (Watson 270; cf. R lxvii).

11 *Magh Eódhnain.* Adomnán's plain. Near Bridge of Balgie in Glen Lyon, Perthshire (north of Loch Tay) (W 270).

12 *Muileann Eódhnain.* Adomnán's mill. Near Bridge of Balgie in Glen Lyon, Perthshire (north of Loch Tay) (W 270).

13 *Rowardennan.* On the eastern shore of Loch Lomond, Stirlingshire. It probably means 'point of Adomnán's cape' (?*Rubha Aird Eódhnain*) (W 270).

14 *St Adamnán's Acre.* In Campsie, southern Stirlingshire (W 271).

15 *St Adamnán's Chapel.* At Furvie (Forvie), Aberdeenshire (W 271).

16 *St Eunan's Tree; St Eunan's Well.* In Aboyne, Aberdeenshire (W 271).

17 *Sanct Eunendi's Seit* (now *St Arnold's Seat*). In the parish of Tannadice, Angus (formerly Forfarshire) (W 271) .

18 *[Sanda Island.]* Just off the south-east coast of the Mull of Kintyre, Argyllshire – 'a cell and sanctuary of St. Adamnan' (W 270).

19 *Teunan Kirk* (*Saunct Eunan's Kirk*). The former name of the church of Forglen in Banffshire (W 270).

20 *Tobar Eonan.* In Glen Lyon, Perthshire (Anderson 1881, 179).

21 *Tom Eódhnain.* At the church of Insh in Badenoch, south-east Inverness-shire (W 271).

The distribution of the names in the foregoing lists calls for comment. In Ireland they are principally concentrated in north-east Donegal and nearby

Derry, at Skreen, Co. Sligo, and at Tara, Co. Meath, with outriders in south Monaghan and Westmeath. The Scottish pattern is particularly noteworthy, the names being largely concentrated in the Grampian region, the ancient Druim Alban. Why this should be deserves consideration but is a matter which will have to be dealt with elsewhere.

ADDENDUM II
Instances of Mo-Cholmóg

Watson, in his great study (1926, 279), deals with a selection of names involving the personal name *Mo-Cholmóg*, which (as has been mentioned above) is a hypocoristic form of *Colum*. He lists the following:

Cill Mo-Chalmáig. Kilmachalmaig in Bute.
Cill Mo-Chalmáig. Kilmachalmaig, on the Kyle of Sutherland.
Féill Mo-Chalmáig. A fair of this name was held at Moulin in Perthshire.
Innis Mo-Cholmáig. Inchmahome, in the Lake of Menteith, Stirlingshire.
Port Mo-Cholmáig. Portmahomack, near Tain, Easter Ross (Johnston 1934, 227).

Johnston (1934, 277) also has mention of *Kilmachalmag* in Kincardineshire. In addition, we may note *Tech Mo-Cholmócc*, which is the medieval form of a place-name which would now be rendered *Steach Cholmóg* in Irish. It is the name of a townland and parish-name in the barony of Lower Kells, in north Co. Meath, Staholmog (see *LL* 367c and 368c: VI, lines 50971 and 51200-1 respectively).

ACKNOWLEDGEMENTS

I wish to record my sincere gratitude to my former colleagues in the Placenames Branch, Ordnance Survey, Phoenix Park, Dublin, for granting me access to the fruits of their researches on several of the place-names listed here; I am also grateful to my colleagues of the Northern Ireland Place-Name Project, based in the Celtic Department, Queen's University, for furnishing me with the results of their work on some of the Ulster place-names treated of above. I wish to thank the Editor for his meticulous reading and checking of this article, for providing a number of references and for saving me from numerous errors and oversights. Needless to remark, I alone am responsible for whatever shortcomings remain. Another person to whom I am most deeply indebted (as will be clear to anyone who even glances through the gazetteer of names) is the long-dead scholar and clergyman, William Reeves, on whose astoundingly rich edition of Adomnán's *Vita Columbae* I have drawn again and again. It is truly one of those books which will endure.

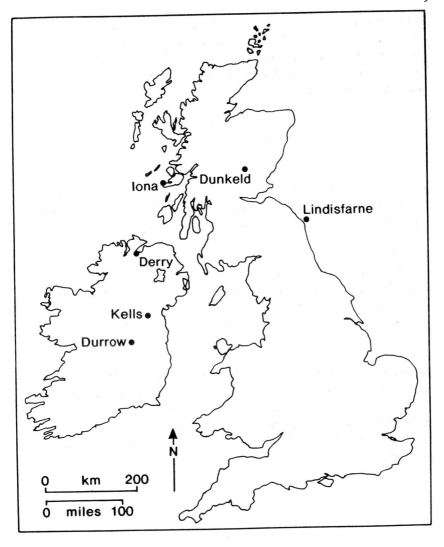

Map 1 Focal points of Columban geography.

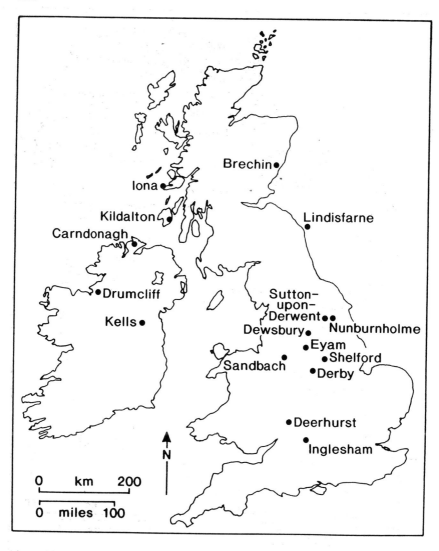

Map 2 Virgin and Child iconography: relevant places.

Map 3 *Insignia Columbae*: relevant places in Ireland.

222

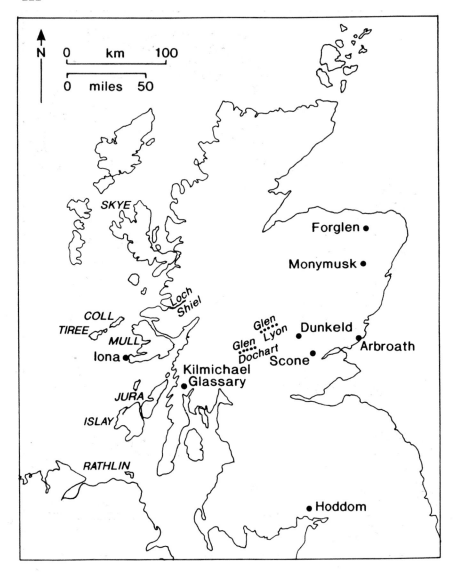

Map 4 *Insignia Columbae*: relevant places in Scotland.

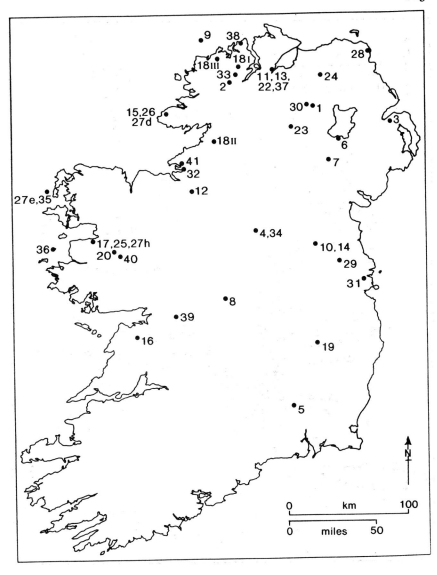

Map 5 *Colum Cille* in Irish place-names (List I).

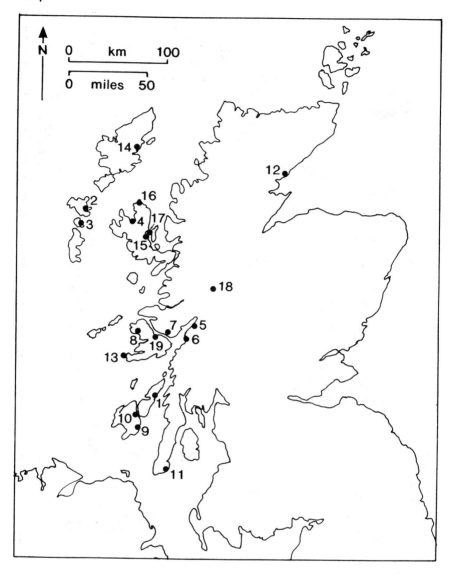

Map 6 *Colum Cille* in Scottish place-names (List II).

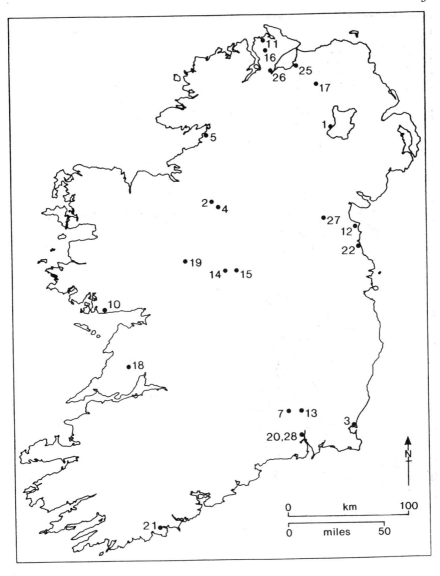

Map 7 *Colum* in Irish place-names (List III).

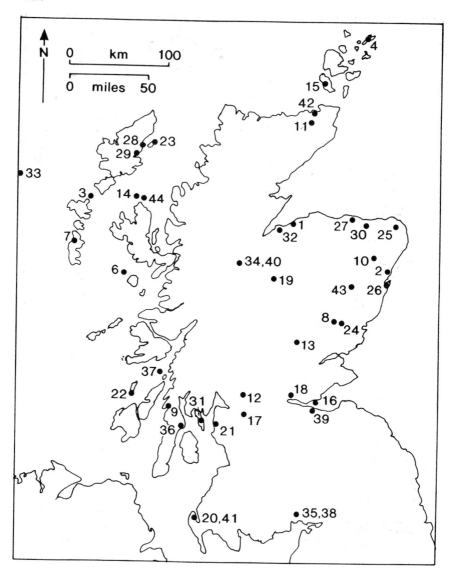

Map 8 *Colum* in Scottish place-names (List IV).

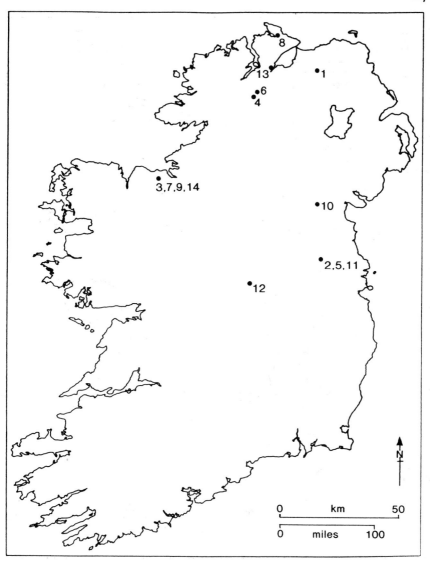

Map 9 *Adomnán* in Irish place-names (List V).

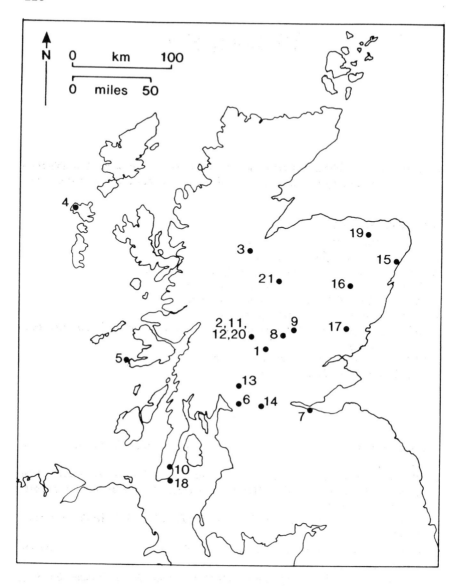

Map 10 *Adomnán* in Scottish place-names (List VI).

Bibliography

References in the Bibliography are divided into two sections: those cited by abbreviation and those cited by surname; the following abbreviations are used within references

BAR British Archaeological Reports
CMCS Cambridge Medieval Celtic Studies
DIAS Dublin Institute for Advanced Studies
JRSAI Journal of the Royal Society of Antiquaries of Ireland
PRIA Proceedings of the Royal Irish Academy
PSAS Proceedings of the Society of Antiquaries of Scotland
RSAI Royal Society of Antiquaries of Ireland
TDGNHAS Transactions of the Dumfriesshire and Galloway Natural History and Antiquarian Society
UJA Ulster Journal of Archaeology (3rd series)
ZCP Zeitschrift für celtische Philologie

SECTION I

AA Road Book = The Automobile Association 1963 *Illustrated Road Book of Ireland.* Dublin

AFM = O'Donovan, J (ed & trans) 1856 *Annala Rioghachta Eireann, Annals of the Kingdom of Ireland by the Four Masters, From the Earliest Period to the Year 1616,* 7 vols (2nd edn). Dublin.

AI = Mac Airt, S (ed & trans) 1951 *The Annals of Inisfallen (MS. Rawlinson B.503).* Dublin.

ALC = Hennessy, W M (ed & trans) 1871 *The Annals of Loch Cé,* 2 vols. London (repr Dublin 1939).

ATig = Stokes, W (ed & trans) The Annals of Tigernach. *Revue Celtique* 16 (1895), 374-419; 17 (1896), 6-33, 119-263, 337-420; 18 (1897), 9-59, 150-97, 267-303, 374-90 (repr in 2 vols, Felinfach 1993).

AU = Mac Airt, S & Mac Niocaill, G (eds & trans) 1983 *The Annals of Ulster (to A.D. 1131).* Dublin.

AU¹ = Mac Carthy, B (ed & trans) 1893-95 *Annala Uladh, Annals of Ulster,* vols II-III. Dublin.

BAAS 1852 = British Association for the Advancement of Science *Descriptive Catalogue of the Collection of Antiquities ... Exhibited in the Museum, Belfast.* Belfast.

BAd = Herbert, M & Ó Riain, P (eds & trans) 1988 *Betha Adamnáin: The Irish Life of Adamnán (Irish Texts Soc 54).* London.

BB = Atkinson, R 1887 *The Book of Ballymote* (facsimile edn). Dublin.

BCC = O'Kelleher, A & Schoepperle, G (eds & trans) 1918 *Betha Colaim Chille, Life of Columba, Compiled by Maghnas Ó Domhnaill in 1532*. Chicago (repr Dublin 1994).

CCSL = *Corpus Christianorum, Series Latina*, 1953-. Turnhout.

CE = Herbermann, C G, Pace, E A, Pallen, C B, Shahan, T J & Wynne, J J (eds) 1910 *The Catholic Encyclopedia*, vol 7. New York.

CPR = Griffith, M C (ed) 1966 *Calendar of the Irish Patent Rolls* [of James I]. Dublin.

CS = Hennessy, W M (ed & trans) 1866 *Chronicum Scotorum. A Chronicle of Irish Affairs, from the Earliest Times to A.D. 1135*. London.

CSEL = *Corpus Scriptorum Ecclesiasticorum Latinorum*. 1866-. Vienna.

DACL = Cabrol, F & Leclercq, H (eds) 1948 *Dictionnaire d'Archéologie Chrétienne et de Liturgie*, vol 14, 2. Paris.

DDA [*De Diversis Artibus*] = Hawthorne, J G & Smith C S (trans) 1979 *Theophilus, On Divers Arts*. New York.

DIL = Royal Irish Academy 1983 *Dictionary of the Irish Language* (compact edn). Dublin.

DLS = Meehan, D (ed & trans) 1958 *Adamnan's De Locis Sanctis* (*Scriptores Latini Hiberniae* 3). Dublin.

FAI = Radner, J N (ed & trans) 1978 *Fragmentary Annals of Ireland*. Dublin.

FGB = Dinneen, P S (ed) 1927 *Foclóir Gaedhilge agus Béarla, An Irish-English Dictionary*. Dublin (repr 1970).

Fiants = Anon (ed) 1875-90 *The Irish Fiants of the Tudor Sovereigns*, I-IV. Dublin (repr 1994).

GMIL = Du Cange, C 1886 *Glossarium Mediae et Infimae Latinitatis*. Paris.

HE = *Historia Ecclesiastica Gentis Anglorum*: see Colgrave & Mynors 1969; McClure & Collins 1994; Sherley-Price 1955.

ILCC = Herbert, M 1988 Edition [and translation] of the Irish life of Colum Cille. In Herbert 1988, 211-86.

LC = Colgrave, B (ed & trans) 1940 *Two Lives of Saint Cuthbert*. Cambridge.

LDO = Lewis, C T & Short, C 1966 *A Latin Dictionary*. Oxford.

LL [*Leabhar Laighneach*] = Best, R I, Bergin, O, O'Brien, M A & O'Sullivan, A (eds) 1954-83 *The Book of Leinster, Formerly Lebar na Núachongbála*, 6 vols. Dublin.

LU = Best, R I & Bergin, O J (eds) 1929 *Lebor na hUidre, Book of the Dun Cow*. Dublin.

MIA = Ó hInnse, S (ed & trans) 1947 *Miscellaneous Irish Annals (A.D. 1114-1437)*. Dublin.

MLLM = Niermeyer, J F 1954 *Mediae Latinitatis Lexicon Minus*. Leiden.

NCE = Catholic University of America 1967 *New Catholic Encyclopaedia*, vol 12. New York.

OSLD = *Ordnance Survey Letters ... Co Donegal* (1835). Typed copies. 1926. Bray.

OSLF = *Ordnance Survey Letters ... Co Fermanagh* (1834-5). Typed copies. 1926. Bray.

OSLG = *Ordnance Survey Letters ... Co Galway*, 3 vols (1838-9). Typed copies. 1927. Bray.

OSLL = *Ordnance Survey Letters ... Co Londonderry* (1834). Typed copies. 1926. Bray.

OSLM = *Ordnance Survey Letters ... Co Mayo*, 2 vols (1838). Typed copies. 1926.
Bray.

OSM = Day, A & McWilliams, P (eds) 1995 *Ordnance Survey Memoirs of Ireland*, vol 31, *Parishes of County Londonderry* XI, *1821, 1833, 1836-7, South Londonderry*. Belfast.

OSNB = *Ordnance Survey Name Books*. MSS in Ordnance Survey Office, Dublin.

PL = Migne, J-P (ed) 1844-64 *Patrologiae Cursus Completus, Series Latina*, 221 vols. Paris.

RCAHMS 1971 = The Royal Commission on the Ancient and Historical Monuments of Scotland, *Argyll, An Inventory of the Ancient Monuments*, vol 1, *Kintyre*. Edinburgh.

RCAHMS 1982 = The Royal Commission on the Ancient and Historical Monuments of Scotland, *Argyll, An Inventory of the Monuments*, vol 4, *Iona*. Edinburgh.

RCAHMS 1984 = The Royal Commission on the Ancient and Historical Monuments of Scotland, *Argyll, An Inventory of the Monuments*, vol 5, *Islay, Jura, Colonsay & Oronsay*. Edinburgh.

RCAHMS 1988 = The Royal Commission on the Ancient and Historical Monuments of Scotland, *Argyll, An Inventory of the Monuments*, vol 6, *Mid Argyll and Cowal*. Edinburgh.

TI = General Register Office 1877 *Census of Ireland, 1871. Alphabetical Index to the Townlands and Towns of Ireland*. Dublin.

UM = Macalister, R A S 1942 *The Book of Uí Maine* (facsimile edn). Dublin.

VC = *Vita Columbae*: see Anderson & Anderson 1961; Anderson 1991; Fowler 1894; 1895; Gregory 1995; Reeves 1857; 1874; Sharpe 1995.

SECTION II

Alexander, J J G 1978 *Insular Manuscripts 6th to the 9th Century* (*A Survey of Manuscripts Illuminated in the British Isles* 1). London.

— 1990 The illumination. In Fox, P (ed) *The Book of Kells, MS 58, Trinity College Library Dublin: Commentary*, 265-305. Lucerne.

Allen, J R & Anderson, J 1903 *The Early Christian Monuments of Scotland*, 3 parts. Edinburgh (repr with an Introduction by I Henderson, 2 vols, Balgavies, 1993).

Anderson, A O 1922 *Early Sources of Scottish History, A.D. 500 to 1286*, 2 vols. Edinburgh/London.

— & Anderson, M O (eds & trans) 1961 *Adomnan's Life of Columba*. Edinburgh/London.

Anderson, J 1881 *Scotland in Early Christian Times*. Edinburgh.

Anderson, M O 1973 *Kings and Kingship in Early Scotland*. Edinburgh.

— 1982 Dalriada and the creation of the kingdom of the Scots. In Whitelock, D et al 1982, 106-32.

— (ed & trans) 1991 *Adomnán's Life of Columba* (rev edn). Oxford.

Armstrong, E C R 1909 Note on a bronze ring-pin. *JRSAI* 39 (1909), 297.

— 1916 Appendix I. The shrine of the Cathach. In Lawlor 1916, 390-96.

— 1922 Irish bronze pins of the Christian period. *Archaeologia* 72 (1922), 71-86.

Atkinson, N 1994 *The Coming of Christianity to Angus* (*Book of the Society of Friends of Brechin Cathedral* 43). Brechin.

Backes, M & Dölling, R 1969 *Art of the Dark Ages*. New York.

Backhouse, J, Turner, D H & Webster, L (eds) 1984 *The Golden Age of Anglo-Saxon Art, 966-1066*. London.

Bailey, R N 1978a *The Durham Cassiodorus (Jarrow Lecture)*. Jarrow.

— 1978b The chronology of Viking age sculpture in Northumbria. In Lang 1978a, 173-204.

— 1996 *England's Earliest Sculptors*. Toronto.

— & Cramp, R 1988 *Corpus of Anglo-Saxon Stone Sculpture*, vol II, *Cumberland, Westmorland and Lancashire-North-of-the-Sands*. Oxford.

Balaam, N 1981 The vallum. In Reece 1981, 5-14.

Bannerman, J 1974 *Studies in the History of Dalriada*. Edinburgh.

— 1989 The king's poet and the inauguration of Alexander III. *Scottish Historical Review* 68, 2 (1989), 120-49.

— 1993 *Comarba Coluim Chille* and the relics of Columba. *Innes Review* 44, 1 (1993), 14-47.

Barber, J 1981a Excavations on Iona, 1979. *PSAS* 111 (1981), 282-380.

— 1981b Some observations on early Christian footwear. *J Cork Historical & Archaeological Society* 86 (1981), 103-6.

Battiscombe, C F 1956a Introduction. In Battiscombe 1956b, 1-98.

— (ed) 1956b *The Relics of Saint Cuthbert*. Oxford.

Baumgarten, R 1984 The geographical orientation of Ireland in Isidore and Orosius. *Peritia* 3 (1984), 189-203.

Bell, J n.d. MS Notebook. Glasgow University Library Farmer Coll 332 (National Library of Ireland MS 2781 (photocopy)).

Belting, H 1994 *Likeness and Presence: A History of the Image Before the Era of Art*. Chicago.

Bergman, R P 1990 The earliest Eleousa: a Coptic ivory in the Walters Art Gallery. *J Walters Art Gallery* 48 (1990), 37-56.

Bernard, J H & Atkinson R (eds & trans) 1898 *The Irish Liber Hymnorum*, 2 vols (*Henry Bradshaw Soc* 13-14). London.

Best, R I 1927 The birth of Brandub son of Eochaid and of Aedan son of Gabran. In [Loomis, R S] (ed) *Medieval Studies in Memory of Gertrude Schoepperle Loomis*, 381-90. Paris/New York.

— & Lawlor, H C (eds & trans) 1931 *The Martyrology of Tallaght* (*Henry Bradshaw Soc* 68). London.

Betham, W 1826 *Irish Antiquarian Researches*, part I. Dublin.

Betten, F S 1918 St. Boniface and the doctrine of the Antipodes. *American Catholic Quarterly Review* 43 (1918), 654-63.

— 1923 Knowledge of the sphericity of the earth during the earlier middle ages. *Catholic Historical Review* 3 (1923), 74-90.

Bhreathnach, E 1996 The documentary evidence for pre-Norman Skreen, County Meath. *Riocht na Midhe* 9, 2 (1996), 37-45.

Bieler, L (ed & trans) 1963 *The Irish Penitentials* (*Scriptores Latini Hiberniae* 5). Dublin.

— (ed & trans) 1979 *The Patrician Texts in the Book of Armagh* (*Scriptores Latini Hiberniae* 10). Dublin.

Binchy, D A (ed & trans) 1938 Bretha Crólige. *Ériu* 12 (1938), 1-77.

Black, G F 1946 *The Surnames of Scotland: Their Origin, Meaning and History*. New York.

Bohncke, S 1981 The pollen diagram from Ditch 1. In Barber 1981a, 346-8.

Bonner, G, Rollason, D & Stancliffe, C (eds) 1939 *St Cuthbert, His Cult and His Community to AD 1200*. Woodbridge (repr 1995).

Borsje, J 1996 *From Chaos to Enemy: Encounters with Monsters in Early Irish Texts*. Turnhout.

— & Ó Cróinín, D 1995 A monster in the Indian Ocean. *Nederlands Theologisch Tijdschrift* 49 (1995), 1-11.

Bourke, C 1980 Early Irish hand-bells. *JRSAI* 110 (1980), 52-66.

— 1983 The hand-bells of the early Scottish church. *PSAS* 113 (1983), 464-8.

— 1985 A crozier and bell from Inishmurray and their place in ninth-century Irish archaeology. *PRIA* 85C (1985), 145-68.

— 1993 *Patrick, The Archaeology of a Saint*. Belfast.

— (ed) 1995 *From the Isles of the North, Early Medieval Art in Ireland and Britain*. Belfast.

Bradley, J 1982 'Medieval' Samian ware - a medicinal suggestion. *UJA* 44-45 (1981-82), 196-7.

— 1993 Moynagh Lough: an Insular workshop of the second quarter of the 8th century. In Spearman & Higgitt 1993, 74-81.

Bramwell, D 1981 Report on bones of birds. In Reece 1981, 45-6.

Braun, J 1932 *Das christliche Altargerät*. Munich.

Brewer, J N 1826 *The Beauties of Ireland: being Original Delineations, Topographical, Historical, and Biographical, of each County*, vol II. London.

Brown, C G & Harper A E T 1984 Excavations on Cathedral Hill, Armagh, 1968. *UJA* 47 (1984), 109-161.

Brown, M P 1994 Echoes: the Book of Kells and southern English manuscript production. In O'Mahony 1994, 333-43.

Bruce, J C 1880 *A Descriptive Catalogue of Antiquities, Chiefly British, at Alnwick Castle*. Newcastle upon Tyne.

Brüning, G 1917 Adamnans Vita Columbae und ihre Ableitungen. *ZCP* 11 (1917), 213-304.

Calvert, J A 1978 *The Early Development of Irish High Crosses and their Relationship to Scottish Sculpture in the Ninth and Tenth Centuries*. Ph D thesis, University of California at Berkeley (publ Ann Arbor 1983).

Campbell, E 1996 Trade in the Dark-Age West; a peripheral activity. In Crawford, B E (ed) *Scotland in Dark Age Britain*, 79-91. Aberdeen.

Campbell, M & Sandeman, M L S 1962 Mid Argyll: a field survey of the historic and prehistoric monuments. *PSAS* 95 (1961-62), 1-125.

Carey, J 1989 Ireland and the Antipodes: the heterodoxy of Virgil of Salzburg. *Speculum* 64 (1989), 1-10.

Carney, J. 1961 *The Problem of St. Patrick*. Dublin.

— (ed & trans) 1964 *The Poems of Blathmac Son of Cú Brettan* (*Irish Texts Soc* 47). Dublin (repr 1989).

— 1983 'A maccucáin, sruith in tiag'. *Celtica* 15 (1983), 25-41.

Carter, S 1993 Report on the micromorphology of the buried peat from area 4. In McCormick 1993, 91-2.

Chadwick, O 1968 *John Cassian*. Cambridge.

Child, H (ed) 1985 *The Calligrapher's Handbook*. London.

Clancy, T O & Márkus, G (eds & trans) 1995 *Iona, The Earliest Poetry of a Celtic Monastery*. Edinburgh.

Clayton, M 1990 *The Cult of the Virgin Mary in Anglo-Saxon England*. Cambridge.

Cochrane, R 1891 The Clonmacnois brooch. *JRSAI* 21 (1890-91), 318-9.

Colgrave, B 1940 = *LC*

— (ed & trans) 1927 *The Life of Bishop Wilfrid by Eddius Stephanus*. Cambridge.

Colgrave, B & Mynors, R A B (eds & trans) 1969 *Bede's Ecclesiastical History of the English People*. Oxford (repr 1991).

Conneely, D 1993 *St Patrick's Letters, A Study of their Theological Dimension*. Maynooth.

Coy, J & Hamilton-Dyer, S 1993 The bird and fish bone. In McCormick 1993, 100-101.

Cramp, R 1974 Tradition and innovation in English stone sculpture of the tenth to the eleventh centuries. *Kolloquium über spätantike und frühmittelalterliche Skulptur, Heidelberg 1972*, 139-48. Mainz.

— 1977 Schools of Mercian sculpture. In Dornier, A (ed) *Mercian Studies*, 191-231. Leicester.

— 1984 *Corpus of Anglo-Saxon Stone Sculpture*, vol I, 2 parts, *County Durham and Northumberland*. Oxford.

Crawford, H S 1923 A descriptive list of Irish shrines and reliquaries, part I. *JRSAI* 53 (1923), 74-93.

Crosthwaite, J C (ed) 1844 *The Book of Obits and Martyrology of the Cathedral Church of the Holy Trinity, commonly called Christ Church, Dublin*. Dublin.

Cubitt, C 1990 *Anglo-Saxon Church Councils c.650-c.850*. Unpublished Ph D thesis, University of Cambridge.

Curle, C 1940 The chronology of the early Christian monuments of Scotland. *PSAS* 74 (1939-40), 60-116.

Cutler, A 1987 The cult of the Galaktotrophousa in Byzantium and Italy. *Jahrbuch der österreichischen Byzantinistik* 37 (1987), 335-50.

Daniélou, J 1956 *The Bible and the Liturgy*. Notre Dame.

Day, J 1985 *God's Conflict with the Dragon and the Sea*. Cambridge.

— 1992 Leviathan. In Freedman 1992, vol 4, 295-6.

De Fleury, C R 1889 *La Messe, Études Archéologiques sur ses Monuments*, vol VIII. Paris.

De hÓir, É 1968 As cartlann na logainmneacha: Moone. *Dinnseanchas* 3, 2 (1968), 55-7.

— 1975 Sracfhéachaint ar logainmneacha Bhaile Átha Cliath. *Studia Hibernica* 15 (1975), 128-42.

De Paor, L 1993 *St Patrick's World, The Christian Culture of Ireland's Apostolic Age*. Blackrock.

Deshman, R 1989 Servants of the mother of God in Byzantine and medieval art. *Word and Image* 5, 1 (1989), 33-70.

Dillon, M 1946 *The Cycles of the Kings*. Oxford.

Dobbs, M E 1938 The origin of the surname 'Mulholland'. *UJA* 1 (1938), 115-17.

Doherty, C 1980 Exchange and trade in early medieval Ireland. *JRSAI* 110 (1980), 67-89.

— 1982 Some aspects of hagiography as a source for Irish economic history. *Peritia* 1 (1982), 300-28.

— 1987 The Irish hagiographer: resources, aims, results. In Dunne, T (ed) *The*

Writer as Witness: Literature as Historical Evidence (Historical Studies 16), 10-22. Cork.

Dore, J N 1992 Pottery. In McCormick, F Early Christian metalworking on Iona: excavations under the 'infirmary' in 1990. *PSAS* 122 (1992), 211-12.

Dunbar, J G & Fisher, I 1995 *Iona, A Guide to the Monuments.* Edinburgh.

Duncan, A A M 1981 Bede, Iona, and the Picts. In Davis, R H C & Wallace-Hadrill, J M (eds) *The Writing of History in the Middle Ages: Essays Presented to Richard William Southern,* 1-42. Oxford.

Dynes, W 1981 Imago leonis. *Gesta* 20, 1 (1981), 35-41.

Earwood, C 1993 *Domestic Wooden Artefacts in Britain and Ireland from Neolithic to Viking Times.* Exeter.

Eberle, L (trans) 1977 *The Rule of the Master.* Kalamazoo.

Edwards, N 1990 *The Archaeology of Early Medieval Ireland.* London.

Enright, M J 1985 Royal succession and abbatial prerogative in Adomnán's Vita Columbae. *Peritia* 4 (1985), 83-103.

Erichsen, J & Brockhoff, E (eds) 1989 *Kilian, Mönch aus Irland - aller Franken Patron, 689-1989. Katalog der Sonder-Ausstellung zur 1300-Jahr-Feier des Kiliansmartyriums, 1. Juli 1989 - 1. Oktober 1989.* Würzburg.

Fairbrother, A D 1981 Macro plant samples from Ditch 1. In Barber 1981a, 370-75.

Fanning, T 1981 Excavation of an early Christian cemetery and settlement at Reask, County Kerry. *PRIA* 81C (1981), 67-172.

Fisher, I 1994 The monastery of Iona in the eighth century. In O'Mahony 1994, 33-47.

Flanagan, D 1982 A summary guide to the more commonly attested ecclesiastical elements in place-names. *Bulletin of the Ulster Place-Name Society* 2nd ser, 4 (1981-82), 69-75.

— 1982 Béal Feirste agus áitainmneacha laistigh. In Mac Aodha, B S (ed) *Topothesia: Aistí in Onóir T. S. Ó Máille,* 45-64. Galway.

— & Flanagan, L 1994 *Irish Place Names.* Dublin.

Flint, V I J 1984 Monsters and the Antipodes in the early middle ages and the Enlightenment. *Viator* 15 (1984), 65-80.

Fontaine, J (trans) 1960 *Isidore de Seville: Traité de la Nature.* Bordeaux.

Forbes, A P (ed & trans) 1874 *Lives of S. Ninian and S. Kentigern (The Historians of Scotland* 5). Edinburgh (repr Felinfach 1989).

Fowler, E & Fowler P J 1988 Excavations on Tòrr an Aba, Iona, Argyll. *PSAS* 118 (1988), 181-201.

Fowler, J T (ed) 1894 *Adamnani Vita S. Columbae.* Oxford.

— (trans) 1895 *Adamnani Vita S. Columbae. Prophesies, Miracles and Visions of St. Columba.* London.

Freedman, D N (ed) 1992 *The Anchor Bible Dictionary,* 6 vols. New York.

Fry, T (ed) 1981 *The Rule of St Benedict.* Collegeville.

Fuchs, R & Oltrogge, D 1994 Colour material and painting technique in the Book of Kells. In O'Mahony 1994, 133-71.

Gaborit-Chopin, D (ed) 1978 *Elfenbeinkunst im Mittelalter.* Berlin.

— 1991 *Le Trésor de Saint-Denis.* Paris.

Gibson, E (trans) 1894 The works of John Cassian, the *Institutes* and *Conferences.* In Schaff, P & Wace H (eds) *Nicene and Post-Nicene Fathers,* 2nd ser, vol 11, 161-641. Oxford (repr Grand Rapids 1978).

Graham-Campbell, J 1981 The bell and the mould. In Reece 1981, 23-5.

Granger-Taylor, H 1989 The weft-patterned silks and their braid: the remains of an Anglo-Saxon dalmatic of c. 800? In Bonner et al 1989, 303-27.

Grant, R M (trans) 1997 *Irenaeus of Lyons*. London.

Gregory, J (trans) 1995 [Life of Columba]. In Marsden, J *The Illustrated Life of Columba*, 69-121, 133-81, 191-219. Edinburgh.

Grether, H G 1992 Abyss. In Freedman 1992, vol 1, 49.

Grimal, P 1986 Oceanus. In Maxwell-Hyslop, E T (ed) *The Dictionary of Classical Mythology*, 315. Oxford.

Gwynn, A & Hadcock, R N 1970 *Medieval Religious Houses, Ireland*. London (repr Blackrock 1988).

Gwynn, E (ed & trans) 1924 *The Metrical Dindshenchas*, part IV. Dublin (repr 1991).

—— & Purton, W J 1912 The Monastery of Tallaght. *PRIA* 29C (1911-12), 115-79.

Haggarty, A M 1988 Iona: some results from recent work. *PSAS* 118 (1988), 203-13.

Hamlin, A 1977 A recently discovered enclosure at Inch Abbey, County Down. *UJA* 40 (1977), 85-8.

Harbison, P 1992 *The High Crosses of Ireland, An Iconographical and Photographic Survey*, 3 vols (*Römisch-Germanisches Zentralmuseum Forschungsinstitut für Vor- und Frühgeschichte, Monographien*, 17). Bonn.

Hardiman, J 1846 *A Chorographical Description of West or H-Iar Connaught, Written A.D. 1684 by Roderic O'Flaherty, Esq.* Dublin.

Hawkes, J 1989 *The Non-Crucifixion Iconography of Pre-Viking Sculpture in the North of England*. Unpublished Ph D thesis, 2 vols, University of Newcastle upon Tyne.

—— 1995a A question of judgement: the iconic programme at Sandbach, Cheshire. In Bourke 1995, 213-19.

—— 1995b The Wirksworth slab: an iconography of humilitas. *Peritia* 9 (1995), 246-89.

—— forthcoming. Programmes of salvation: the iconography of the Iona crosses.

Heine, R (trans) 1982 *Origen. Homilies on Genesis and Exodus*. Washington DC.

Heist, W W (ed) 1965 *Vitae Sanctorum Hiberniae, Ex Codice olim Salmanticensi nunc Bruxellensi*. Brussels.

Hencken, H 1950 Lagore crannog: an Irish royal residence of the 7th to 10th centuries A.D. *PRIA* 53C (1950), 1-247.

Henderson, G 1987 *From Durrow to Kells, The Insular Gospel-books 650-800*. London.

Henderson, I 1982 Pictish art and the Book of Kells. In Whitelock et al 1982, 79-105.

—— 1983 Review of RCAHMS 1982. *Medieval Archaeology* 27 (1982), 235-8.

—— 1986 The 'David Cycle' in Pictish art. In Higgitt 1986, 87-123.

—— 1987 The Book of Kells and the snake-boss motif on Pictish cross-slabs and the Iona crosses. In Ryan 1987, 56-65.

Hennessy, W M & Kelly, D H (eds & trans) 1875 *The Book of Fenagh*. Dublin (repr 1939 = *Irish Manuscripts Commission Reflex Facsimiles* II).

Henry, F 1965 *Irish Art in the Early Christian Period (to 800 A.D.)*. London.

—— 1967 *Irish Art during the Viking Invasions (800-1020 A.D.)*. London.

—— 1970 *Irish Art in the Romanesque Period (1020-1170 A.D.)*. London.

—— 1974 *The Book of Kells,.Reproductions from the Manuscript in Trinity College Dublin*. London/New York.

Herbert, M 1988 *Iona, Kells, and Derry, The History and Hagiography of the Monastic Familia of Columba*. Oxford (repr Blackrock 1996).

— 1989 The preface to *Amra Coluim Cille*. In Ó Corráin, D, Breatnach, L & McKone, K (eds) *Sages, Saints and Storytellers, Celtic Studies in Honour of Professor James Carney*, 67-75. Maynooth.

— & McNamara, M (eds) 1989 *Irish Biblical Apocrypha, Selected Texts in Translation*. Edinburgh.

Herity, M 1993 The forms of the tomb-shrine of the founder saint in Ireland. In Spearman & Higgitt 1993, 188-95.

Herren, M (ed & trans) 1974 *The Hisperica Famina*: I. *The A-Text* (*Pontifical Institute of Medieval Studies, Studies and Texts* 31). Toronto.

Higgins, J G 1987 *The Early Christian Cross Slabs, Pillar Stones and Related Monuments of County Galway, Ireland*, 2 vols (*BAR International Ser* 375). Oxford.

Higgitt, J (ed) 1986 *Early Medieval Sculpture in Britain and Ireland* (*BAR British Ser* 152). Oxford.

— 1989 The iconography of St Peter in Anglo-Saxon England, and St Cuthbert's coffin. In Bonner et al 1989, 267-85.

Hill, D 1981 *An Atlas of Anglo-Saxon England*. Oxford.

Hillgarth, J N 1984 Ireland and Spain in the seventh century. *Peritia* 3 (1984), 1-16.

Hogan, E 1910 *Onomasticon Goedelicum*. Dublin/London.

Holmer, N M 1942 *The Irish Language in Rathlin Island, Co. Antrim*. Dublin.

Holzherr, G 1994 *The Rule of St Benedict* (Glenstal Abbey translation). Blackrock.

Home Lorimer, D 1994 Human bones. In O'Sullivan 1994b, 347-53.

Hubert, J, Porcher, J & Volbach, W F 1969 *Europe in the Dark Ages*. London.

Hughes, K 1971 Evidence for contacts between the Churches of the Irish and English from the Synod of Whitby to the Viking age. In Clemoes, P & Hughes, K (eds) *England Before the Conquest, Studies in Primary Sources Presented to Dorothy Whitelock*, 49-67. Cambridge.

Hull, V (ed & trans) 1968 Apgitir Chrábaid: the Alphabet of Piety. *Celtica* 8 (1968), 44-89.

Hurley, V 1982 The early Church in the south-west of Ireland: settlement and organisation. In Pearce, S M (ed) *The Early Church in Western Britain and Ireland* (*BAR British Ser* 102), 297-332. Oxford.

Hurst D (trans) 1990 *Forty Homilies of Gregory the Great*. Kalamazoo.

Hynes, J 1931 St Caillin. *JRSAI* 61 (1931), 39-54.

Ivens, R J 1987 The early Christian monastic enclosure at Tullylish, Co. Down. *UJA* 50 (1987), 55-121.

James, E 1982 Ireland and western Gaul in the Merovingian period. In Whitelock et al 1982, 362-86.

Jamieson, J 1890 *A Historical Account of the Ancient Culdees of Iona and their Settlements in Scotland, England and Ireland*. Glasgow.

Jancey, M 1994 *Mappa Mundi: The Map of the World in Hereford Cathedral* (rev edn). Hereford.

Jervise, A 1860 Remarks on the round tower of Brechin. *PSAS* 3 (1858-60), 28-35.

Johnston, J B 1934 *Place-Names of Scotland*. London.

Jones, A H M, Grierson, P & Crook, J A 1957 The authenticity of the *Testamentum S Remigii*. *Revue Belge de Philosophie et d'Histoire* 35 (1957), 356-73.

Jones, C W 1969 Some introductory remarks on Bede's Commentary on Genesis. *Sacris Erudiri* 19 (1969), 115-98.

Joyce, P W 1869 *Irish Names of Places*, vol 1. Dublin (repr 1995).

Joynt, M (trans) 1927 *The Life of St Gall*. London.

Kelly, D 1993 The relationships of the crosses of Argyll: the evidence of form. In Spearman & Higgitt 1993, 219-29.

— 1995 The Virgin and Child in Irish sculpture. In Bourke 1995, 197-204.

Kelly, F (ed) 1973 A poem in praise of Columb Cille. *Ériu* 24 (1973), 1-34.

Kelly, J F 1982 The Gallic resistance to Eastern asceticism. *Studia Patristica* 17 (1982), 506-10.

Kendal, A 1970 *Medieval Pilgrims*. New York.

Kenney, J 1929 *The Sources for the Early History of Ireland: Ecclesiastical, An Introduction and Guide*. New York (repr Shannon 1968).

Kessler, H L 1977 *The Illustrated Bibles from Tours*. Princeton.

Kinder-Carr, C 1978 *Aspects of the Iconography of St Peter in the Medieval Art of Western Europe to the Early Thirteenth Century*. Unpublished Ph D thesis, Case Western Reserve University.

Kitzinger, E 1956 The coffin-reliquary. In Battiscombe 1956b, 202-304.

Konstan, D 1987 Oceans. In Eliade, M (ed) *Encyclopaedia of Religion*, vol 11, 53-6. London.

Krusch, B (ed) 1902 *Passiones Vitaeque Sanctorum Aevi Merovingici* (*Monumenta Germaniae Historica, Scriptorum Rerum Merovingicarum* 4). Leipzig/Hannover.

Lambert, P-Y 1991 Le vocabulaire du scribe irlandais. In Picard, J-M (ed) *Ireland and Northern France, AD 600-850*, 157-67. Blackrock.

Lane, A & Campbell, E 1988 The pottery. In Haggarty 1988, 208-12.

Lang, J (ed) 1978a *Anglo-Saxon and Viking Age Sculpture and its Context: Papers from the Collingwood Symposium on Insular Sculpture from 800 to 1066* (*BAR British Ser* 49). Oxford.

— 1978b Continuity and innovation in Anglo-Scandinavian sculpture. In Lang 1978a, 145-72.

— 1986 Principles of design in free-style carving in the Irish Sea province: c 800 to c 950. In Higgitt 1986, 153-74.

— 1990 The painting of pre-Conquest sculpture in Northumbria. In Cather, S, Park, D & Williamson, P (eds) *Early Medieval Wall Painting and Painted Sculpture in England* (*BAR British Ser* 216), 135-46. Oxford.

— 1991 *Corpus of Anglo-Saxon Stone Sculpture*, vol III, *York and Eastern Yorkshire*. Oxford.

Lasko, P 1972 *Ars Sacra 800-1200*. Harmondsworth.

Lawlor, H C 1925 *The Monastery of Saint Mochaoi of Nendrum*. Belfast.

Lawlor, H J 1916 The Cathach of St. Columba. *PRIA* 33C (1916), 241-443.

Lazareff, V 1938 Studies in the iconography of the Virgin. *Art Bulletin* 20 (1938), 26-65.

Leask, H G 1955 *Irish Churches and Monastic Buildings*, I, *The First Phases and the Romanesque*. Dundalk (repr 1977).

Legner, A 1982 *Deutsche Kunst der Romanik*. Munich.

Lehmann, R (ed) 1964 *Fled Dúin na nGéd* (*DIAS Mediaeval & Modern Irish Ser* 21). Dublin.

Lehmann-Brockhaus, O 1955 *Lateinische Schriftquellen zur Kunst in England, Wales und Schottland vom Jahre 901 bis zum Jahre 1307*, vol 1. Munich.

— 1956 *Lateinische Schriftquellen zur Kunst in England, Wales und Schottland vom Jahre 901 bis zum Jahre 1307*, vol 2. Munich.

Leveto, P D 1990 The Marian theme of the frescos in Santa Maria at Castelseprio. *Art Bulletin* 72 (1990), 393-413.

Lewis, S 1837 *A Topographical Dictionary of Ireland*, 2 vols. London.

Lewis, T J 1992 Dead, abode of the. In Freedman 1992, vol 2, 101-5.

Lindsay, W M (ed) 1911 *Isidori Hispalensis Episcopi Etymologiarum sive Originum, Libri XX*, 2 vols. Oxford (repr 1985).

Lines, M 1992 *Sacred Stones and Sacred Places*. Edinburgh.

Logan, P 1980 *The Holy Wells of Ireland*. Gerrards Cross.

Lowe, C E, Craig, D & Dixon, D 1991 New light on the Anglian 'minster' at Hoddom. *TDGNHAS* 66 (1991), 11-35.

Luce, A A, Simms, G O, Meyer, P & Bieler, L, 1960 *Evangeliorum Quattuor Codex Durmachensis*, 2 vols. Olten/Lausanne/Freiburg i. Br.

Macalister, R A S 1909 *The Memorial Slabs of Clonmacnois, King's County* (*RSAI Extra Vol* 1907-8). Dublin.

— 1928 The cross of St. John, Iona. *Antiquity* 2 (1928), 215-17.

— 1949 *Corpus Inscriptionum Insularum Celticarum*, vol II. Dublin.

Mac Arthur, E M 1995 *Columba's Island, Iona from Past to Present*. Edinburgh.

MacBain, A 1922 *Place Names: Highlands and Islands of Scotland*. Stirling.

McCann, J (trans) 1980 *Life of Benedict* (*Dialogues* II). Manchester.

McCloskey, J 1821 Parishes of Ballynascreen, Desertmartin and Kilcronaghan, County Londonderry. In *OSM* 111-44.

McClure, J & Collins, R (eds) 1994 *The Ecclesiastical History of the English People; The Greater Chronicle; Bede's Letter to Egbert*. Oxford.

McCormick, F 1981 The animal bones from Ditch 1. In Barber 1981a, 313-18.

— 1987 *Stockrearing in early Christian Ireland*. Unpublished Ph D thesis, Queen's University of Belfast.

— 1992 Early faunal evidence for dairying. *Oxford J Archaeology* 11 (1992), 201-9.

— 1993 Excavations at Iona, 1988. *UJA* 56 (1993), 78-108.

MacDonald, A 1973 'Annat' in Scotland: a provisional review. *Scottish Studies* 17 (1973), 135-46.

— 1984 Aspects of the monastery and monastic life in Adomnán's Life of Columba. *Peritia* 3 (1984), 271-302.

— 1995 A fruit tree at Durrow. *Hallel* 20, 1 (1995), 10-14.

McGrath, F 1979 *Education in Ancient and Medieval Ireland*. Dublin.

Mackenzie, W C 1931 *Scottish Place-Names*. London.

Mac Lean, D 1985 *Early Medieval Sculpture in the West Highlands and Islands of Scotland*. Unpublished Ph D thesis, 2 vols, University of Edinburgh.

— 1986 The Keills cross in Knapdale, the Iona School and the Book of Kells. In Higgitt 1986, 175-97.

— 1991 Iona, Armenia and Italy in the early medieval period. In Zekiyan, B L (ed) *Atti del Quinto Simposio Internazionale di Arte Armena - 1988*, 559-68. Venice.

— 1993 Snake-bosses and redemption at Iona and in Pictland. In Spearman & Higgitt 1993, 245-53.

MacLysaght, E 1967 Seventeenth century Hearth Money Rolls with full transcript relating to Co. Sligo. *Analecta Hibernica* 24 (1967), 1-89.

— 1980 *The Surnames of Ireland* (5th edn). Dublin.

— 1982 *More Irish Families*. Dublin.

McNeill, C 1943 The Perrott papers. *Analecta Hibernica* 12 (1943), 3-65.

MacNeill, E 1930 The Vita Tripartita. *Ériu* 11 (1930), 1-41.

Mac Niocaill, G (ed) 1961 *Notitiae as Leabhar Cheanannais 1033-1161*. Dublin.

McRoberts, D 1961 The ecclesiastical significance of the St Ninian's Isle treasure. *PSAS* 94 (1960-61), 301-13.

Manning, C 1986 Archaeological excavation of a succession of enclosures at Millockstown, Co. Louth. *PRIA* 86C (1986), 135-81.

— 1994 *Clonmacnoise*. Dublin.

Martin, M 1703 *A Description of the Western Islands of Scotland*. London (repr Stirling 1934).

Massie, J 1898 Abyss. In Hastings, J (ed) *Dictionary of the Bible*, vol 2, 20. Edinburgh.

Meehan, B 1994 *The Book of Kells*. London.

Meehan, D 1958 = *DLS*.

Meyer, K (ed & trans) 1899 Gein Branduib maic Echach ocus Aedáin maic Gabráin inso sís. *ZCP* 2 (1899), 134-7.

Michelli, P E 1986 Four Scottish crosiers and their relation to the Irish tradition. *PSAS* 116 (1986), 375-92.

— 1996 The inscriptions on pre-Norman Irish reliquaries. *PRIA* 96C (1996), 1-48.

Mulchrone, K 1937 *The Book of Lecan, Leabhar Mór Mhic Fhir Bhisigh Leacain (Facsimiles in Collotype of Irish Manuscripts* II). Dublin.

— (ed) 1939 *Bethu Phátraic, The Tripartite Life of Patrick*. Dublin.

Müller-Lisowski, K (ed & trans) 1923 Texte zur Mog Ruith Sage. *ZCP* 14 (1923), 145-63.

Munch, G S 1987 Borg in Lofoten. A chieftain's farm in arctic Norway. In Knirk, J E (ed) *Proceedings of the Tenth Viking Congress, Larkollen, Norway, 1985* (*Universitetets Oldsaksamlings Skrifter, Ny Rekke* 9), 149-70. Oslo.

Murphy, D (ed) 1896 *The Annals of Clonmacnoise, being Annals of Ireland from the Earliest Period to A.D. 1408* (*RSAI Extra Vol* 1893-95). Dublin.

Murphy, G 1956 *Early Irish Lyrics, Eighth to Twelfth Century*. Oxford.

Nees, L 1983 The colophon drawing in the Book of Mulling: a supposed Irish monastery plan and the tradition of terminal illustration in early medieval manuscripts. *CMCS* 5 (1983), 67-91.

Nicolson, N 1988 *The Counties of Britain, A Tudor Atlas by John Speed*. London.

Ní Dhonnchadha, M 1982 The guarantor list of *Cáin Adomnáin*, 697. *Peritia* 1 (1982), 178-215.

Nieke, M 1993 Penannular and related brooches: secular ornament or symbol in action? In Spearman & Higgitt 1993, 128-34.

Noddle, B A 1974 Report on the animal bones found at Dun Mor Vaul. In MacKie, E W *Dun Mor Vaul: An Iron Age Broch on Tiree*, 187-200. Glasgow.

— 1981 A comparison of mammalian bones found in the 'midden deposit' with others from the Iron Age site of Dun Bhuirg. In Reece 1981, 38-44.

Nordhagen, P J 1962 The earliest decorations in Sta Maria Antiqua and their date. *Acta ad Archaeologiam et Artum Historiam Pertinentia* 1 (1962), 53-79.

O'Brien, M A 1962 *Corpus Genealogiarum Hiberniae*, vol I. Dublin.

— 1973 Old Irish personal names. *Celtica* 10 (1973), 211-36.

Ó Ceallaigh, S 1951 *Gleanings from Ulster History*. Cork/Dublin (repr with contributions by N Whitfield & N Ó Muraíle, Draperstown 1994).

Ó Colm, E 1971 *Toraigh na dTonn*. Dublin.

Ó Concheanainn, T 1973 The scribe of the Leabhar Breac. *Ériu* 24 (1973), 64-79.

Ó Corráin, D 1972 *Ireland Before the Normans*. Dublin.

— 1986 Brian Boru and the Battle of Clontarf. In De Paor, L (ed) *Milestones in Irish History*, 31-40. Dublin.

— 1989 Prehistoric and early Christian Ireland. In Foster, R F (ed) *The Oxford Illustrated History of Ireland*, 1-52. Oxford/New York.

— 1994 The historical and cultural background of the Book of Kells. In O'Mahony 1994, 1-32.

Ó Cróinín, D 1995 *Early Medieval Ireland 400-1200*. London/New York.

Ó Cuív, B 1986 *Aspects of Irish Personal Names*. Dublin.

Ó Donnchadha, T 1931 *Leabhar Cloinne Aodha Buidhe*. Dublin.

O'Donovan, J 1844 *The Genealogies, Tribes and Customs of Hy-Fiachrach*. Dublin.

— (ed & trans) 1846a The Irish charters in the Book of Kells. *Miscellany of the Irish Archaeological Society* 1 (1846), 127-58.

— (ed & trans) 1846b Covenant between Mageoghegan and the Fox, with brief historical notices of the two families. *Miscellany of the Irish Archaeological Society* 1 (1846), 179-197.

Ó Fiaich, T 1986 *Gaelscrínte san Eoraip*. Dublin.

Ó Floinn, R 1990 A fragmentary house-shaped shrine from Clonard, Co. Meath. *J Irish Archaeology* 5 (1989-90), 49-55.

— 1995a Sandhills, silver and shrines - fine metalwork of the medieval period from Donegal. In Nolan, W, Ronayne, L & Dunlevy, M (eds) *Donegal, History & Society*, 85-148. Dublin.

— 1995b Clonmacnoise: art and patronage in the early medieval period. In Bourke 1995, 251-60.

O'Grady, S H (ed) 1892 *Silva Gadelica*, I. London.

O' Keeffe, T 1995 The Romanesque portal at Clonfert Cathedral and its iconography. In Bourke 1995, 261-9.

O'Laverty, J 1878 *An Historical Account of the Diocese of Down and Connor, Ancient and Modern*, vol I. Dublin.

O'Loughlin, T 1992a 'Aquae super caelos' (Gen 1:6-7): the first faith-science debate. *Milltown Studies* 29 (1992), 92-114.

— 1992b Unexplored Irish influences on Eriugena. *Recherches de Théologie Ancienne et Médiévale* 59 (1993), 23-40.

— 1992c The exegetical purpose of Adomnán's *De Locis Sanctis*. *CMCS* 24 (1992), 37-53.

— 1993a The earliest world maps known in Ireland. *History Ireland* 1, 1 (1993), 7-10.

— 1993b The quincentenary of Schedel's map of the Creation: a turning point in the development of the modern mind. *Milltown Studies* 31 (1993), 30-52.

— 1994a The library of Iona in the late seventh century: the evidence from Adomnán's *De Locis Sanctis*. *Ériu* 45 (1994), 33-52.

— 1994b The Latin version of the Scriptures in Iona in the late seventh century: the evidence from Adomnán's *De Locis Sanctis*. *Peritia* 8 (1994), 18-26.

— 1995a Adomnán the Illustrious. *Innes Review* 46 (1995), 1-14.

— 1995b The waters above the heavens: Isidore and the Latin tradition. *Milltown Studies* 36 (1995), 104-17.

— 1996 'The gates of hell': from metaphor to fact. *Milltown Studies* 38 (1996), 98-114.

O'Mahony, F (ed) 1994 *The Book of Kells, Proceedings of a Conference at Trinity College Dublin, 6-9 September 1992*. Aldershot.

O'Meadhra, U 1979 *Early Christian, Viking and Romanesque Art, Motif-Pieces from Ireland* (*Theses and Papers in North-European Archaeology* 7) Stockholm/Atlantic Highlands.

O'Neill, T 1984 *The Irish Hand*. Mountrath.

— 1989 Book-making in early Christian Ireland. *Archaeology Ireland* 3, 3 (1989), 96-100.

O'Reilly, J 1987 The rough-hewn cross in Anglo-Saxon art. In Ryan 1987, 153-8.

— 1993 The Book of Kells, folio 114r: a mystery revealed yet concealed. In Spearman & Higgitt 1993, 106-14.

— 1994 Exegesis and the Book of Kells: the Lucan genealogy. In O'Mahony 1994, 344-97.

— 1995 Introduction. In Connolly, S (trans) *Bede: On the Temple*, xvii-lv. Liverpool.

Ó Riain, P 1983 Cainnech *alias* Colum Cille, patron of Ossory. In de Brún, P, Ó Coileáin, S & Ó Riain, P (eds) *Folia Gadelica*, 20-35. Cork.

— 1985 *Corpus Genealogiarum Sanctorum Hiberniae*. Dublin.

O'Sullivan, D 1989 The plan of the early Christian monastery on Lindisfarne: a fresh look at the evidence. In Bonner et al 1989, 125-42.

O'Sullivan, J 1994a Excavations beside Sruth a' Mhuilinn ('the Mill Stream'), Iona. *PSAS* 124 (1994), 491-508.

— 1994b Excavation of an early church and a women's cemetery at St Ronan's medieval parish church, Iona. *PSAS* 124 (1994), 327-65.

Pattison, I R 1973 The Nunburnholme cross and Anglo-Danish sculpture in York. *Archaeologia* 104 (1973), 209-34.

Paxton, F S 1990 *Christianising Death*. Ithaca.

Pearson, G W, Pilcher, J R, Baillie, M G L, Corbett, D M & Qua, F 1986 High-precision 14C measurement of Irish oak to show the natural 14C variation from AD 1840 - 5210 BC. In Stuiver, M & Kra, R S (eds) *International 14C Conference, 12th Proceedings* (= *Radiocarbon* 28, 2b (1986)), 911-34.

Pender, S (ed) 1939 *A 'Census' of Ireland (c. 1659)*. Dublin.

— (ed) 1951 The O Clery Book of Genealogies. *Analecta Hibernica* 18 (1951), 1-194.

Picard, J M 1982 The purpose of Adomnán's *Vita Columbae*. *Peritia* 1 (1982), 160-77.

— 1984 Bede, Adomnán, and the writing of history. *Peritia* 3 (1984), 50-70.

— 1985 Structural patterns in early Hiberno-Latin hagiography. *Peritia* 4 (1985), 67-82.

Plummer, C (ed) 1907 Betha Farannáin. From MS. Nr. 4190-4200 ff. 91v-94v, Bibliothèque Royale, Brussels. *Anecdota from Irish Manuscripts* 3, 1-7.

— (ed) 1910 *Vitae Sanctorum Hiberniae*, 2 vols. Oxford (repr 1968).

— (ed & trans) 1922 *Bethada Náem nÉrenn, Lives of Irish Saints*, 2 vols. Oxford (repr 1968).

— 1926 On the colophons and marginalia of Irish scribes. *Proceedings of the British Academy* 12 (1926), 11-44.

Price, L 1967 *The Place-Names of Co. Wicklow*, VII - *The Baronies of Newcastle and Arklow*. Dublin.

Purser, J 1992 *Scotland's Music, A History of the Traditional and Classical Music of Scotland from Earliest Times to the Present Day*. Edinburgh/London.

Radford, C A R 1942 The early Christian monuments of Scotland. *Antiquity* 16

(1942), 1-18.

— 1953 Hoddom. *TDGNHAS* 31 (1952-53), 194-7.

— 1954 Two reliquaries connected with south-west Scotland. *TDGNHAS* 32 (1953-54), 115-23.

— 1961 Pre-Conquest sculpture in Derbyshire. *Archaeological J* 118 (1961), 209-10.

— 1976 The church of St Alkmund, Derby. *Derbyshire Archaeological J* 96 (1976), 26-61.

Raftery, J (ed) 1941 *Christian Art in Ancient Ireland*, vol II. Dublin.

Raw, B 1966 The Inglesham Virgin and Child. *Wiltshire Archaeological & Natural History Magazine* 61 (1966), 43-6.

Redknap, M 1977 Excavation at Iona Abbey, 1976. *PSAS* 108 (1976-77), 228-53.

Reece, R 1981 *Excavations in Iona 1964 to 1974* (*Institute of Archaeology Occasional Publication* 5). London.

— & Wells, C 1981 Martyrs' Bay. In Reece 1981, 63-102.

Reeves, W 1847 *Ecclesiastical Antiquities of Down, Connor, and Dromore*. Dublin.

— (ed) 1857 *The Life of St. Columba, Founder of Hy*. Dublin/Edinburgh.

— (ed) 1874 *Life of Saint Columba, Founder of Hy* (*The Historians of Scotland* 6 (with translation supervised by A P Forbes and appendices compiled by W F Skene)). Edinburgh (translation repr Felinfach 1988).

Renwick, R & Lindsay, J 1921 *History of Glasgow*, vol I. Glasgow.

Reymond, P 1958 *L'Eau, Sa Vie, et Sa Signification dans L'Ancien Testament*. Leiden.

Rice, D T 1963 *Art of the Byzantine Era*. London.

Richardson, H 1993 Remarks on the liturgical fan, flabellum or rhipidion. In Spearman & Higgitt 1993, 27-34.

Ritchie, A 1989 *Picts*. Edinburgh.

Robertson, W N 1975 St John's cross, Iona, Argyll. *PSAS* 106 (1974-75), 111-23.

Rosenthal, E 1969 Some observations on Coptic influence in western early medieval manuscripts. In Lehmann-Haupt, H (ed) *Homage to a Bookman*, 51-74. Berlin.

Roth, H 1979 *Kunst der Völkerwanderungszeit* (*Propyläen Kunstgeschichte, Supplement-Band* 4). Frankfurt/Berlin/Vienna.

Routh, R E 1937 A corpus of the pre-Conquest carved stones of Derbyshire. *Archaeological J* 94 (1937), 1-42.

Ryan, J 1931 *Irish Monasticism, Origins and Early Development*. Dublin (repr 1993).

Ryan, M (ed) 1983 *Treasures of Ireland, Irish Art 3000 B.C. - 1500 A.D.* Dublin.

— (ed) 1987 *Ireland and Insular Art A.D. 500-1200*. Dublin.

— 1988 Fine metalworking and early Irish monasteries: the archaeological evidence. In Bradley, J (ed) *Settlement and Society in Medieval Ireland, Studies Presented to F. X. Martin, o. s. a.*, 33-48. Kilkenny.

— 1994 The Book of Kells and metalwork. In O'Mahony 1994, 270-79.

Rynne, C 1992 Milling in the 7th century - Europe's earliest tide mills. *Archaeology Ireland* 6, 2 (1992), 22-4.

Scaife, R G & Dimbleby, G W 1990 Landscape changes on Iona. *Bulletin of the Institute of Archaeology* 27 (1990), 25-61.

Schiller, G 1971 *Iconography of Christian Art*, vol I. London.

— 1980 *Ikonographie der christlichen Kunst*, vol IV, 2. Gütersloh.

Scott, A B & Martin, F X (eds & trans) 1978 *Expugnatio Hibernica, The Conquest of Ireland, by Giraldus Cambrensis* (*A New History of Ireland, Ancillary Publications* 3). Dublin.

Selassie, S H 1981 *Book-Making in Ethiopia*. Leiden.

Sharpe, R (trans) 1995 *Adomnán of Iona, Life of St Columba*. Harmondsworth.

Shepherd, D G 1969 An icon of the Virgin: a sixth-century tapestry panel from Egypt. *Bulletin of the Cleveland Museum of Art* 56 (1969), 90-120.

Sherley-Price, L (trans) 1955 *Bede, A History of the English Church and People*. Harmondsworth (rev edn 1990).

Shiel, R 1988 The soils. In Haggarty 1988, 207-8.

Sieger, J D 1987 Visual metaphor as theology: Leo the Great's sermon on the Incarnation and the arch mosaics at S. Maria Maggiore. *Gesta* 26, 2 (1987), 83-91.

Simington, R C (ed) 1937 *The Civil Survey*, III *(Donegal, Derry and Tyrone)*. Dublin.

Simpson, W D 1963 The early Romanesque tower at Restenneth priory, Angus. *Antiquaries J* 43 (1963), 269-83.

Smith, J A 1878 Notes on medieval 'kitchen middens' recently discovered in the monastery and the nunnery on the island of Iona. *PSAS* 12 (1876-78), 103-17.

Smith, R 1923 *British Museum, A Guide to the Anglo-Saxon and Foreign Teutonic Antiquities in the Department of British and Mediaeval Antiquities*. London.

Smyth, A P 1972 The earliest Irish annals: their first contemporary entries, and the earliest centres of recording. *PRIA* 72C (1972), 1-48.

— 1984 *Warlords and Holy Men, Scotland AD 80-1000*. London.

Smyth, M 1986 The physical world in seventh century Hiberno-Latin texts. *Peritia* 5 (1986), 201-34.

Somerville, O 1993 Kite-shaped brooches. *JRSAI* 123 (1993), 59-101.

Spearman, R M & Higgitt, J (eds) 1993 *The Age of Migrating Ideas, Early Medieval Art in Northern Britain and Ireland*. Edinburgh/Stroud.

Speiser, E A 1964 *Genesis: The Anchor Bible,* I. New York.

Stancliffe, C 1990 Irish saints' lives. In Fontaine, J & Hillgarth J N (eds) *The Seventh Century, Change and Continuity*, 87-115. London.

— 1995 Oswald, 'most holy and most victorious king of the Northumbrians'. In Stancliffe, C & Cambridge, E (eds) *Oswald, Northumbrian King to European Saint*, 33-83. Stamford.

Staniforth, M (trans) 1968 *Early Christian Writings*. Harmondsworth.

Steer, K A & Bannerman, J W M 1977 *Late Medieval Monumental Sculpture in the West Highlands*. Edinburgh.

Stevenson, J (ed) 1995 *The 'Laterculus Malalianus' and the School of Archbishop Theodore*. Cambridge.

Stevenson, R B K 1955 Pictish art. In Wainwright, F T (ed) *The Problem of the Picts*, 96-128. Edinburgh.

— 1956 The chronology and relationships of some Irish and Scottish crosses. *JRSAI* 86 (1956), 84-96.

— 1971 Sculpture in Scotland in the 6th-9th centuries AD. *Kolloquium über spätantike und frühmittelalterliche Skulptur, Universität Heidelberg, 1970*, 65-74. Mainz.

— 1974 The Hunterston brooch and its significance. *Medieval Archaeology* 18 (1974), 16-42.

— 1983 Further notes on the Hunterston and 'Tara' brooches, Monymusk reliquary and Blackness bracelet. *PSAS* 113 (1983), 469-77.

Stokes, W (ed & trans) 1887 *The Tripartite Life of Patrick, with other Documents relating to that Saint*, 2 vols. London.

— (ed & trans) 1895 *Félire Húi Gormáin, The Martyrology of Gorman (Henry Bradshaw*

Soc 9). London.

— (ed & trans) 1905 *Félire Óengusso Céli Dé, The Martyrology of Oengus the Culdee* (*Henry Bradshaw Soc* 29). London (repr Dublin 1984).

— & Strachan, J 1903 *Thesaurus Palaeohibernicus*, vol II. Dublin (repr 1975).

Swan, L 1983 Enclosed ecclesiastical sites and their relevance to settlement patterns of the first millennium A.D. In Reeves-Smith, T & Hamond, F (eds) *Landscape Archaeology in Ireland* (*BAR British Ser* 116), 269-94. Oxford.

Swarzenski, H 1967 *Monuments of Romanesque Art* (2nd edn). Chicago.

— 1969 A medieval treasury. *Apollo* 90 (1969), 484-93.

Thomas, C 1971 *The Early Christian Archaeology of North Britain*. Oxford.

Thurneysen, R (ed & trans) 1933 Die Flöte von Mac Díchoeme. *ZCP* 19 (1933), 117-24.

Todd, J H (ed & trans) 1867 *Cogadh Gaedhel re Gallaibh, The War of the Gaedhil with the Gaill*. London.

Toner, G 1996 *Place-Names of Northern Ireland*, vol 5, *County Derry* I, *The Moyola Valley*. Belfast.

Trost, V 1991 *Skriptorium*. Stuttgart.

Tweddle, D 1996 *Corpus of Anglo-Saxon Stone Sculpture*, vol IV, *South-Eastern England*. Oxford.

Van Hamel, A G (ed) 1932 *Lebor Bretnach*. Dublin.

— (ed) 1941 *Immrama* (*DIAS Mediaeval & Modern Irish Ser* 10). Dublin.

Van Stone, M 1994 Ornamental techniques in Kells and its kin. In O'Mahony 1994, 234-42.

Walker, G S M (ed & trans) 1957 *Sancti Columbani Opera* (*Scriptores Latini Hiberniae* 2). Dublin.

Walsh, P (ed) 1948 *The Life of Aodh Ruadh Ó Domhnaill*, vol I (*Irish Texts Soc* 42). Dublin (repr 1970).

Waterer, J W 1968 Irish book-satchels or budgets. *Medieval Archaeology* 12 (1968), 70-82.

Waterman, D M 1959 Late Saxon, Viking, and early medieval finds from York. *Archaeologia* 97 (1959), 59-105

Watkins, C 1970 Studies in Indo-European legal language, institutions, and mythology. In Cardona, G, Hoenigswald, H M & Senn, A (eds) *Indo-European and Indo-Europeans*, 231-54. Philadelphia.

Watson, W J 1926 *The History of the Celtic Place-Names of Scotland*. Edinburgh/London (repr Shannon 1973).

Watt, D E R (general ed) 1989 = MacQueen J & MacQueen W (eds & trans) *Scotichronicon by Walter Bower*, vol 2. Aberdeen.

Way, A 1848 Notices of ancient ornaments and appliances of sacred use. The flabellum, flabrum, muscatorium, muscifugium, alara or ventilabrium. *Antiquaries J* 5 (1848), 201-6.

Webster, L & Backhouse, J (eds) 1991 *The Making of England, Anglo-Saxon Art and Culture AD 600-900*. London.

Wensinck, A J 1918 *The Ocean in the Literature of the Western Semites*. Amsterdam.

Werner, M 1972 The Madonna and Child miniature in the Book of Kells. *Art Bulletin* 54 (1972), 1-23, 129-39.

Wheeler, A 1981 Report on the fish bones from the monastic midden. In Reece 1981, 47-8.

Whitaker, E C (trans) 1960 *Documents of the Baptismal Liturgy*. London.

White, N (ed) 1943 *The Extents of Irish Monastic Possessions*. Dublin.

Whitelock, D, McKitterick, R & Dumville, D (eds) 1982 *Ireland in Early Mediaeval Europe, Studies in Memory of Kathleen Hughes*. Cambridge.

White Marshall, J & Walsh, C 1994 Illaunloughan. *Archaeology Ireland* 8, 4 (1994), 24-8.

Whitfield, N forthcoming The Waterford kite-brooch and its place in Irish metalwork. In Hurley, M F, Scully, O B and McCutcheon, S W J (eds) *Hiberno-Norse and Medieval Waterford, Excavations 1986-1992*.

Wilde, W R 1861 *A Descriptive Catalogue of the Antiquities of Animal Materials and Bronze in the Museum of the Royal Irish Academy*. Dublin.

Williams, E V 1985 *The Bells of Russia, History and Technology*. Princeton.

Wilson, D 1863 *Prehistoric Annals of Scotland*, 2 vols. Edinburgh.

Wilson, D M 1973 The treasure. In Small, A, Thomas, C & Wilson, D M (eds) *St. Ninian's Isle and its Treasure*, 2 vols (*Aberdeen University Studies Ser* 152), 45-148. Oxford.

— 1983 A bone pin from Sconsburgh, Dunrossness. In O'Connor, A & Clarke D V (eds) *From the Stone Age to the 'Forty-Five, Studies Presented to R B K Stevenson*, 343-9. Edinburgh.

Winterbottom, M (ed & trans) 1978 *Gildas. The Ruin of Britain and Other Works*. London/Chichester.

Wittkower, R 1942 Marvels of the East: a study in the history of monsters. *J Warburg & Courtauld Institutes* 5 (1942), 159-97.

Wood-Martin, W G 1889 *History of Sligo, County and Town*, vol II. Sligo.

Wölfflin, E 1900 Campana, Glocke. Species, Spezerei. *Archiv für lateinische Lexicographie und Grammatik* 11 (1900), 537-44.

Woulfe, P 1923 *Sloinnte Gaedheal is Gall, Irish Names and Surnames*. Dublin.

Youngs, S (ed) 1989 *'The Work of Angels'. Masterpieces of Celtic Metalwork, 6th-9th Centuries AD*. London.

Zanchin, G, Rossi, P, Isler, H & Maggioni, F 1996 Headache as an occupational illness in the treatise 'De morbis artificium diatriba' of Bernardino Ramazzini. *Cephalagia* 16 (1996), 79-86.

Zarnecki, G, Holt, J & Holland, T (eds) 1984 *English Romanesque Art 1066-1200*. London.

List of Contributors

Thomas O'Loughlin, Dept of Theology & Religious Studies, University of Wales, Lampeter

Aidan MacDonald, Dept of Archaeology, University College, Cork

Finbar McCormick, Dept of Archaeology & Palaeoecology, Queen's University, Belfast

Tim O'Neill, Sandymount, Dublin

Jennifer O'Reilly, Dept of Medieval History, University College, Cork

Jane Hawkes, Dept of English Literary & Linguistic Studies, University of Newcastle, Newcastle upon Tyne

Raghnall Ó Floinn, Irish Antiquities Division, National Museum of Ireland, Dublin

Cormac Bourke, Dept of Archaeology & Ethnography, Ulster Museum, Belfast

Nollaig Ó Muraíle, Dept of Celtic, Queen's University, Belfast

Maura Pringle, School of Geosciences, Queen's University, Belfast

Index